Reframing Academic Leadership

Reframing
Academic
Leadership

Lee G. Bolman, Joan V. Gallos

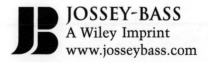

JOSSEY-BASS
A Wiley Imprint
www.josseybass.com

Published by Jossey-Bass
A Wiley Imprint
989 Market Street, San Francisco, CA 94103-1741—www.josseybass.com

Readers should be aware that Internet Web sites offered as citations and/or sources for further information may have changed or disappeared between the time this was written and when it is read.

Jossey-Bass books and products are available through most bookstores. To contact Jossey-Bass directly call our Customer Care Department within the U.S. at 800-956-7739, outside the U.S. at 317-572-3986, or fax 317-572-4002.

Jossey-Bass also publishes its books in a variety of electronic formats. Some content that appears in print may not be available in electronic books.

Quotations from speeches of Arizona State University President Michael Crow in Chapter 7 used by permission of Michael Crow.

Library of Congress Cataloging-in-Publication Data
Bolman, Lee G.
    Reframing academic leadership / Lee G. Bolman, Joan Gallos.—1st ed.
      p. cm.—(The Jossey-Bass higher and adult education series)
    Includes bibliographical references and index.
    ISBN 978-0-7879-8806-7 (hardback)
    978-0-4709-2925-4 (ebk)
    978-0-4709-2932-2 (ebk)
    978-0-4709-2933-9 (ebk)
      1. Educational leadership.   2. Education, Higher.   I. Gallos, Joan V.   II. Title.
LB2806.B583   2011
378.1'01—dc22

2010042999

Printed in the United States of America
FIRST EDITION
HB Printing   10 9 8 7 6 5 4

The Jossey-Bass Higher and
Adult Education Series

Contents

To our family
Those who have paved the way:
Florence and Eldred Bolman
Elizabeth and John Gallos

Those who enliven the present and determine the future:
Bradley Garrison Bolman
Christopher John Gallos Bolman
Scott Parker Bolman
Lori, Barry, and Jazmyne Holwegner
Shelley, Christine, and Foster Woodberry
Edward, Cat, and James Parker Noel
. . . and Douglas McGregor

Preface

We wrote this book for readers who care deeply about higher education, appreciate its strengths and imperfections, and are committed to making it better. If you are comfortable with the status quo and aspire to no more than a paycheck, *or* if you believe that nothing short of revolution can save a dying industry, this is not your book. If you strive to be a leader with impact and a significant force for good, we hope you find in these pages a readable, intellectually provocative, and pragmatic approach to your work and its possibilities.

There are multiple roads to careers in higher education administration. Some leaders in student affairs, advancement, business, operations, and other nonfaculty posts bring extensive training in their fields and in higher education administration. Other administrators are scholars and educators who have made a conscious choice in response to disappointment with the pace and focus of faculty life or an honest assessment of their interests and strengths. Then there are the many accidental leaders for whom an administrative career just seems to happen. A nudge from somewhere combines with a willingness to serve—to fill an unanticipated administrative gap, to take one's turn as a division chair, to use one's talents to salvage a program or launch a needed project. Before long, service turns into more than a temporary assignment. Many an interim becomes permanent after a year or so on the job. This sets in motion a series of choices, consequences, and rewards that can turn an initial administrative foray into a longer commitment. Sometimes the small detour becomes a longer journey down a road with no turning back: years away from teaching require retooling for the classroom, and scholarship once put on hold gets ever harder to restart as fields march forward.

The administrative world is different from faculty life, and it offers many rewards. Academic leadership is a highly social endeavor. The collaboration and partnerships needed to get things done foster a sense of community, connection, and shared purpose often missing in the isolation of the classroom, research desk, or laboratory. Much as we may complain about it, a calendar filled with meetings and events has its charms. Administrative life offers a pace, rhythm, and structure that focus one's time and energy. Deadlines and academic calendars encourage discipline and closure. And there is deep excitement and satisfaction in seeing tangible and measurable outcomes from one's efforts. A new degree program, dormitory, or sports complex has a durability and sense of completeness that are not always as easy to find in teaching and research.

But along with its benefits, academic leadership brings challenges and even heartaches, particularly in an era of political controversy, public doubts, technological changes, demographic shifts, mission drift (Kezar et al., 2005), and financial crisis. Higher education administration is demanding work that tests the mind, soul, and stamina of all who attempt it. We know because we've done it, and we have worked with many others over the years to help them learn to do it better. We have studied the factors that make the work so difficult, written about them, and benefitted from the research of colleagues. Colleges and universities constitute a special type of organization; and their complex mission, dynamics, personnel structures, and values require a distinct set of understandings and skills to lead and manage them well. That is what this book aims to provide: ideas, tools, and encouragement to help readers make better sense of their work and their institutions, feel more confident, and become more skilled and versatile in handling the vicissitudes of daily life.

Our approach builds from multiple sources. One is our experience both working in and teaching higher education leadership for
more years than either of us likes to acknowledge. One or both
of us have served as tenured faculty member, alumni affairs officer,
principal investigator, academic program director, campus accreditation coordinator, department chair, dean, and special assistant to
a university president. We have studied, lived, and worked in elite
private and urban public institutions. We have years of experience
teaching higher education leadership to aspiring professionals in
graduate courses and to experienced administrators in executive
programs and summer institutes. We hope this book reflects all that
we have learned from our students, colleagues, and experiences.

Throughout the book are cases and examples drawn from our own
experiences and from the experience of the many thousands of academic leaders with whom we have worked over the years. Except for
a few clearly labeled public examples, the cases are amended and well
disguised. Many are composites created, like good teaching cases, to
illustrate dynamics regularly seen across institutions and situations.
You're likely to encounter more than one example that sounds a lot
like something that happened at your institution not so long ago,
but that is purely coincidental. In higher education, it can truly be
said, "What has been will be again, what has been done will be done
again; there is nothing new under the sun" (Eccl. 1:9, NIV).

Outline of the Book

The chapters in Part One (Leadership Epistemology: When You
Understand, You Know What to Do) develop a central theme
in the book: thinking and learning are at the heart of effective
leadership. The opening chapter (Chapter One: Opportunities
and Challenges in Academic Leadership) uses a very public case
of a leader under fire to explore the institutional factors that make
leadership complex in colleges and universities. Our next chapter
(Chapter Two: Sensemaking and the Power of Reframing) explores
how we come to know and understand our world and the people in

it, and how our thinking can limit or enhance our vision, choices, and strategies. Chapter Three (Knowing What You're Doing: Learning, Authenticity, and Theories for Action) extends the discussion of sensemaking to the specific issue of learning from experience and from our relationships with others. Starting from a key premise that leadership is in the eye of the beholder, it discusses how leaders can learn more about their tendencies, strengths, and gaps.

Part Two of the book (Reframing Leadership Challenges) focuses on the big picture: how to understand the institutional landscape and translate intentions into effective action. We take on four of the knottiest concerns endemic to higher education administration and use a variety of case examples to provide concepts and guidelines for both diagnosis and action. Chapter Four (Building Clarity and Capacity: Leader as Analyst and Architect) addresses the leader's role in institutional structure and design, as well as the challenges in building linkages that enable people to work together in academic institutions that often seem designed for disconnection and dissension. Chapter Five (Respecting and Managing Differences: Leader as Compassionate Politician) tackles head-on how leaders can best handle a reality they would often prefer to avoid: enduring differences and the ubiquity of conflict in higher education. Chapter Six (Fostering a Caring and Productive Campus: Leader as Servant, Catalyst, and Coach) examines the complexity and importance of managing people in ways that foster creativity and commitment. Chapter Seven (Keeping the Faith and Celebrating the Mission: Leader as Prophet and Artist) uses a contemporary case at a well-known public university to explore ways that academic leaders can bring meaning and vision to their institution by embracing skills and strategies often associated with spiritual leaders and spirited artists.

Part Three of this volume (Sustaining Higher Education Leaders: Courage and Hope) focuses on the deeply personal relationship between higher education leaders and their work. The six chapters are written to sustain (or awaken) leaders' search for the best in themselves and in their institutions, and

each offers pragmatic advice on how to handle recurrent challenges that can derail even the most skilled. Chapter Eight
(Managing Conflict) explores a perennial hazard of administrative life: conflict. Effective academic administrators manage it
so as to foster creative problem solving, build commitment, and
make wise trade-offs among competing institutional objectives.
We offer tips for how to generate lasting solutions from thorny
situations by orchestrating disagreements so that things don't get
too hot or too cold for progress. Chapter Nine (Leading from the
Middle) examines the opportunities and challenges of working
with multiple constituencies. When academic leaders are buffeted by conflicting demands from every direction, what helps
them cope? Chapter Ten (Leading Difficult People) addresses
ways to productively handle the rogues' gallery of idiosyncratic
folks who sometimes seem over-represented in higher education.
People problems regularly top the list of challenges that can easily overwhelm leaders' coping strategies and psychic resources
and produce harm for both academic administrators and their
institutions. Chapter Eleven (Managing Your Boss) addresses the
important but often neglected issue of how to influence and work
effectively with a boss and other top players in the institutional
hierarchy. Leadership is sometimes equated to managing people
who report to you, but wise academic leaders understand that
leading is every bit as important. Chapter Twelve (Sustaining
Health and Vitality) addresses the reality that administrative life
can tax a leader's well-being. The chapter offers a series of steps
academic leaders can take to sustain their stamina and balance.
Chapter Thirteen (Feeding the Soul) explores the ethical and
spiritual dimensions of higher education leadership: the role of
faith, calling, and a deep sense of self as essentials for steering
academic institutions and programs to greatness. We conclude
with an Epilogue (The Sacred Nature of Academic Leadership)
that challenges higher education leaders to find and embrace the
sacred nature of their work.

Acknowledgments

We have been helped by far more people than we will ever succeed in acknowledging. We are blessed with a large circle of remarkable friends and colleagues, and they have taught us much. We begin with Terry Deal, a valued teacher, wonderful collaborator, and beloved friend to us both. Terry's ideas and influence are everywhere in this book—and elsewhere in our lives. Terry, for example, taught Joan never to sacrifice a good story for the sake of mere accuracy, which has given Lee many opportunities to play straight man to both his wife's and his longtime coauthor's penchant for storytelling. Terry taught Lee to plunge joyously into the nonrational, requiring Joan to develop tolerance for such things as drag races in dueling tuk-tuks through the streets of Thailand. Thanks, TD. We love you.

Equally significant is Chris Argyris, an extraordinary teacher and wonderful friend who was instrumental in both our decisions to make a career of studying organizations and leadership. Our first-born is named Chris, so no more need be said about the place that Chris Argyris holds in our hearts. Other highly valued individuals have enriched our lives and careers in important ways; and we send special nods of affection and appreciation to Bob Marx, Sandy Renz, Amy Sales, Ed Schein, Beth K. Smith, and Joan Weiner.

Academic leadership is a lot easier to study than to provide, and there are special people who have given us opportunities to learn that lesson firsthand. They include Eleanor Brantley Schwartz, Marvin Querry, Gordon Lamb, Marjorie Smelstor, Martha Gilliland, Bill Eddy, Homer Erickson, Karyl Leggio, Guy Bailey, Gail Hackett, Leo Morton, and Teng-Kee Tan at the University of Missouri-Kansas City (UMKC); and William Bowen and Dave Rahr at Princeton. Our forays into academic administration have enabled us to understand the challenges in drinking water from a fire hose, and we have learned much from the experience. We appreciate the trust, support, and leadership lessons from these consummate professionals; and we are honored to call so many our friends.

We have been fortunate to work with and for many other gifted and dedicated higher education leaders, and we have learned from their examples. They include Richard M. Cyert at Carnegie-Mellon; Derek Bok, Patricia Albjerg Graham, Walter McCann, Jerome T. Murphy, George Weathersby, Blenda Wilson, and Paul Ylvisaker at Harvard; Bill Porter at MIT; and Bill French, Ron MacQuarrie, Agapito Mendoza, and Brenda Tonyes among others at UMKC. We remember with fondness those who are deceased. Most of those on our list are still very much alive and active in service to the profession.

We have learned from and tested many of our ideas with students at UMKC, Harvard, Babson, Carnegie-Mellon, and UMass-Boston over the years, as well as with participants in many workshops, programs, and institutes across the world. We are particularly grateful to the many participants we have taught in summer programs under the auspices of the Harvard Institutes for Higher Education (HIHE). These talented academic leaders trusted us with their professional stories, some of which are the basis for case examples in this book. We are grateful to many of our HIHE colleagues, including Carlos Cortés, Jim Fisher, Tom Fryer, Charles Ping, Maureen Sullivan, and Joe Zolner.

We are particularly grateful to Dr. Judith McLaughlin, director of the Higher Education Program and Educational Chair of the Seminar for New Presidents at the Harvard Graduate School of Education, for taking time from a busy life to read the manuscript and offer extremely thoughtful and helpful comments. Three insightful deans, Brian Schmisek of the University of Dallas, Michael Stevenson of Northern Arizona University, and Julie Guiliani of Florida State College at Jacksonville, and Professor Bradford Kirkman-Liff of Arizona State University generously read earlier chapter drafts and provided very helpful comments. Thanks as well to Fernando León Garcia, Rector of the CETYS University system in Mexico, for his very helpful insights. We owe gratitude to the *wine and cheese soiree* attendees from UMKC— Doranne Hudson, Sandra Kruse-Smith, Paula Shipper, Lanny

Solomon, Peter Witte, and Kimberly Young—who provided valuable feedback on the manuscript. The book is better as a result of all the input. Our administrative assistant, Bruce Kay, deserves special thanks for his warm and unflappable approach to work, coupled with high levels of organization, artistry, and follow-through. Bruce provided important administrative support to the project; and he joyously took on the work of sorting out glitches in references, footnotes, charts, and procards. We love Bruce and are thankful that he postponed his full retirement to stay with us this year.

We've been blessed over the years with many wonderful colleagues. At Harvard, they included Cliff Baden, Millie Blackman, Louis B. "By" Barnes, Walter Broadnax, Kent Chabotar, Dick Chait, David Cohen, John Collins, Linda Corey Cyr, Dan Fenn, Jack Gabarro, Ron Heifetz, Jim Honan, Greg Jackson, Fred Jacobson, Susan Moore Johnson, Rosabeth Kanter, John Kotter, Bob Kegan, Dave Kuechle, Paul Lawrence, Marvin Lazerson, Dick Light, Sarah Lawrence Lightfoot, Larry Lynn, Marty Marshall, Marcy Murninghan, David Riesman, Irv Rubin, Fritz Steele, Bill Torbert, and Carol Weiss. At Babson, Allan Cohen, J. B. Kassarjian, and Jeff Timmons stood out. The list is long from UMKC and includes Arif Ahmed, Terry Applebaum, Raj Arora, Erma Artist, Sandy Bretz, Rita Cain, Nancy Day, Samee Desai, Dave Donnelly, Larry Garrison, Fred Hayes, Dick Heimovics, Bob Herman, Tusha Kimber, Clancy Martin, Mary Morgan, Brent Never, Johanna Nilsson, Brian Paul, Nick Peroff, Steve Pruitt, David Renz, Leon Robertson, Marilyn Taylor, Kami Thomas, and Doug Toma among others.

The Organizational Behavior Teaching Society has been a learning base and professional sanctuary for us both. We treasure this network of dedicated educators that includes respected learning buddies like Darlyne Bailey, Regina Bento, Diana Bilimoria, Jon Billsberry, David Bradford, Kim Cameron, Andre Delbecq, Jonah Friedman, Jeanie Forray, Roy Lewicki, Dorothy Marcic, Chris Poulson, Bob Quinn, Jean Ramsey, Peter Vaill, Karl Weick, and others. The members of the famous Brookline Group—Dave

Brown, Tim Hall, Todd Jick, Bill Kahn, Phil Mirvis, and Barry Oshry—continue to be a source of learning, inspiration, and camaraderie.

We have been hanging around Jossey-Bass so long that it feels like family. Our editor David Brightman is a committed educator and editor—and a patient soul who amiably tolerated a missed deadline or two. Thank you, David, for all you and your production staff have done to bring this project to fruition. Kathe Sweeney, now executive editor of Business, Nonprofit and Public Management, and J-B publisher Cedric Crocker among others have believed in us for a long time. Please know that it matters.

We dedicate this book to our family. Our two sons, Brad and Chris, are talented young men who enrich our lives. We love them, and we're deeply proud of them both. Chris made the transition from Wall Street to the global world of solar energy—and we know he has a very bright future (if you'll pardon the pun). His love of learning and his artistry at work and in his music impress us. We wish him well in his first book project. Brad deserves a special nod as the last in the roost—and the child who lived with the daily ups, downs, and sideways of this book project. As we chugged along on this manuscript, he moved quicker on the writing front, producing a wealth of AP papers, independent studies, two academic articles, college essays, debate cases, successful scholarship applications, and the first six chapters of his autobiographical novel. His depiction of the fictional professorial parents had us roaring, while his writing speed, capacity for literary allusions, and beautiful prose kept us humble. Lee's older children contribute their own brands of artistry and grace to the family. Theater, music, teaching, and our sweet new grandchild, Foster, fill the lives of Shelley and Christine Woodberry. Scott Bolman is the jet-setter as international lighting designer extraordinaire. Lori and Barry Holwegner anchor the Western contingent and take good care of spelling bee champion, granddaughter Jazmyne. Edward and Cat Noel round out the portrait with Hollywood and cartoon mastery, and budding-filmmaker

James holds the distinction of senior grandchild. Finally, we continue our tradition of giving a nod to some wayward canine who has served as a loyal distraction from writer's block. This book's award goes to the gorgeous yet impish, sock-eating, bed-loving mega-cockapoo, Douglas McGregor. Family life in all its richness is grand!

The two of us, like many others, stumbled unplanfully into academic life and later into academic administration. As children, neither of us imagined a university paycheck in our future. None of our parents were college graduates, and all were chronically puzzled about whether what we did qualified as real work. Elizabeth and John Gallos and Florence and Eldred Bolman are no longer with us, but we know they would have been tickled to see this joint venture and to see themselves saluted in it. We honor their encouragement and support—and love of learning that we hope we have passed along to our children—by adding their names to our acknowledgments.

It was some three decades ago that we made our first attempt to write together. It resulted in an unpublished manuscript that may still lie buried in a file drawer somewhere. It is not accidental that we waited a long time before again testing whether book writing and a viable marriage are remotely compatible. The moments during this project of what we might euphemistically call dramatic tension confirm both our wisdom in waiting and our passions for writing and teaching. But it was worth it for us to persist this time, and we hope for you as well. We're proud of what we've been able to do together, and we reconfirm our commitments to each other and to our shared interests. Onward!

About the Authors

Lee G. Bolman holds the Marion Bloch/Missouri Chair in Leadership at the Henry W. Bloch School of Business and Public Administration at the University of Missouri-Kansas City, where he has also served as department chair and interim dean. He holds a B.A. in history and a Ph.D. in organizational behavior from Yale University.

He has written numerous books on leadership and organizations with coauthor Terry Deal, including *Reframing Organizations: Artistry, Choice, and Leadership* (4th ed., 2008); *The Wizard and the Warrior: Leading with Passion and Power* (2006); *Leading with Soul: An Uncommon Journey of Spirit* (2nd ed., 2001); *Escape from Cluelessness: A Guide for the Organizationally Challenged* (2000); *Modern Approaches to Understanding and Managing Organizations* (1984); *Reframing the Path to School Leadership: A Guide for Principals and Teachers* (2nd ed., 2010); and *Becoming a Teacher Leader* (1994). His books have been translated into more than ten languages; and his publications also include numerous cases, chapters, and articles in scholarly and professional journals.

Bolman consults and lectures worldwide to corporations, public agencies, universities, and schools. Prior to assuming his current position, he taught at Carnegie Mellon and then for more than twenty years at Harvard, where he served as director and principal investigator for the National Center for Educational Leadership and for the Harvard School Leadership Academy. He has also served as educational chair for two Harvard executive programs—the Institute for Educational Management (IEM) and the Management Development Program (MDP)—and was the founder of MDP.

In 2003, Bolman received the David L. Bradford Outstanding Educator Award from the Organizational Behavior Teaching Society for his lifetime contributions to teaching and learning in the organizational sciences.

Joan V. Gallos is currently professor of Leadership, University of Missouri Curators' Distinguished Teaching Professor, and director of the Executive MBA program at the Henry W. Bloch School of Business and Public Administration at the University of Missouri-Kansas City, where she has also served as professor and dean of Education, coordinator of university accreditation, special assistant to the chancellor for strategic planning, and director of the Higher Education Graduate Programs. Gallos holds a bachelor's degree *cum laude* in English from Princeton University and master's and doctoral degrees in organizational behavior and professional education from the Harvard Graduate School of Education.

She has published widely on issues of professional effectiveness, organizational change, and leadership development. She is the editor of *Organization Development* (2006) and of *Business Leadership* (2nd ed., 2008); coauthor of *Teaching Diversity: Listening to the Soul, Speaking from the Heart* (1997); creator of a wide variety of published management education teaching and training materials, including the instructional guides for the *Jossey-Bass Reader* series in management; and author of numerous articles and chapters in scholarly and professional journals. She is also the former editor-in-chief of the *Journal of Management Education*.

Gallos lectures and consults in the United States and abroad on leadership and organization development. She has served as a Salzburg Seminar Fellow; as president of the Organizational Behavior Teaching Society; on a large number of national and regional advisory boards, such as the Forum for Early Childhood Organization and Leadership Development, the Kauffman and Danforth Foundations' Superintendents Leadership Forum, the national steering committee for the New Models of Management Education project (a joint effort of the Graduate Management Admissions Council and the Association to Advance Collegiate Schools of Business), and the W. K. Kellogg Foundation College Age Youth Leadership Review Team; and on civic and nonprofit boards in greater Kansas City, including as a founding board member for Actors Theater of Kansas City and for the Kansas City Library Foundation.

She has received numerous awards for her writing, teaching, and professional service, including both the Sage of the Society and the Distinguished Service awards from the Organizational Behavior Teaching Society for the breadth of her contributions to excellence in the field of management education; the Fritz Roethlisberger Memorial Award for the best article on management education (and finalist for the same prize in subsequent years); and the Radcliffe College/Harvard University Excellence in Teaching award. She also served as founding director of the Truman Center for the Healing Arts, based in Kansas City's public teaching hospital, which received the 2004 Kansas City Business Committee for the Arts Partnership Award as the best partnership between a large organization and the arts.

Joan Gallos and Lee Bolman have worked together for more than thirty-three years on a variety of teaching, training, and consulting projects for universities, corporations, nonprofits, and government agencies. This is their first book together.

Reframing Academic Leadership

Part I

Leadership Epistemology
When You Understand, You Know What to Do

The three chapters in Part One develop a central theme in the book: thinking and learning are at the heart of effective academic leadership. Colleges and universities are complex institutions that put a premium on sensemaking: the ability to decode messy and cryptic events and circumstances. One source of that complexity is the reality that academic institutions are inhabited by people and are designed to foster human creativity and development, which means that all the mysteries of the psyche, human groups, learning, personal and professional growth, and human relationships are central to the everyday work of academic administrators. Effectiveness in such a world requires both self-knowledge and intellectual tools that enable leaders to understand and decipher the ambiguous situations they regularly face in order to make sensible choices about what to do.

Chapter One digs into the institutional characteristics that make academic leadership unique, rewarding, and tough, with a preview of how this book can help leaders cope. Chapter Two examines everyday epistemology: how leaders come to know and understand their world and work, and how their humanity can limit or enhance their choices, tactics, and strategies. Chapter Three extends the discussion of sensemaking to the issue of learning from experience and from relationships with others. Leaders can never prepare for all that they may face. Strong capacities for ongoing learning and self-reflection are indispensable.

1

Opportunities and Challenges in Academic Leadership

It was front page news in America and around the globe when Lawrence H. Summers resigned the presidency of Harvard University in 2006 after a stormy five-year tenure. Despite his impressive résumé (wunderkind economist, one of the youngest professors ever tenured at Harvard, Secretary of the Treasury under President Bill Clinton, and more), Summers had the shortest term of any Harvard president since a long-forgotten incumbent died in office in 1862. Just about everyone agreed that his rise and fall was a tragedy of Shakespearean proportions, but there was debate about whether Summers was more like Othello and a victim of betrayal by threatened insiders or like King Lear and a casualty of his own foolishness and ego. "The greatest president in Harvard history has been forced to resign by the Faculty of Arts and Sciences," thundered a disgusted member of Harvard's class of 1949. Not so, said many faculty members who saw Summers as "a brash, imperious leader who ran roughshod over the nation's most-lauded faculty and got what he deserved" (Wilson, 2006).

Much of the commentary treated the story as specific to Summers and Harvard, but it is much more than that. It is an emblematic tale containing vital lessons for contemporary academic leaders. Not because Harvard and its president are typical of American higher education or because Harvard's perch atop the prestige hierarchy makes it what most institutions would like to be. This saga has much to teach because the similarities among colleges and universities—and what it takes to lead them—are as important and pervasive as their differences. Every institution of higher education is unique, but all have much in common. That's why variants of the same story—a talented and aggressive leader undone by faculty opposition—played out almost simultaneously in institutions as different as an elite private university in New England, a church-related university in the South, an urban public institution in the Midwest, and a community college in the Northwest. Welcome to the reality of academic leadership!

Opportunities and Challenges

The basic issues that can cripple university presidents are built into the daily lives of higher education administrators at every level, from chief executive to department chair and in support functions as well as in core academic units. That's because no one person or group can ever control very much at a college or university. Presidents, provosts, and deans are often seen by underlings as imperial figures who bestride their world like a colossus, but experienced administrators are usually more impressed by the limits of their own influence and authority. Outsiders, particularly corporate executives, often ask why universities can't be run more like businesses. They envision the superlative levels of speed, efficiency, and unity of effort that they like to think typify their corporate worlds—and wonder why higher education holds on to arcane practices like faculty governance and cumbersome collegial decision-making processes. But business provides abundant examples of failure as well as success. The 2008 meltdown in the financial sector, for example, took much of the world's economy with it; and it took Enron only a year to change from first to worst, evolving from one of America's most admired companies to the poster child for everything that's wrong in the corporate world. The series of errors and misjudgments that led to BP's 2010 oil spill catastrophe in the Gulf of Mexico would have been comic had the results not been so tragic. One study estimates that one-half to three-quarters of all American managers are incompetent in the sense that their skills don't match the demands of their work (Hogan, Curphy, & Hogan, 1994). But most of them probably don't even recognize the mismatch: the less competent people are, the more they overestimate their performance, partly because they don't know good performance when they see it (Kruger & Dunning, 1999).

This is not to say that business cannot serve as a fertile source of management ideas and innovation. Colleges and universities have some of the same elements found in almost any organization: goals, structures, administrative hierarchies, coordinating mechanisms, cultures, employees, vendors, and powerful stakeholders, to name a few. Leaders in higher education should learn from advances in other sectors whenever they can. Not every managerial wheel needs to be reinvented.

But the differences between business and higher education do matter (Birnbaum, 2001). Higher education's distinctive combination of goals, tasks, employees, governance structures, values, technologies, and history makes it not quite like anything else (Altbach, Gumport, & Johnstone, 2001; Thelin, 2004). It is different first because of its educational mission—a complex and variable mix of teaching, research, service, and outreach. Creating, interpreting, disseminating, and applying knowledge through multiple means for many different audiences and purposes is exciting and significant work, but it is not a simple job—nor is it one in which outcomes are easy to observe or assess.

> The "production process" in higher education is far more intricate and complicated than that in any industrial enterprise. . . . Students vary enormously in academic aptitude, in interests, in intellectual dispositions, in social and cultural characteristics, in education and vocational objectives, and in many other ways. Furthermore, the disciplines and professions with which institutions of higher education are concerned require diverse methods

of investigation, intellectual structures, means of relating methods of inquiry and ideas to personal and social
values, and processes of relating knowledge to human
experience. Learning, consequently, is a subtle process,
the nature of which may vary from student to student,
from institution to institution, from discipline to discipline, from one scholar or teacher to another, and from
one level of student development to another. (Berdahl &
McConnell, 1999, p. 71)

It is no surprise then that teaching and research are complex
enterprises, requiring significant financial and intellectual capital. In today's world, academic leaders at all levels and in both the
private and the public sectors scramble to find talent, resources,
donors, income-generating projects, and tuition dollars in an
intensely competitive environment. Colleges and universities
must respond to a host of forces. They face pressures from multiple fronts to become more accountable, businesslike, and market-
oriented in service to individuals, government, and industry. They
have to cope with profound changes in technology, major demographic and global shifts in student populations, formidable new
competitors in for-profit and virtual universities, and widespread
concerns that higher education lags in giving today's citizens and
tomorrow's workforce the twenty-first-century skills and values
they need. In the wake of the 2008 financial meltdown, for example, budgets at many institutions were decimated by precipitous
drops in endowments or state funding at a time when student
demand for courses and services kept growing. Academic leaders are under tremendous pressure to initiate change (Fullan &
Scott, 2009) and to embrace an entrepreneurial mindset in order
to keep pace with rapidly evolving conditions—and they need to
find a path that avoids either of two unproductive extremes.
Those who move too slowly will fall behind speedier competitors;
but those who move too precipitously will sow confusion, breed

discontent, and undercut their institution's traditional purpose, contributions, and strength (Newman, Couturier, & Scurry, 2004).

Higher education's mission requires that many of its key employees be teachers and scholars whose contributions depend on their unique expertise, dedication, and capacity for professional judgment. As in many other specialized professions, much of their performance can be assessed only by their peers. Their expertise supports faculty claims that they are uniquely qualified to make decisions about the core teaching and research activities of the institution. Faculty thus attain levels of individual autonomy and collective power beyond most employees in other sectors. The faculty role in institutional governance varies by institution; but it consistently creates challenges and dilemmas for administrators, who often find themselves in a turbulent and contested in-between zone, chronically buffeted by the conflicting concerns, viewpoints, and agendas of faculty, students, other administrators, governing boards, and a variety of important external constituents.

This governance conundrum gives rise to distinctive assets and liabilities in higher education. The same processes that foster individual creativity, initiative, and flexibility also buttress institutional inertia. The same safeguards and freedoms protect both the highly productive and the ineffective. The same arrangements that give faculty substantial control of their own affairs and contributions can lead to departments or schools that get sicker every year as personal and intellectual conflicts lead educated professionals to behave much like squabbling children or bullying mobs (Twale & DeLuca, 2008). Colleges and universities are centers of learning and hope. They are also complex organizational beasts—and the work of academic leaders in taming and directing them only becomes harder as demands increase while public support erodes (London, 2002).

A major national survey, for example, asked more than five hundred academic leaders to provide analogies that capture their daily life at work (Scott, Coates, & Anderson, 2008). Among the most popular were familiar classics like herding cats and juggling. Others were more creative and idiosyncratic: trying to nail jelly to the ceiling while putting out spot fires with one's feet, hanging wallpaper with one arm in a gale, pushing a pea uphill with one's nose, rowing without an oar, and driving nails into a wall of pudding (little resistance, messy, but no results). Taken together, these images add up to a familiar portrait of complicated and chaotic work in which great effort produces scant impact. They also point to the need for understanding and for solid preparation in order to tackle the complexity and to strengthen leadership skills and resolve.

But such preparation is rare in the context of academic norms and higher education career paths. Research on department chairs, for example, confirms that most assume their role with no prior administrative experience or training (Gmelch & Miskin, 1993, 2004). The same dearth of preparation is true across administrative ranks (Debowski & Blake, 2004). A study of two thousand academic leaders in the United States surveyed between 1990 and 2000 found that only 3 percent had received any type of leadership training or preparation (Gmelch, 2002). Additional research in the United States and abroad aligns with these findings (Fullan & Scott, 2009; Aziz, Mullins, Balzer, Grauer, Burnfield, Lodato, et al., 2005; Debowski & Blake, 2004). With the work of colleges and universities so difficult yet vital to the lives of individuals, communities, industries, and nations, findings like these are cause for deep concern. They were also a driving force behind the development of this book.

Purpose of the Book

Reframing Academic Leadership is designed to serve all who labor in the academic trenches to bring quality teaching, research, and service to those who need it. It offers perspectives for understanding the unique dynamics of the academy as well as realistic and practical ideas and strategies to get the cats to follow, the jelly to stick, and the pea to move uphill—without too many scraped or bent noses. It was written to challenge readers to reflect on their experience and to consider new ways of thinking and leading. You may already know or suspect that what got you where you are now may not be enough going forward.

Leadership preparation for higher education is of two kinds, and this book is written to offer both. One is intellectual: the acquisition of a conceptual road map, if you will, that helps academic leaders see more clearly what they're up against and what options they have. Leadership sage and former university president Warren Bennis captured this mission well when he noted, "When you understand, you know what to do" (Bennis, 2003, p. 55). Knowledge is power; and academic leaders empower themselves when they know where they are, where they want to go, and what will get them there.

A second mode of preparation is more personal and behavioral. Leadership requires individual qualities like courage, passion, confidence, flexibility, resourcefulness, and creativity—the foundations of healthy leadership resolve and stamina. Academic leaders strengthen those in themselves when they compare their worldview with what others see and when they understand how the mindsets they have formed from their everyday experiences close them off to options and to new learning. Higher education cases that are sprinkled through the book offer opportunities to think about what you might have done—or done differently—in similar situations. Leadership success rests in the quality of the choices made by leaders, and leaders make better choices when they are mindful about their thought processes and actions. Research and experience tell us that academic leaders go awry for two reasons: (1) they see a limited or inaccurate picture—they miss important cues and clues in their environment—and as a result take the wrong course; and (2) they fail to take people along with them—they move too fast, too unilaterally, or without full appreciation of the power of cultural norms and traditions to enable others to buy into their plans. Larry Summers at Harvard is a case in point. The goal of this book is to reduce your risk of falling into similar traps by helping you expand the ideas and understandings that you bring to your work and the self-awareness essential for using them effectively.

You can enhance your capacities to sidestep the snares through better understanding of three overarching issues: (1) links among thinking, learning, and effective action; (2) major challenges and dynamics in the academy; and (3) strategies for sustaining yourself and your leadership. We've organized the book into three parts to provide you what you need to know about each. Part One (Leadership Epistemology: When You Understand, You Know What to Do) explores leaders' ways of knowing. Leading is a social process that involves relationships of influence, learning, and exchange. How leaders think about others and their situations, learn from their experiences, and translate that into effective action make all the difference. Informed choice requires knowing self, others, and context. Part Two (Reframing Academic Leadership Challenges) takes a big-picture look at academic leadership and addresses four recurrent challenges for campus administrators: how to bring institutional clarity, manage differences, foster productive working relationships, and enact a powerful vision. It lays out a framework for action: what you need to do to get things done. Part Three (Sustaining Higher Education Leaders: Courage and Hope) strengthens academic leaders for the inevitable twists, turns, and bumps in the road. Courage and confidence come from knowing how to handle thorny situations and from recognizing that there is hope and possibility on the other side of challenge.

Our approach builds from our work as higher education teachers, scholars, and administrators and from the experiences of the many other academic leaders with whom we have worked, consulted, and studied. We draw on ideas and concepts from a variety of sources, including work on organizational learning (for example,

Argyris & Schön, 1996; Senge, 1990), professional effectiveness (for example, Argyris & Schön, 1974; Schön, 1983, 1987), cognition (for example, Groopman, 2007; Langer, 1989), and academic leadership (for example, Birnbaum, 1992; McLaughlin, 1996; Padilla, 2005). Our perspectives in this book are deeply informed by a conceptual framework, developed by Bolman and Deal (1984), that has been important to our individual and collective work[1] and that leads us to argue it is easier to understand colleges and universities when you learn to think of them simultaneously as machines, families, jungles, and theaters. Each of those images corresponds to a different *frame* or perspective that captures a vital and distinctive slice of institutional life. The capacity to embrace multiframe thinking is at the core of the model of academic leadership effectiveness developed in this volume.

The image of the machine, for example, serves as a metaphor for the task-related facets of organizations. Colleges and universities are rational systems requiring rules, roles, and policies that align with campus goals and purpose. Academic leaders succeed when they create an appropriate set of campus arrangements and reporting relationships that offer clarity to key constituents and facilitate the work of faculty, students, staff, and volunteers.

Successful academic leaders . . .

1. Create campus arrangements and reporting relationships that offer clarity and facilitate work

2. Create caring and productive campus environments that channel talent and encourage cooperation

3. Respect differences, manage them productively, and respond ethically and responsibly to the needs of multiple constituencies

4. Infuse everyday efforts with energy and soul

The family image focuses on the powerful symbiotic relationship between people and organizations: individuals need opportunities to express their talents and skills; organizations need human energy and contribution to fuel their efforts. When the fit is right, both benefit. Effective academic leaders create caring and productive campus environments where all find ways to channel their full talents to the mission at hand and to work cooperatively with important others.

The jungle image encapsulates a world of enduring differences: diverse species or tribes participating in a complex dance of cooperation and competition as they maneuver for scarce resources and for influence. Diversity of values, beliefs, interests, behaviors, skills, goals, and worldviews often spawns destructive campus conflict. It is also the wellspring of creativity and innovation—and hope for the future of higher education. Skilled academic administrators are compassionate politicians who respect differences, manage them productively, and respond ethically and responsibly to the needs of multiple constituencies without losing sight of institutional goals and priorities.

Finally, the theater image captures university life as an ongoing drama: individuals coming together to create context, culture, commitment, and meaning as they play their assigned roles and bring artistry and self-expression into their work. Good theater fuels the moral imagination, and successful campus leaders infuse everyday efforts with energy and soul.

Multiframe thinking is necessary because colleges and universities are messy and difficult organizations that require from their leaders simultaneous attention to vastly different sets of needs. Academic institutions require a solid organizational architecture—rules, roles, policies, procedures, technologies, coordinating mechanisms, environmental linkages—that channels resources and human talents to support institutional goals and purpose. At the same time, they need workplace relationships and a campus environment that motivate and foster high levels of satisfaction, cooperation, and productivity. Innovation comes from managing the enduring differences and political dynamics at the center of university life that can spark misunderstandings, disagreements, and power struggles. Finally, every institution needs a culture that aligns with its values, inspires individual and collective efforts, and provides the symbolic glue to coordinate diverse contributions. In such a complex institutional world, multiframe thinking keeps university administrators alert and responsive to the demands of the whole while avoiding a narrow optic that oversimplifies a complex reality—and sends academic leaders blindly down the wrong path, squandering resources, time, and credibility along the way.

Strong academic leaders are skilled in the art of *reframing*—a deliberate process of shifting perspectives to see the same situation in multiple ways and through different lenses. Experience, training, and developmental limitations leave too many leaders with a limited range of perspectives for making sense of their work. The dearth of training and preservice preparation for college and university leaders only exacerbates this gap. As a result, academic leaders can stay stuck in their comfort zones—shielded from experiences that challenge them to see beyond current preferences and to embrace more complicated socioemotional, intellectual, and ethical reasoning (Gallos, 1993a and b, 2005). When things turn out badly, they blame circumstances, the environment, a lack of resources, or other people, unaware that limits in their own thinking have restricted their options and undermined their efforts. More versatile habits of mind enable academic leaders to think in more powerful and comprehensive ways about their own leadership and about the complexities and opportunities in leading colleges and universities.

Above all, our goal is to encourage optimism, confidence, and clarity of purpose. Academic leadership is a noble enterprise—and a challenging one. It is too difficult and too important for the faint of heart or light of mind. We may never fully escape error and imperfection, but we can do better—and we need to. Educating students, creating knowledge, and serving society demand all the intellect, skill, and commitment that academic leaders can muster. This book can help. Read it thoughtfully, yet playfully. Engage the ideas. Argue with them. Test them against your experiences. Try them out at work. As reward for your efforts, you will find that you expand your thinking, strengthen your resolve, clarify your purpose, and deepen your commitment and capacity to achieve your full potential as an academic leader.

Note

1. Readers can trace the evolution in our thinking about leadership effectiveness by exploring our other work, such as Bolman and Deal (1984, 2006, 2008a and b, 2010), and Gallos (1991, 1997, 2003, 2006, 2008c).

2

Sensemaking and the Power
of Reframing

Nancy Turner was delighted to participate in a summer institute for new college presidents. The timing was perfect. She had just begun her term as president of North Valley Community College. She was optimistic but not naive, and she was eager for input. Nancy knew she faced big challenges. North Valley was respected in its region and in the community college world—strong and varied vocational programs and a solid record of sending students to four-year institutions. "A firm foundation gives me room to build," Nancy reassured herself on accepting the presidency. But she also knew there were many clouds on the horizon.

North Valley had suffered budget cuts in recent years due to the economic downturn and to declining state appropriations. Faculty and staff had seen no raises in two of the prior three years, and morale on campus bordered on dismal. North Valley's chief academic officer and dean of instruction, Bill Hartley, was widely unpopular on campus, partly because he had been the point person in the push by Nancy's predecessor to increase teaching loads in response to budget shortfalls. Nancy knew she needed a strong partnership with the chief academic officer to get things rolling in the right direction. She was leery, however, of aligning herself too quickly or closely with a controversial campus figure.

"Take it slow" was the advice of Nancy's mentor and former boss. The advice resonated with Nancy's own style. Plus, she wanted more time to get to know Bill. His close-to-the-chest style seemed unusually cool, and Nancy wondered how much was due to Bill's weariness after years of battling campus opposition and how much was due to his disappointment that she, not he, had been selected as president.

"Well, the board chose me," mused Nancy with some measure of satisfaction. "At least, most of them did." Nancy had to admit that the board's split vote still troubled her.

"Forget about it," her board chair advised. "Those people were making a statement in support of our faculty, not voting against you. A few well-connected faculty got to their friends on the board and tried to hold up the hiring process until next year's state appropriations were announced. And that gang has a history of disagreeing with the rest of the board anyway. We just vote them down and get on with our work," he added with a smile. "Trust me. We're confident that you're the one to lead this campus out of its malaise." Nancy wanted to believe him.

Only weeks after moving into her new office, Nancy found herself sitting around a table, discussing her situation with five other new presidents at the summer institute. She laid out her situation as objectively as she could, then asked, "If you were me, where would you start? How can I get this presidency off on the right foot?" Her colleagues jumped in with enthusiasm, as Nancy expected. She was surprised, however, that everyone gave her different advice.

"Get a vision and fast! You're the captain of the ship, and you better know where you're steering it. Rally the campus around a sense of direction," suggested the first president.

"I disagree," said the second. "You don't want a one-woman show. You want a strategic planning process that involves the campus in setting priorities. Without that, no one has a basis for decision making. And involving folks in a campuswide activity is good for morale."

"Maybe," began the third, "but you know what Jim Collins says in *Good to Great* [2001]: First you have to have the right people on the bus. Nancy, you need a team that you can count on. Fire that chief academic officer, and get people who can build programs without taking it out of faculty hides. Go it alone, and you'll collapse from trying to carry the whole campus on your shoulders."

"Interesting," said the fourth, "that no one suggested what I see as job number one: start with the faculty and work on morale and communications. Get out there. Hold faculty dialogue meetings. Get communications lines open and functioning. Tell everyone your picture of the college. Listen to theirs. Let them ask questions. Ask questions yourself. Good working relationships with the faculty are the key to a successful presidency."

"Nope," said a fifth emphatically. "Start with your board. If they're not with you, you can't go anywhere."

Lively debate ensued as the group explored what Nancy should do. Each president provided additional examples and information to buttress his or her perspective. They referenced Barack Obama and Jack Welch, while offering quotes from best-selling leadership books and gurus. Nancy was impressed by her colleagues' intelligence and gratified by all the input. But the discussion never arrived at the convergent picture she had hoped for. The diversity of views and variety of suggestions raised a question about whether there was anything else that she and her colleagues had missed. Five experienced academic leaders offered five different leadership paths, each convinced he or she was right. Nancy was intrigued by issues she hadn't thought about. She was clearer about her options—she could choose among multiple roads going forward, each with its own pluses and minuses. But she felt little closer to answering her original question: "Where do I begin?" All the counsel seemed to produce more uncertainty than clarity. "I still don't know where I'm going," laughed Nancy. "But I'm afraid that it's going to be a bumpy ride."

Nancy's situation illustrates an important truth and theme in this book. Sensemaking is the difficult art at the heart of academic leadership. We'd all like instant clarity about the complexities that we face and a clean slate to begin our academic leadership, but we are rarely that fortunate. Academic leaders bring their own ways of studying and interpreting what they see. They step midstream into institutions that have evolved distinctive histories, cultures, and traditions. Ideas about how to lead are based on implicit and often deeply buried belief systems about what's important and how things work. Those beliefs vary, as we see in the different scenarios offered to Nancy. A key challenge for Nancy and any academic leader is how to make sense of complex circumstances, recognize available choices, choose the best path forward, and convey all that to others in a compelling manner. Whether we call this executive wisdom, sound judgment, reflective practice (Schön, 1983), or learning from experience, the lesson is clear. Effectiveness requires untangling the conundrums of the academy and the realities of your current situation, and then translating both into sensible choices and actions for self and others. Like all leaders, Nancy needs to know if she is seeing the right picture or if she has tuned in to the wrong channel. Knowing this is not always as easy and straightforward as one would wish.

Cluelessness is a perennial risk, even for very smart people. Sometimes, the information that leaders need is hard to get. Other times, they ignore or misinterpret data right before their eyes. A look at the basics of sensemaking offers insights into why that is so.[1]

Sensemaking involves three basic steps: notice something, decide what to make of it, and determine what to do about it. Humans are pretty good at all three, but we do them so automatically that we tend to overlook three important—and limiting—features of the process.

1. *Sensemaking is incomplete and personal.* Humans can attend to only a portion of the information and experiences available to them. Individuals' values, education, past experience, cognitive capacities, physical abilities, and developmental limitations

influence what they see. Leaders register some things, ignore others, and draw conclusions—and these steps occur quickly and often tacitly. For that reason, the everyday theories that higher education administrators construct feel so obvious and real to them that they are understood more as Truth and the way the world really is than as the individual creations and interpretations that they are. The five college presidents advising Nancy are cases in point. The tacit nature of the human sensemaking process can blind academic leaders to available alternatives and to gaps and biases in their framing (Argyris, 1982). It also leaves them feeling little incentive to question their interpretations or retrace any of their steps from data selection through action.

2. *Sensemaking is interpretive.* When thrown into life's ongoing stream of experiences, people create explanations of what things mean—and often assume that others see things the same way or are wrong if they don't. Each of the presidents advising Nancy offered different advice, and each felt confident that his or her perspective was right.

3. *Sensemaking is action oriented.* People's personal interpretations contain implicit prescriptions for how they and others should respond. If you conclude, for example, that your unit's budget problems result from overspending, then you'll probably cut expenses. If you see the problem as inadequate allocations from central administration, then you might lobby for more. If you bemoan inattention to revenue generation, you'll turn to new program development. If it's embezzlement, a call to the campus police is in order. Think about Nancy Turner. If she accepts that strong support from faculty is key to her success, then building and sustaining those relationships is vital. If she concludes that the campus expects her to lead off with a compelling vision, she'll get to work on the big picture. You can see the ease and the potential complications in all this for academic leaders. They're off and running before they're even sure what's most important and where they should really be heading.

Sensemaking is a personal search for meaning, governed by tacit criteria of plausibility and *satisficing* (March & Simon, 1958) rather than accuracy. "We carve out order by leaving the disorderly parts out," concludes eminent psychologist William James (Richardson, 2006, p. 5). Human nature is such that a "good enough" explanation of the situation will stop our search for other alternatives, even early in the hunt. We need not find *the* truth or *the* best of all possible solutions. We just want something that's good enough by our tacit standards to let us move forward and get things done. And we're rarely aware that this is what we are doing.

Jerome Groopman, a Harvard Medical School professor, studied how doctors think (Groopman, 2000, 2007).[2] His work reminds us how easily and naturally humans satisfice even in life-and-death situations. It also illustrates the costs. Multiple studies of autopsies, for example, find that about 15 percent of all diagnoses are wrong, but usually not because of gaps in medical expertise (Groopman, 2007). More often, errors results from flawed sensemaking: ignoring information and test results that contradict whatever notion the doctor has already settled on.

What's at stake for academic leaders is illustrated in a story from Groopman's work (2007). He tells about a patient he calls Ann Dodge. At age twenty, Ann developed a serious eating disorder—every meal produced pain, nausea, vomiting, and diarrhea. Over time, she saw some thirty doctors in a variety of specialties, and there was general agreement. Ann had a psychiatric condition, anorexia nervosa with bulimia. The problem was in her mind, the doctors concluded, but still very dangerous and potentially deadly. Doctors prescribed a series of treatments, including diet, drugs, and talk therapy. Her doctor told her to consume 3,000 calories a day, mostly in easily digested carbohydrates like pasta. Over fifteen years, she kept getting worse. In 2004, Ann was hospitalized four times in a mental health facility in hopes that close supervision of her food intake might enable her to gain weight. Nothing worked.

Finally, at her boyfriend's insistence, Ann traveled to Boston to see a highly recommended gastroenterologist, Dr. Myron Falchuk. Ann was reluctant, and her primary care doctor advised that the trip was unnecessary since her problem was so well understood. But Ann went anyway. Falchuk had reviewed Ann's records and knew what all the doctors had concluded. But he put the information aside—literally pushing the tall stack of folders and reports to the far side on his desk—and asked Ann to tell him her whole story again. As she did, Falchuk listened with a fresh mind and felt the story didn't quite add up. Something was missing from the picture. In particular, he wondered why Ann wasn't gaining weight if, as she insisted, she really was consuming as much as 3,000 calories a day. Well, he wondered, what if she couldn't digest what she was eating? He did more tests, and eventually concluded that Ann suffered from celiac disease—an intolerance of the gluten commonly found in grains like wheat, rye, and barley. Ann Dodge was being poisoned by the pasta diet her physicians had prescribed to save her. As soon as she shifted to a gluten-free diet, she began to gain weight. In Ann's view, Dr. Falchuk was a miracle worker. From our perspective, Dr. Falchuk illustrates the power and importance of reframing in helping us transcend the limits in our automatic sensemaking.

Here's the point. When a doctor encounters a new patient, he or she tries to frame the patient by matching symptoms and selected pieces of information to patterns that the doctor has learned through experience and training. The process is quick and automatic: it begins with the first look at the patient when the physician enters the examining room. Doctors frame patients all the time.

> "I'm sending you a case of diabetes and renal failure," or "I have a drug addict here in the ER with fever and a cough from pneumonia." Often a doctor chooses the correct frame and all the clinical data fit neatly within it.

> But a self-aware physician knows that accepting the frame as a given can be a serious error. (Groopman, 2007, p. 22)

Expert clinicians can often determine what's going on with a patient in twenty seconds. It's simple pattern recognition, honed by training and experience. But sometimes they get it wrong. One source of error is anchoring: doctors can lock on to the first answer that seems right. "Your mind plays tricks on you," says Groopman, "because you see only the landmarks you expect to see and neglect those that should tell you that in fact you're still at sea" (2007, p. 65). Another source of distortion is a doctor's own needs and feelings. Operating under time pressures and wanting to be help-ful, physicians want to arrive at a diagnosis and prescription as quickly as possible. They feel competent and successful when they do. The same is true for academic administrators. Look at how readily Nancy Turner's colleagues offered her advice. They wanted to help. She expected nothing less.

Like physicians, daily life for academic leaders presents them with a continuous stream of complex and ambiguous stimuli. Like their medical counterparts, higher education professionals live in a world of time pressures, work overload, and high expectations. To make sense of diverse forms and sources of information, higher education administrators do what doctors do. They frame each situation by matching it with a familiar pattern. That means aca-demic leaders depend on the completeness of the information they gather, on the depth and accuracy of their frames, and on their ability to appropriately apply those frames to make accurate sense of the current situation. Whether academic leaders realize it or not, they always have choices about how to frame and interpret their world—and their choices are fateful. If, for example, Nancy Turner focuses her energies on recruiting a new chief academic officer while faculty morale continues to plummet—and news of the growing dissatisfaction bombards sympathetic board members—she may find herself in a deep hole before she can benefit from a stronger top leadership team.

A central mistake for leaders in any context is to lock into limited and flawed views of their world. We see reframing—the conceptual core of the book—as an antidote. *Reframing* is the deliberate process of looking at a situation carefully and from multiple perspectives, choosing to be more mindful about the sensemaking process by examining alternative views and explanations. Nancy's colleagues each framed her situation differently, and each got at a vital piece of a larger puzzle. Each bit of advice expressed the personal frame, the mental map, of its maker—and that is the beauty and utility in strategies that seek feedback from diverse others. Each colleague stretched Nancy's original views of her campus and of her leadership options. Together they offered Nancy a larger understanding of her challenges than any one alone might have. In the language of this book, they helped Nancy to reframe.

Research has shown that leaders often miss significant elements in decoding the situations and opportunities that they face (Bolman & Deal, 2008b; Weick, 1995). They will nonetheless do the best they can with what they have. The risk is that they'll do what Ann Dodge's early doctors did—focus on selected cues and fit what they see into a familiar pattern, even if it isn't quite right. Like Ann's doctors, they may insist that their answer is correct and that there's no need for further input or investigation—even if the diagnosis leads to options that don't work. In those cases, they will often conclude that the problem rests in the behavior of others, just as Ann Dodge's doctors blamed her for not following their advice rather than asking if their advice was flawed. Academic administrators may do no physical harm when they frame a situation incorrectly, but they can still damage their credibility, their careers, and their institutions. We're all in trouble when our sensemaking fails us.

Learning for Effective Action

From the outside, it may seem that effective leaders have an uncanny ability to read situations quickly. Many do, but they weren't born that way. They acquired their capacity from practice and experience. Effective leaders have learned powerful thought processes that enable them to register what is going on, reflect on it, assemble it quickly into a conscious pattern, and see the big picture. What Malcolm Gladwell (2005) calls the *blink* phenomenon is a learned form of rapid cognition. There is no shortcut to developing this kind of quick judgment—it takes effort, time, practice, and feedback.

Academic leaders can develop their skills in reframing—train themselves to see their role, work, and institution more broadly and from different perspectives. The images of academic leadership developed in this book are a good place to start. By learning how to think and act in such diverse roles as institutional architect, politician, servant, coach, prophet, artist, and diplomat, you can expand your mental maps and cognitive frameworks. The images build on more than a century of theorizing about organizations and about human behavior in them, and capture much of what we know about organizations as rational systems, human enterprises, political arenas, and theaters of worklife (Bolman & Deal, 2008b).

Paradoxically, learning to make deep, accurate, and quick situational diagnoses requires slowing down. When you are feeling overwhelmed by everything coming at you, slowing down is counterintuitive and hard to do. But it is vital. The next time that happens, stop and ask yourself some questions. What's happening here structurally—how do institutional rules, roles, and policies contribute? What are the people issues at play? What are the political dynamics, and who are the key constituents to consider and reach? What's the meaning of this situation and of the options to me and to significant others? With practice, the process of reframing takes on the characteristics of any well-learned skill: quick, automatic, largely tacit. Such skills emerge from active learning and from practice, and we suggest five strategies to help the process along. None is rocket science, but all are easier to espouse than to do well and consistently.

To build your reframing skills . . .

1. Embrace the life of a reflective practitioner

2. Be aggressive in seeking growth opportunities

3. Actively and regularly solicit input from others

4. Anticipate and practice the future through data gathering and scenario building

5. Step outside your comfort zones and "break frame"

Embrace the Life of a Reflective Practitioner

A consistent research finding on professional effectiveness is that those who learn best, lead best. "Leadership and learning," according to John F. Kennedy, "are indispensable to each other" (Kennedy, 1963). Publicly modeling engagement in learning as a daily professional imperative is a mode of leadership in and of itself (Preskill & Brookfield, 2009). For higher education administrators, this suggests developing skills as a reflective practitioner (Schön, 1983). Leadership problems in higher education are complicated and rarely have one "right" answer. No one can anticipate and prepare for all that might arise on a college campus, but we can all get better at learning from our experiences. Skillful academic leadership depends on reflection-in-action (Schön, 1987): the capacity for leaders to think deeply before taking action, to reflect on how things are going as they act, and to continue learning throughout their professional careers. Over time, reflecting on what we do also teaches us about our preferences, comfort zones, predictable responses, and trigger points. It's easier to break habits when we know what they are.

Be Aggressive in Seeking Growth Opportunities

One of the best ways to learn is to take on new challenges and to be deliberate in determining how you will use these opportunities to build leadership capacities. Leadership is more a performing art than a science. Like artists, leaders can enhance their skills by regularly practicing their craft and honing their talents. A key quality among successful executives is a dogged tenacity in learning about themselves as leaders and managers and in seeking rich and varied opportunities for professional development (McCall, Lombardo, & Morrison, 1988). "Learning is not attained by chance," reminds Abigail Adams (1780), "it must be sought for with ardor and attended to with diligence." Don't be afraid to experiment—stretching oneself broadens life and work skills. It can be risky: you may not learn as quickly as needed, and you can find yourself in over your head. Think carefully before you leap, and then keep an open mind. We learn from failure as well as success, and sometimes learning is even easier when the going is rough (Dotlich, Noel, & Walker, 2008).

Actively and Regularly Solicit Input from Others

We are all human and limited in our framing of the world around us. But that need not derail our leadership effectiveness. Constituents can teach us a lot about leading and about our organizations if we encourage them. They can offer alternative ways to view situations and help to identify our frame gaps and tendencies, as Nancy Turner's story illustrates. Skillful leaders routinely seek information and advice from diverse others. They thank them for their honesty through nondefensive listening, and they acknowledge constituent contributions to successful outcomes. Such conversations will broaden our perspectives and diagnostic skills.

We learn about the preferences and tendencies of those around us and strengthen our capacities to work with them. The respect that we show others in seeking their participation and involvement will only deepen their commitment to our organization and to our leadership success.

Anticipate and Practice the Future: Data Gathering and Scenario Building

The future is hard to anticipate, but that doesn't mean that we shouldn't try. A powerful way for academic leaders to clarify their thinking and to test assumptions is to develop their own scenarios or stories about how specific leadership choices might play out over time. Scenario building has been used in industry for a long time—a way to "rehearse the future" and anticipate the impact of a host of forces. There's plenty of advice out there on how to build scenarios if you want a more structured method (for example, de Geus, 1991; Schwartz, 1991; van der Heijden, 2005). Strategic planners approach the process as though a science. Or it can be a more informal and playful process of looking ahead (Heracleous & Jacobs, 2008). Our goal is to encourage you to craft alternative stories for yourself about possible futures based on different choices and assumptions. Your organizational sagas may identify interesting plot twists, winners, and losers—things you'd want to know before facing them at work!

Take Nancy Turner's case. Her colleagues suggested a number of different leadership paths. She might pick a few and construct alternative scenarios about each. She could envision one story, for example, where she started with creating a vision, and another where she started by getting the right team in place. Playing each out, she might find that one seems much more promising, that her two paths converge eventually, or even that she can see ways to do both at the same time. In any event, the process of projecting will help her to think and to communicate more clearly about possible futures for her college. She will be better able to predict and to prepare for the twists and turns of different paths going forward. She will also lessen the risk of losing her way—or her footing—in the face of unanticipated challenges.

Step Outside Your Comfort Zone and Break Frame

Albert Szent-Gyorgyi, the Hungarian-born, American biochemist who won the Nobel Prize in 1937, got it right when he noted, "Discovery consists of seeing what everybody has seen and thinking what nobody has thought" (Good, 1965, p. 000). Reframing is a step on the road to important discoveries for academic leaders. Expanding one's frame of reference requires knowledge about alternative perspectives, appreciation for their potential contribution, and opportunities to practice looking at the same situation through multiple lenses. It also takes personal courage to break frame—to step out of one's comfort zone and away from the crowd in seeking new options, proposing new explanations, or testing alternative responses. Frame-breaking can move mountains, and at times leadership requires just that. Consider a news story about a home intrusion that flashed across the wires in the summer of 2007 (Klein, 2007).

Imagine that you are with a group of friends enjoying dinner on the patio of a home in Washington, D.C. As you are finishing the jumbo shrimp and enjoying an excellent bottle of French wine, an armed, hooded intruder suddenly appears and points a gun at the head of a young female guest. "Give me your money," he says, "or I'll start shooting." If you're at that table, what do you do? Quietly hand over your wallet? Look for some way to resist? Something else?

You could try to break frame. That is exactly what one of the guests did when this happened on that warm July evening. As everyone around her froze, Cristina "Cha Cha" Rowan spoke up. "We were just finishing dinner," she blurted out. "Why don't you have a glass of wine with us?"

The young intruder hesitated for a moment then took a sip of the Chateau Malescot St-Exupéry and said, "Damn, that's good wine."

The father of the young woman being held at gunpoint encouraged the intruder to finish the whole glass, and Rowan offered him the bottle. The robber, with his hood down now, took another sip and then a piece of food from the table. He put his gun away in the pocket of his sweatpants.

"I may have come to the wrong house," the intruder said before apologizing and backing away, carrying only the glass of wine.

"I was definitely expecting there would be some kind of casualty," said the young girl's father. "He was very aggressive at first. Then it miraculously just changed. His whole emotional tone turned."

In one stoke, Cha Cha Rowan broke frame, transforming the situation for herself and others from "We might all be killed" to "Let's offer our guest some wine." Pretty dramatic. Sure. But there's learning here for us all. Sometimes we just need a new perspective—and an opportunity to step back, take stock, and know that we have options. With calm and renewed confidence, we may find a route that gets us to a better place than we were before. An occasional skeptic has asked if the story is true. The news accounts say yes; but even if apocryphal, this tale still makes its point. When you see what everyone else sees but think differently about it, you're on the path to finding more interesting possibilities and becoming a better, more creative leader.

Summary

Sensemaking is at the heart of leadership, and it is particularly vital in the complex and confusing world of higher education. It is a personal, interpretive, action-oriented process involving three basic steps: noticing things, interpreting them, and deciding what to do about them. Intuitively and automatically, we do this by trying to match current information and circumstances to learned patterns or frames. Often, that process works well enough—our take on the situation at hand tells us what to do, and we get results that are close enough to what we had hoped for. But sometimes, we get it wrong—we miss what's really happening, frame incorrectly, misinterpret our options, and go down a path to failure. When the world doesn't quite make sense and our actions keep producing the wrong results, it is time to reframe: to examine the world from alternative perspectives, looking for new ways to understand and for new strategies to move ahead.

Notes

1. For a deeper discussion of the links between sensemaking and effective action, see Gallos (2008c).

2. Relevant Groopman articles published in the *New Yorker* and other popular press outlets can be found at http://www.jeromegroopman .com/.

3

Knowing What You're Doing

Learning, Authenticity, and
Theories for Action

Sarah didn't want to be department chair, but she reluctantly agreed to take the job. None of her colleagues wanted it, and "someone had to do it." Now she wondered if she had made a mistake. A few of the "dinosaurs"—all male and all more senior than Sarah—seemed resistant to the idea that a younger woman could be in any sense their "boss." Sarah had tried to be cordial and supportive with everyone, but now she had to face the task she dreaded most: annual performance reviews. She stared glumly at one folder in particular: the performance materials for Professor George Hamden, a senior member of the department who held a distinguished endowed chair.

George was a charming curmudgeon—witty, articulate, opinionated, and quick to criticize anything he didn't like. Loved by some, feared by others, he regularly undermined Sarah in department meetings with his entertaining but acerbic comments on almost any new idea or initiative that she brought to the floor. But what troubled her now was Hamden's deteriorating performance. "The truth is," Sarah thought to herself, "he's been going downhill the last few years. His last publication was four years ago, and it wasn't very good. He says he's got great work in progress, but where's the evidence? His teaching evaluations are down, and students are complaining that sometimes he doesn't even show up to class."

Sarah felt that the previous chair had ducked the problem—giving George a higher rating than his record deserved. She was tempted to follow suit and avoid a confrontation. But that felt like a compromise of her integrity. Sarah also remembered the dean's admonition that the school was not Lake Wobegon and that he didn't want chairs telling him that "all the professors are above average"—especially those whose records indicate that they are not.

Sarah's musing about her dilemma was interrupted by a knock on the door. George was here for his assessment conference. She had to do her best. We'll eavesdrop on an abridged version of the conversation between Sarah and George. As you read, note that the left column shows what they said to one another. The right column shows what Sarah tells us was happening in her mind as the meeting progressed.

Sarah's Meeting with George

What was said:	Sarah's thoughts and feelings:
S: George, thanks very much for coming. I'm glad we have this chance to talk.	Start friendly and positive.
G: I hope I'll be glad as well.	I wish I thought that was possible.
S: Of course. George, you know I have great respect for you, and I appreciate all you've done for the department over the years.	Play to his ego, and maybe we can have a productive meeting. But I'm not optimistic.
G: I'm delighted to hear that.	So far so good?
S: But it's because I have so much respect, I have to be honest. George, you must realize that your performance has slipped a bit in the last few years.	Try to be as gentle as possible, but tell him the truth.
G: (pauses, frowns, then smiles) What makes you feel qualified to make such a judgment?	He's trying to change the subject. Let's stick to the facts.

What was said:	Sarah's thoughts and feelings:
S: This isn't about my personal judgment. It's about the evidence. You don't have any recent publications. Your teaching . . .	Stay calm. Be objective. Stick to the facts.
G: (*interrupting*) If you look at my output over the years, I'm sure you can easily see that it compares favorably to anyone in the department. I should certainly hope you're not trying to compare my reputation with your own.	If only he were as good as he thinks he is. He's an annoying, arrogant windbag. I need to stay calm.
S: (*as calmly and amiably as possible*) I'd never compare myself to you, George, and of course you have good reason to be proud of all you've done. But this isn't about your whole career; it's an annual assessment.	He wants to talk about me instead of facing up to his own performance. Try to get back on track. Stay focused.
G: (*acidly*) Perhaps when you've matured a bit more, you'll realize that the only sensible way to look at scholarship is over the long term.	There he goes again. This is infuriating.
S: (*her voice rising*) I didn't ask to be department chair, but I am. I'm just trying to do my job.	I'm losing it!
G: Yes, well, I suppose you're doing your job about as well as you can.	I don't like him, and I hate this job!
S: (*heatedly*) George, it would help if you would open your mind and listen to someone else for a change! The evidence shows that . . .	I've lost it.
G: There's no reason I should tolerate someone shouting and insulting me. I believe this meeting has already gone longer than productive. (He rises and leaves the office.)	What a disaster! He was totally uncooperative, but he'll blame me and tell all his buddies how unfair I was.
S: (*watches George leave*)	I should do something, but I have no idea what.

Sarah's intentions were honorable. She had a job to do. She expected it to be difficult, even painful, but it still turned out worse than she feared. She and George both left feeling that the meeting was an unpleasant failure. As the meeting spun out of control, Sarah struggled without success to control the conversation and her own feelings. At the end, she felt angry and helpless. Sarah and George each contributed to the disaster and each blamed the other. But neither felt responsible for the dismal denouement. Sarah left the meeting feeling worse about George and about herself; the same is likely true of George. More significant, neither party learned anything that might help them do better in conversations like this or with each other in the future.

Skilled Incompetence: Understanding Theories for Action

In Chapter Two, we argued that sensemaking and learning from experience are at the heart of leadership effectiveness. In looking at how Sarah prepared for and conducted her meeting with George, we can see an example of how everyday sensemaking can go awry and lead well-intentioned administrators into a quagmire while preventing them from having any idea how they could have avoided it. Sadly, scenes like this are all too common in the life of academic leaders. The Sarahs of the world dig their way into holes with unproductive strategies that they have come by honestly. The Georges help them shovel. There's a perfect description for this kind of behavior: *skilled incompetence*, the use of automatic, learned behaviors to produce the opposite of what you intend (Argyris, 1986). Why does this happen? It is not because people set out to fail—almost no one does that. But in interactions with others, people often know what they intend without realizing that they're not doing what they think they are. To complicate matters, they often have little or no understanding of the impact of their behaviors on others—and they have not developed habits of the mind to make such inquiry a regular part of their professional practice. As a result, they don't see their responsibility for failed interactions, don't see other options, and often don't recognize the need to search for them. The same ineffective behaviors get repeated again and again. It happens to all of us—more than we realize. It is most common in situations that are the most challenging, and those are often the most important. The result is that academic administrators may handle routine items with aplomb but flounder with the things that really matter. Imagine the consequences of a steady diet of meetings that make things worse for all concerned.

Noted organizational theorists Chris Argyris and Donald Schön offer a framework for understanding this dynamic (Argyris & Schön, 1974, 1996). They argue that individual behavior is controlled by personal "theories for action": mental models that tacitly inform and guide our choices. Argyris and Schön distinguish between two kinds of personal theory. One is *espoused theory*: the accounts individuals provide whenever they try to describe their behavior ("Here's what I did . . ."), explain the reason for it ("I did that because . . ."), or predict it ("What I'll do in that meeting is . . ."). The other is their *theory-in-use*: the internal decision rules or implicit programs that guide how they behave. Others hear us talk about our espoused theories, but they see our theories-in-use. Problems ensue when the two kinds of theory don't match.

Argyris and Schön studied thousands of professionals and managers, finding significant discrepancies between their espoused theories and their theories-in-use. In other words, individuals are often poor at describing and understanding the impact of their own actions. Would-be leaders typically saw themselves as more rational, open, concerned for others, and democratic than they were seen by their colleagues—or by the researchers. And such blindness was persistent because as a rule, people didn't know they were blind and didn't learn very well from their experience.

Argyris and Schön concluded that a major block to learning was a cycle of self-protective, interpersonal behavior that they labeled Model I. Their research showed that this program for action is ubiquitous: almost everyone uses it, even though few people realize that they do.

Model I Assumptions

Lurking in Model I is a set of core assumptions that the world is dangerous and so we better not let our guard down. These assumptions cause individuals to follow predictable steps in their attempt to protect themselves in their interactions with others. We can see this progression in the exchanges between Sarah and George.

1. *Assume that the problem is caused by the other person(s).* Sarah sees herself as earnest, selfless, and principled, simply trying to do a good job under difficult circumstances. She expects the meeting to be challenging despite her best efforts because George is routinely exasperating. Her implicit assumption is "George is the problem, and I have to be the solution."

2. *Develop a private, unilateral diagnosis and solution—and then act on them.* Sarah sees at least two problems. The first is George's work performance, which she hopes to discuss with him. The second is that she expects George to be defensive, unpleasant, and possibly belligerent in response to feedback on his performance. But it does not occur to Sarah to discuss that concern with George or to enlist his thoughts on how they can have a productive conversation about difficult issues. Sarah's strategy instead is threefold: start positive; flatter George; and stay cool, rational, and factual. We have no direct evidence of what George was thinking in advance of the meeting, but it is likely he too was pessimistic. His consistent sarcasm and criticism convey little confidence in Sarah's leadership. This means that they both expected failure and that both saw their pessimism as undiscussable.

3. *Get the others to change and be who you want them to be.* Use one or more of three basic strategies to accomplish the makeover: (1) facts, logic, and rational persuasion (argue the merits of your point of view); (2) indirect influence (ease in, ask leading questions, cajole or manipulate the other person); or (3) direct critique (tell the other person directly what he or she is doing wrong and how he or she should change). Sarah made a half-hearted and somewhat clumsy stab at easing into the conversation with George. The results were less than stellar. She then shifted to facts and logic, arguing the merits of her case. George riposted with disparagement of Sarah's reputation and experience. It was all downhill from there.

4. *If the other person resists or becomes defensive, it confirms the initial diagnosis that the other is the cause of the problem.* George's reactions and resistance to discussion of his performance proved to Sarah that her pessimism was justified and her diagnosis was spot on: George was as defensive and exasperating as expected. It is likely that Sarah's raised voice and rising emotionality confirmed George's perception that she was in over her head.

5. *Respond to resistance with some combination of intensifying pressure and protecting the other person or with rejection.* Sarah responded to George's resistance by intensifying the pressure when she told him to open his mind and "listen to someone else for a change." That led George to reject her before she could figure out what to do next—or to reject him first.

6. *If your efforts are less successful than hoped, it is the other person's fault.* Sarah sees the meeting as a failure and regrets that she couldn't do anything to make it go better. In her mind, it's still George's fault: he kept "trying to change the subject," and he was "infuriating," "arrogant," and "totally uncooperative." Sarah does not see how her behavior might have encouraged or allowed George to act in the very ways she feared he would.

Model II Assumptions

Model I survives because it enables us to get things done, but at a price that often includes wasted energy, strained relationships, and bad decisions. We continue to pay the price because we don't see our contributions to the bad results—and even if we do, we often don't know a better option. Argyris and Schön (1974) propose Model II as an alternative for more effective interactions. The basic precepts of Model II include:

1. *Emphasize common goals and mutual interests.* Even in a situation as difficult as Sarah's meeting with George, shared goals are possible. They both want to be effective, and neither will benefit from mutual destruction. Creating a shared agenda is a good starting point. Sarah could, for example, have said, "George, you've been in meetings like this before. What do you hope we can accomplish, and how should we proceed to make sure that happens?"

2. *Communicate openly, publicly test assumptions, and be willing to discuss the undiscussables.* Sarah dreads the meeting because she believes George will respond negatively to any questions about his performance. Her reasoning puts her in a hole from the beginning because she begins the meeting feeling anxious and fearful and ties herself in knots. She does not realize that she has built her approach to George around an effort to avoid what she suspects is unavoidable—an unpleasant battle with George. Model II suggests that Sarah openly test her assumption with George. She might say, for example, "George, let me tell you what I dread. If I raise questions about your work, you'll get angry and the meeting will go downhill. Should I be worried about that?" Such directness may seem surprising and risky. But Model II argues that Sarah has little to lose and much to gain. Even if George does not respond positively to her question, she is following a simple, but surprisingly useful precept: "When in doubt, try telling the truth." That

would give George fuller information about her thinking and might enable them to talk about the elephant in the room. It is typically easier to address something that you can discuss than something you can't.

3. *Combine advocacy with inquiry.* Advocacy includes statements that communicate what an individual thinks, knows, wants, or feels. Inquiry seeks to learn what others think, know, want, or feel. Successful exchanges need a balance of both. Figure 3.1 presents a simple model of the relationship between advocacy and inquiry and a way to think about the meaning of our choices in using both.

Model II emphasizes high advocacy coupled with high inquiry. It asks academic leaders to express openly what they think and feel and to actively seek understanding of others' thoughts and feelings. The Sarah and George meeting consisted almost entirely of advocacy versus advocacy. Sarah tried to persuade George to look at evidence of his declining performance. George tried to persuade Sarah through his attacks that such a conversation was not a good idea. Neither showed any interest in learning about the other's point of view. Sarah never asks George for his perspectives and avoids or rejects almost everything he says. George does largely the same: the only question he asks ("What makes you feel qualified to make such a judgment?") is an attack rather than a request for information. Sarah saw George as dominating and arrogant without realizing that he could easily feel the same about her.

		Inquiry	
		Low	High
Advocacy	High	Dominant, persuasive	Collaborative, engaged
	Low	Passive, withdrawn	Questioning, manipulative

Figure 3.1   Advocacy and Inquiry.

Model II counsels Sarah to be open with George about her thoughts while testing her assumptions about him and the situation in order to learn about both. This is difficult. Openness carries risks, and it is hard to be effective when you are ambivalent, anxious, or frightened. It gets easier as you become more confident that you can cope with other people's responses and that you have a range of workable options for doing so. How do you build both? Practice. Experiment in low-risk situations and test out new strategies. Write out and rehearse in advance new responses to situations that are likely to trigger nonproductive reactions. Role-play with a coach or a trusted colleague. Sarah's ability to handle the difficult conversation with George depends on her confidence in herself and in her interpersonal skills. Beliefs can be self-fulfilling. If she tells herself that it is too dangerous to be open and that she does not know how to deal with difficult people, she will probably be right. A more optimistic prediction, however, can also be self-fulfilling.

Learning and Effective Action: Habits of Learning for Daily Practice

The larger lesson from Sarah's meeting with George is not that a particular meeting didn't go very well. We are all imperfect humans, and academic administrators work in a complex and challenging environment: it's inevitable we'll get things wrong. If we recognize and learn from those mistakes, things generally work out better over the long run. But Sarah didn't learn, and the same is often true for other leaders. Why might that be so?

Learning about ourselves and our effectiveness can be a deceptively simple process: we act, assess the results, and decide what to do next. When the connection between act and outcome is easy to see, we learn quickly. Most of us learned to ride a bicycle— a set of skills too complex and subtle to be rendered in simple English—because the feedback was immediate, consistent, and clear. Some things worked, others didn't—and we learned to distinguish which was which. Decades later, for example, one of the authors still has vivid memories of crashing painfully into a wooden barrier after rolling downhill before fully mastering the intricacies of the coaster brake. He only made that mistake once.

Learning is harder in interpersonal transactions because they are complex and fast-changing, feedback from others is elusive and ambiguous, and the same behaviors that work in one situation may fail in another. In her meeting with George, Sarah knew he wasn't responding as she would have preferred, but she had to infer her impact from George's comments, which were anything but direct. It was easier to conclude that George was annoying than to see how she might be fostering the very thing she hoped to avoid. George offered little to help her see otherwise.

Interpersonal learning is also difficult because egos and defenses get in the way. Chris Argyris reminds us that in threatening or emotionally awkward encounters we automatically seek to protect ourselves against vulnerability, embarrassment, or the appearance of incompetence (Argyris, 1990, 1994). The result is a recipe for anti-learning about something we need to understand: how our choices and actions fail us. In the complex world of higher education today, such blindness is potentially fatal. Leadership lies in the eyes of the beholder—and if academic leaders don't know how their constituents see them, they're in trouble. They need information to recognize when they are off course,

---

Four Habits of Learning for Leadership Effectiveness

1. Be proactive and persistent in seeking feedback from others.

2. Test assumptions and attributions.

3. Work on balancing advocacy and inquiry.

4. Learn about your theories-in-use.

as well as strategies for improving their ability to learn from experience. Both enable them to bring more confidence and authenticity to their leadership. We suggest four learning routines that academic leaders can build into daily practice.

Be Proactive and Persistent in Seeking Feedback from Others

We see our leadership from the inside. We know what we intend. Since we are all sometimes blind to the gap between our espoused theories and theories-in-use, feedback from those who know and work with us is the only way to determine whether our intentions match our actions. Few academic leaders, for example, seek such input from faculty—often because they fear what they would find out. The result is that many crash into walls of faculty mistrust or anger that they don't see until too late. Two basic principles of interpersonal feedback can remedy that.

Ask and You Shall Receive

This sounds simple and obvious, but it's surprisingly rare. Feedback mostly occurs in structured, high-stakes situations, like Sarah's annual review meeting with George, or when debriefing major failures or special events. Experience makes people leery of offering feedback at other times unless they're sure the recipient wants it. Asking is the easiest way to encourage them. It takes persistence and skill in framing the right questions. If you simply ask a colleague, "What did you think about my report/ speech/ . . . ?," the first responses will often amount to vague reassurance ("Seemed fine to me") because comforting platitudes feel safe. But they don't help. You'll need to keep at it to get the kind of information necessary to expand your learning opportunities. Help others help you by following up with more specific probes:

"What do you think worked best?"

"What could I have done better?"

"What would you suggest I do to strengthen it?"

"What message do you think the audience took away?"

People are reluctant to risk telling us more than we want to know. Persistence makes requests for honest feedback clear and credible.

Stay Appreciative

The risk of asking for feedback is that you may be disappointed in what you hear. If that's true, say so—the other person will sense it anyway. But don't defend your actions or explain why the feedback is wrong. You don't have to believe or act on everything that others tell you, but you want to hear them and respond in ways that encourage them to keep communicating. Be sure to thank anyone who tries to help. If you respond to feedback by rejecting it, criticizing it, or inducing guilt, the flow of future offerings will dry up quickly.

Skilled and confident academic leaders make it a point to regularly seek feedback from peers, subordinates, bosses, and other key stakeholders. Colleagues can also agree to support each other with open feedback. A seasoned coach or mentor is another alternative. Deep learning, the Talmud teaches, is only achieved in company.

Test Assumptions and Attributions

When others do things we find puzzling or infuriating, the temptation is to attribute unfavorable motives and thoughts to them and then to act on those attributions as if they were true. But none of us is 100 percent accurate in interpreting why others do what they do, and we often make difficult situations worse by operating on the basis of untested attributions. A better alternative is to ask others what they mean, what they intend, or how they are thinking.

In Sarah's performance review with George, for example, she believed George was trying to deflect the conversation away from his performance by his comments on her junior status and comparative inexperience. Sarah never mentioned this to George, but she got angry and began to pound harder (and louder) on him. As an alternative, Sarah might have surfaced her assumption with something like, "George, are you wanting to discuss my performance or yours?" If George is playing a game, as Sarah believes, then her question alerts him. His defensive maneuvers may be so automatic and overlearned that the question might help him see what he is doing. George may want to discuss Sarah's performance, and a confident Sarah would want that feedback. She could even ask, "Would it help to discuss your perceptions of me first?" But that is not a substitute for George's annual review.

Testing assumptions in this way can lead to learning for both Sarah and George. Sarah might learn that she can handle difficult people without being controlled by their aggression or her fears. This is important for us all. It is essential for young professionals and for women who, research tell us, are more often the brunt of uncivil behavior in higher education classrooms (Goodyear, Reynolds, & Gragg, 2010; Schmidt, 2010a) and other campus work environments (Freyd & Johnson, 2010; Sadler, n.d.; Riger, n.d.; Twale & De Luca, 2008). George may be acting out gender politics or playing the age-old intellectual game of self-protection through deflection and sarcasm. He may be unaware that not everyone finds his style charming—and that others who view him as hard to handle might choose to exclude him from events and critical conversations. If no one calls George's game, he'll probably keep on playing it. Sarah's question might help George become more aware of his tactics and their consequences.

Work on Balancing Advocacy and Inquiry

Some leaders advocate far more than they inquire. Others do the opposite. Paying attention to your patterns can help you assess the appropriate balance for your purposes. Effective academic leaders are versatile and skilled in both areas. But effectiveness is reflected not only in the amount of each but in the quality of the effort. Quantity is easier to assess—and focusing on balance is a good entry point for academic leaders new to these issues. Improving the quality of advocacy and inquiry is harder. Good advocacy is complex. It is the ability to communicate clearly and persuasively. That means talking about your take on reality and the reasoning behind your diagnoses and decisions without discouraging others from doing the same. Inquiry involves skills in listening, reflecting what you hear to test accuracy, and crafting questions that enable you to learn the things you need to know. You won't get that from asking leading questions that manipulate the answer. Yes/no questions will get you a brief response but may reveal little about what others think, feel, or know. Good inquiry uses questions of *how*, *what*, and *why* to get people talking about things that matter.

Learn About Your Theories-in-Use

The Sarah and George case exemplifies a useful learning tool. Writing a two-sided case in the same format that Sarah used is something you can do before or after an unusually tough situation.[1] Take a piece of paper and divide it in half. Write a short dialogue that reflects what you said (or anticipate saying) and how others responded (or how you think they will) in the left-hand column. Add what you were thinking but didn't (or wouldn't) say in the right. You may be surprised to see what you choose to say and not to say. Write these cases on different situations that you face over time, and you'll get new clarity about your strengths, comfort zones, and flat spots. Keep them as a record of your professional growth.

The two-sided case is a specific form of scenario building that we discussed at the end of Chapter Two. It's a low-risk way to rehearse the future. You'll think more deeply about your intended strategies, how you want to talk with others, and the possible consequences. The case can also tell you how optimistic or pessimistic you are about the situation and reveal what you are reluctant to discuss or make public. Knowing that in advance can enable you to develop and practice new strategies—and build your confidence and communication skills. Remember: the undiscussable issues are often the keys for steering a difficult conversation in a positive direction.

If you use a case to reflect after the fact about what you might have done differently, enlist a trusted friend, coach, or colleague to help. The things we don't know about ourselves are hard for us to see without help from someone else. Case writers almost always struggle to see gaps and options that are transparent to others. Take heart! With practice and persistence, you'll improve the alignment of your actions with your purposes.

Summary

Leadership works when relationships work—and fails when they don't. Leaders' self-awareness and interpersonal skills are central to their effectiveness, but are often insufficient for the challenges of academic leadership. When relationships go awry, leaders often know what they intended, but not what they did to contribute to unsatisfactory outcomes. As a result, they often blame others instead of learning how to do things better. The best leaders are persistent and proactive in reflecting on their behavior and in learning from those around them. They seek feedback, test assumptions, work on balancing advocacy and inquiry, and learn about their own habitual patterns of action.

Note

1. Readers interested in additional information about how to construct or use this kind of case for learning can find details in Argyris and Schön (1974), or Senge (1990a and b).

Part II

Reframing Leadership Challenges

Part Two focuses on the big picture: how to understand the basic requirements for academic leadership and respond to the challenges of institutional complexity. Colleges and universities, like all complex organizations, operate simultaneously on four different levels (Bolman & Deal, 2008b). They need a solid architecture: an appropriate institutional structure with rules, roles, policies, and procedures that channel resources and human talents into activities that support campus goals. At the same time, they must address the complexity of human nature and create work environments that facilitate creativity, satisfaction, and productivity. Enduring differences of all kinds lead to incompatible campus priorities, power struggles, and the ongoing need to manage conflict. Finally, every institution needs a culture that aligns with its purposes and values and provides the symbolic glue to coordinate the activities of many.

Leading in such a demanding environment is not easy; effective academic administrators need diverse skills, strategies, and understandings. The next four chapters are written to provide those. Chapter Four addresses how academic leaders can best structure their work, their institutions, and the processes of change and continuous improvement. Chapter Five encourages leaders to understand, embrace, and productively manage the political dynamics that are an inevitable feature of academic life. Chapter Six discusses the importance of the fit between people and their workplaces. Chapter Seven explores the power of viewing colleges and universities as theaters and temples that ultimately rely on their capacity to build meaning and faith.

The central idea at the heart of these four chapters is that reframing academic leadership—deliberately choosing to look at the requirements for leading colleges and universities from multiple perspectives—is a powerful and essential tool for institutional success. The work of academic leaders is too diverse—and the purposes too important—for a more simplistic approach. Reframing is only possible when we have more than one leadership frame—when we can bring multiple, coherent ways of understanding the complex realities and requirements of the work. Developing skills and confidence across multiple leadership frames prepares academic administrators for the range of situations they will face.

4

Building Clarity and Capacity
Leader as Analyst and Architect

Among the first things that Helen Chu confronted as the new dean of the School of Professional Studies at Midstate University was a campus push to expand distance learning (DL). Midstate was facing another round of funding cuts, and increasing DL enrollments was targeted as a priority for generating new income. The campus had an Office of Distance Learning (ODL) that was facing its own fiscal crisis, with revenues falling short of projections for the third straight year. In Chu's mind, part of ODL's problem was its "Cadillac" strategy: offering high-quality, high-cost courses without having done sufficient market research.

Helen felt her school could do well on its own, developing courses faster, better, and at a lower cost. She worked with one of her department chairs who had significant distance learning experience from his prior institution and developed a tentative plan for a distance curriculum. She ran the idea by ODL's director, who, like her, was a member of the deans' council and reported to the provost. The director raised no objections, and Chu got clearance from the provost to go ahead. When her school launched its first course, Chu hoped for an enrollment of thirty. Instead, she got more than three hundred students and had to scramble to find instructors to handle the load. Financially, the new DL offering was the most successful in Midstate's history—a boon for Chu, her school, and the university. But she soon discovered that the director of Distance Learning was not happy. He argued that Chu was competing with his department and undercutting his ability to ensure quality and consistency in Midstate's DL offerings. She worried that his opposition could undermine a successful and profitable initiative. She wondered what to do.

Helen Chu's case illustrates basic structural challenges facing higher education leaders. How should work be parceled out across roles and units in the institution? Equally important, how will the institution integrate the diverse efforts of individuals, groups, divisions, and departments to ensure quality and alignment with campus mission and goals? Is it better, for example, to centralize or to decentralize distance education at Midstate? And once work is parceled out, how is coordination supposed to happen? Is it a job for the provost's office or something better left to Helen Chu and her DL counterpart? Such questions are central in a structural view of academic leadership (see Table 4.1).

Table 4.1.   A Structural View on Academic Leadership

Metaphor for academic institution	Factory
Images of the academic leader	Institutional architect, analyst, systems designer
Basic leadership task	Divide the work, coordinate the pieces
Leadership logic	Rational analysis
Leadership currency	Clarity
Frame emphasis	Formal roles and relationships
Key leadership assumptions	Specialization increases efficiency
	Clarity and control enhance performance
	Problems result from structural misalignment
Areas of analysis	Rules, roles, policies, procedures, lines of authority, technology, environment

Source: Adapted from Gallos (2006, 2008c).

A structural view looks at colleges and universities as rational entities that can be likened to factories. Like a manufacturing operation, they are designed to transform a variety of inputs into outputs such as educated graduates, journal articles, books, community service, and winning football teams. How can an institution do that in a way that is efficient and effective? That's the job of structural leadership. Someone has to determine the right roles, rules, and arrangements to get all this done. When the structure is wrong, even bright and talented people find it hard to be productive. Take, for example, the case of a professor who arrived one rainy Saturday morning for a weekend class only to find that someone forgot to unlock the building. Fortunately, campus police responded promptly to his call, so that he and his students were drenched but only ten minutes late when they made it into the classroom. But then the professor discovered that the instructional technology wasn't working. After several frustrating minutes trying to set things right, he called tech support only to find that no one answered the phone and that the voicemail box was full. A well-prepared and skilled instructor was frustrated and hampered by routine structural glitches.

In the structural view of academic institutions, college and university leaders play two central roles. They are analysts who carefully study the institution's production processes; and they are institutional architects and systems designers who develop the rules, roles, policies, reporting relationships, and procedures that align efforts with campus goals. When "the characters change but the plot remains the same" (Berg, 1999, p. 116)—and the same undesirable results repeat themselves year after year even though everyone wishes they wouldn't—structure is a likely culprit. The good and bad news about any organizational structure is that it keeps producing what it was designed to produce, even if that is not what anyone wants.

Surprise is a continuing feature of administrative life. Institutional structures need to respond to the uncertainty, but they also contribute to it. Higher education scholar Robert Birnbaum (1988) notes that colleges and universities are loosely coupled, open systems. As open systems, they have permeable boundaries and are vulnerable to the continual pulls and pushes coming from many different directions and audiences. Educational institutions are loosely coupled in the sense that linkages among organizational units and departments "may be infrequent, circumscribed, weak in their mutual effects, unimportant, or slow to respond" (p. 38).

Faculty members, for example, work largely independently of their colleagues, save for occasional attempts at coordination in often chaotic or conflict-filled committees and faculty meetings. Campus advancement officers and student affairs personnel assigned to various schools and units coordinate more closely with their school and unit colleagues than with the central campus leadership designated to direct and oversee those functions. Vertical coordination is also often weakened by large spans of control. A department chair who is responsible for fifty faculty and an additional number of adjunct instructors and staff will find it hard to supervise any of them very closely. A director of residence life may have multiple buildings across a span of campus locations and hundreds of resident assistants and student advisors who operate with only modest oversight. Loose coupling is essential for the autonomy that is typical of campus units and academic work—and vital to an ambiguous mission like the discovery and dissemination of knowledge or the creation of educated and responsible citizens for today's and tomorrow's organizations. There's a reason that everyone on campus often seems to be going off in different directions or crashing into one another—they are. Higher education has evolved an architecture of disconnection. When it's your job to realign things, change them, or pull them together, you can expect to swim upstream. It can be done, but it's rarely quick or easy—and you'll need to know how to read the stream as well as how to swim.

Leaders in any organization, including colleges and universities, inevitably face structural challenges at three levels: (1) structuring

> **Leaders who embrace a structural view . . .**
>
> 1. Structure their own work
>
> 2. Structure their organizations
>
> 3. Structure the change process

their own work; (2) structuring their organization; and (3) structuring the change process. All are challenging, but the likelihood of success is much higher when structure at all three levels is appropriate to the circumstances.

Structuring Your Work

Antonio Machado wrote, "Wayfarer, there is no path. You make the path as you go" (Machado, 1996, pp. 239–240). So it is for academic leaders. When they enter an administrative job, they have to forge a path even as they are trying to figure out where they are, where they and their organizations want to go, and what they must do to get everyone there.

In his classic, *The Effective Executive*, Peter Drucker (2006) wrote that effective leaders do three things well: (1) they manage their time, (2) they focus on results, and (3) they do "first things first" by concentrating on the things that matter. Structuring one's time is a continuing challenge in any administrative job. Leaders cannot do all the things that they would like to do or that others want them to do. Many try—and plunge down a path to exhaustion and failure. Just surviving the early weeks in a new administrative role can be challenging. Hanging in for the long run is even tougher. His experience as a university president led Warren Bennis (1996) to identify an "unconscious conspiracy" of everyone around him to keep him too busy to think or lead. Like a mother bird amid a large brood of open mouths, academic administrators are surrounded by individuals and groups pressing them to give even more. This makes it easy to fill their days fighting fires and reacting to the endless stream of messages, meetings, calls, demands, and projects that comes along. It's a seductive trap, because it's an easy way to feel productive and needed. Administrators get so busy they don't even notice that they've lost track of the big picture and have made little headway on the issues that really matter. Bennis called it his "First Law of Academic Pseudodynamics: routine work drives out nonroutine work and smothers to death all creative planning, all fundamental change in the university" (p. 15).

That's why Drucker's three imperatives—manage your time, focus on results, and first things first—are so critical. Academic leaders who hope to take their organization somewhere need to get control of their schedules, get clear about what's important, and focus on results rather than activity. A first step in getting control of your schedule is getting clear about your most critical priorities in the short, medium, and longer term and identifying the primary outcomes you want to achieve. That lets you regularly line up your priorities against your calendar by asking, What percentage of time is going to what's most important? Where is the rest of the time going? What can I do to get a better alignment? As you achieve clarity about priorities and results, you gain the perspective you need to work in a disciplined, focused way.

Before any meeting goes (or stays) on your calendar, for example, ask which of your priorities it supports and what outcomes it will achieve. If you don't have good answers, drop it—it's probably not worth doing. It's easy in higher education to get seduced by meetings that are interesting and intellectually stimulating but aren't really moving your agenda forward. Still, don't expect perfect alignment between your calendar and your priorities. Predicting the value of meetings is not an exact science, and it's hard to say no to all the people who want a piece of your time. James Lang put it well in describing his first year as head of his school's honors college:

> The most time-consuming part of the job has been that I have become so popular. Everyone wants to have a meeting with me or wants me to attend a meeting: the Academic Council, Faculty Senate, Honors Faculty Council, Student Honors Council, Residential Life, the provost, the associate provost, deans, the Undergraduate Research Committee, faculty members teaching in the program, department chairs and departmental committees. (Lang, 2010)

Clarity about priorities and results does not come quickly or easily, and it is not something you should expect to do on your own. It emerges from asking questions, listening, and engaging in dialogue with your constituents. Even if you feel sure on Day One about where you want to go, it is wise to check your bearings regularly with key stakeholders. Prominent among them are your boss and other superiors. Whoever put you in a job has expectations for how you'll perform it, and you need to know what those are. You will not always agree with your boss, so there will be times when upward influence is critical. But maintaining a productive relationship is vital because you often need things that your boss can provide. If you attend to your boss's agenda and concerns and make his or her life easier, your boss will usually return the favor. As one of our colleagues puts it, "As a faculty member, I get to be a cat; but as an administrator, I have to be a dog—and most times an alpha dog." No academic leader can go very far without bringing people along, and they are much more likely to come along if they understand and see value in going where you want to go.

Structuring Your Organization

At the same time that you work to define purpose and set priorities, it is vital to sort out basic structural elements. Every organization has to answer two fundamental structural questions:

1. The question of *differentiation*: How do we divide up the work?
2. The question of *integration*: How do we coordinate effort once work has been divided?

In studying your academic institution, a good place to begin is with the role system. Who's in what job? What is each of them supposed to be doing? How clear are their job descriptions, role requirements, and criteria for assessment? Who reports to whom? What are the principal lines of communication? The different jobs that people occupy are a basic form of differentiation that provides the advantages of specialization and focus, but always at a price. A basic structural precept is, The more you differentiate, the more you need to invest in integrative devices to pull things together. That is, *unless* you are willing to give different individuals or units ample autonomy and to put heavy reliance on their ability to manage themselves—which is indeed what colleges and universities often do. As you get clearer about who's doing what, you also need to ask how, and how well, all their efforts tie together. What are the integrative mechanisms—rules, procedures, policies, information systems, and so on—that create linkages and provide coherence and reliability? Strong academic leaders keep asking, Is the current structure right? Could it be better? In what ways?

The simplest and most basic integrative device is authority, some of which is built into every administrative role—although never enough. Authority gives you the ability as a boss to give instructions and to make decisions that bind subordinates. It's quick and efficient, and it provides much of the glue that holds groups and organizations together. But authority always has important limits: it works only to the degree that subordinates accept it and choose to cooperate with it. Tenure, academic governance structures, and the collegial culture of the academy magnify those basic limits to authority—and academic leaders are at risk if they overrely on it.

Authority is an asymmetric relationship that works best when bosses know enough to provide helpful guidance and make the right decisions. That is true when they have an information advantage—they know the work and the circumstances well enough to give good directions. Top-down is less effective when subordinates' work requires application of expertise and professional judgment to fluid and unpredictable circumstances. For those times, Drucker (1965) suggests coordination through engagement.

> In making and moving things, partnership with a responsible worker is only the best way to increase productivity. But [the father of Scientific Management Frederick Winslow] Taylor's telling them worked too, and quite well after all. In knowledge and service work, however, partnership with the responsible worker is the only way to improve productivity. Nothing else works at all. (p. 165)

Faculty, in particular, are not always convinced that administrative authority is helpful or worth heeding—and their classic question of "Why do we need all these administrators?" can be interpreted in two ways. One, it's an important structural question about the match between resource allocations and campus priorities. Surplus administrators add costs and smother efficiency. The growing scale and increasingly complex mission of colleges and universities requires additional coordination in some form, but more administrators is not always the best answer. Two, the question gets to the fundamental issues of faculty mistrust of administrative authority (Cohen, 1996) and of how academic leaders can

build influence and credibility with this important campus con-
stituency. Judith Block McLaughlin sees it this way:

> [Do] administrators have authority over faculty? Obvi-
> ously many professors don't see things this way! Rather,
> administrators have to prove their usefulness, to make
> the case for their being needed, or they are viewed as
> entirely illegitimate. Academic administrators largely
> operate with the tacit consent of the faculty and have
> little power over them other than through the occa-
> sional use of rewards. (McLaughlin, 2010)

Administrative authority is most likely to be seen as useful
when it sets broad parameters and manages administrative details
that faculty don't need or want to do themselves, so long as it does
not get in the way of their work.

> Hierarchy is efficient for setting aspirations, making
> decisions, assigning tasks, allocating resources, manag-
> ing people who cannot direct themselves, and holding
> people accountable. Even in the 21st century, we need
> hierarchy to put boundaries around individuals and
> teams. Management must ensure that workers direct
> and organize their own work so that it furthers the inter-
> ests of the shareholders, not just their personal interests.
> (Bryan & Joyce, 2007, p. 25)

So provosts, deans, department heads, and other academic affairs
professionals need to oversee administrative support, set teaching
loads and schedules, assign classrooms, coordinate technology support, and attend to larger campus and unit issues and priorities; but
typically they lack the information and expertise to instruct professors on how or what to teach or on what research to pursue. Therein
rests the structural origin of the weak authority system that is a

distinctive feature of colleges and universities—and an explanation for why attempts to overlay corporate management systems on academic governance fail (Birnbaum, 2001). Outsiders often see this as a puzzling indication of poor management. They wonder how you can run organizations when people don't have to follow orders and you can't easily fire them if they don't. But academic institutions have to rely heavily on the expertise and judgment of highly trained, independent professionals to meet their core mission. The terminal degree looms so high as an academic qualification because it is a proxy for specialized knowledge, professional judgment, unique capabilities, and skill. Colleges and universities are designed, with variations across institutions, to protect the autonomy and the influence of individual faculty members. Both tend to be higher at research universities than at teaching institutions because research is even less amenable to hierarchical control. Managing faculty is akin to leading creative talent[1]—or herding cats. Success rests in structuring a work environment that supports and rewards faculty for what they do best.

At the same time, teaching and research aren't the only work done in higher education. That adds complexity to an institution's structural mix. Many administrative and support jobs are more amenable to routine and hierarchy, and they operate better with more top-down coordination and control than professors are used to. Faculty-staff friction on campus is often fueled by these structural differences. Faculty can see staff as unduly constrained and bureaucratic. Staff often wonder why they have to track their hours and vacation days when faculty seem to come and go as they please.

The limits and contextual constraints on authority make it all the more important that academic administrators use what they have as judiciously and with as much effect as possible. Structurally, they do this by focusing on two primary tasks: (1) they work on getting the right structure in place so as to maximize support and minimize barriers to the work that must be done; and (2) they create structures that pull things together efficiently and effectively. Strong academic leaders recognize that structures change and evolve as people and organizations do, and they are willing to revise the structure when necessary.

Getting Structure Right

Many of the problems that leaders face call for structural responses. Sometimes those solutions are straightforward, as in a case that revolved around nudes and elementary school students. The setting was a college that housed its music and art departments in the same building. It happened one year that the annual exhibition of graduating seniors' art coincided with a concert hosted by the music department for a large group of elementary school students. As those students, accompanied by teachers and parents, proceeded to the auditorium, they noticed the many examples of student art on the walls. Some parents and teachers were shocked to note that the exhibit included paintings and photos of nudes, some in suggestive poses. A firestorm ensued, swirling around classic issues of institutional image, town/gown relations, and academic freedom. It is one of many examples of campus controversies that are easier to avoid with structural fixes in advance than to resolve once the flames of outrage burn hot. Modest coordination between the art and music departments could have alerted administrators of the potential problem. Once aware, they could have found fixes. They might have shielded the young students by rescheduling the exhibit or their visit or by judiciously positioning the art so as to provide a nude-free path to the auditorium.

Many challenges are harder. They require an awareness of organizational design principles and structural options (see, for example, Galbraith, 2002). They also demand the ability to think systemically: What are our goals? How can we best organize to accomplish them? What are the trade-offs in choosing among structural options? What are the possible intended and unintended consequences of our structural choices, particularly over time? Can we think multiple moves ahead on the chessboard? The willingness to experiment in a spirit of continuous improvement also helps. We examine a classic structural issue that reveals the kind of thinking necessary.

Pulling Things Together

A recurring structural challenge is that academic units and sub-units often become insular silos that don't play very well with each other or anyone else. Consider a case where a campus had an information technology department that reported to the vice president for business affairs and an academic technology unit that reported through the provost's office. The two units never worked well together and maintained two completely separate computer systems. The result was high costs, duplication of effort, outmoded systems, and chronic user complaints about unmet needs and poor customer service. If you were asked to study the issue and determine what the campus can do to solve it, what would you do?

Well, why not just merge the competing fiefdoms into one unit, perhaps under a new technology "czar" who is assigned to knock heads if necessary to get the two units to respond to one another and to their users? It's a straightforward structural solution that's relatively easy to implement and aligns with conventional wisdom. It might even work, particularly if the long-range goal is integrating the separate systems. But putting both groups under the same boss doesn't guarantee that they'll work together.

One danger is that the "czar" strategy relies on hierarchy to solve a problem that might originate elsewhere. When you ask why the denizens of each silo aren't responding to each other or to users, you're likely to discover that they're doing their job as they understand it about as well as they know how. If know-how is the issue, they may need training they haven't received. Or maybe the original problem emanates from too much hierarchy: employees in each unit may have fallen into the common structural trap of looking up, not out—they're less focused on cross-departmental collaboration or user concerns than on signals from their respective bosses about what they're supposed to be doing and how they're being judged. The boss in either unit might dispute this, saying, "I've told them we're here to find solutions that best serve our customers." But they won't "get it" unless the boss goes beyond platitudes and creates structures, incentives, and reward systems to channel efforts in desired directions.

What kind of structures? The options for improving lateral coordination include informal processes, electronic coordination, formal groups, and integrative roles. Informal options—spontaneous efforts to build linkages—are often the cheapest and easiest. In the case at hand, such efforts aren't happening or aren't working. But why? A first question is what staff believe their jobs are and what they're being rewarded for. What gets measured and how are staff evaluated? Are there measures of customer service or satisfaction? Rewards or recognition for working across silos? Is there a practice of rotating staff between the two departments? How often are staff from the two units brought together in interdepartmental events? Do the structures of the two units mirror one another so that there are natural linkages among people who do parallel customer service work? Could there be common measures of customer service for both groups? There may be relatively simple ways to make it easier and more rewarding for both units to engage in spontaneous coordination activities.

Another option is electronic coordination, which could make it easier for the two units to communicate and to access shared information. After all, technology is a common strength. Would it be helpful to have a shared database that shows the expertise of the staff in the two departments? A listing of campus problems and requests to each unit? Measures of customer satisfaction for both departments? A third structural option is the creation of formal groups or task forces. Should there be cross-functional teams to study and develop recommendations for better teamwork, customer service, or shared systems planning? A fourth possibility is designating "integrators"—individuals whose job is to manage linkages across organizational units and boundaries. Should someone be assigned to monitor all customer service or to be a liaison between the two silos?

A basic structural proposition is, If you reward A while hoping for B, you'll still get A. Remember, structures do what structures are designed to do, whether we want that or not. If you don't provide incentives and clearly defined routes between where people are and where you want them to go, you're likely to be disappointed. But don't make the common mistake of blaming your staff. Instead, work with them to identify the structural barriers and to design something that makes it easier and more rewarding for them to do their jobs. Restructuring should not be a solitary, top-down exercise. But if you're in charge, you need to take initiative to examine and to resolve structural barriers to high performance.

Structuring the Change Process

A university president's signature initiative, an updated common curriculum for undergraduates, seemed promising when it was initially unveiled to great fanfare. A campuswide committee worked for more than a year to develop the innovative, student-friendly proposal. But another year later, the process seemed to have bogged down in endless faculty debate and conflicts among different schools. If it's your job to get the project back on track, where do you begin?

Every administrative job contains routine tasks where the challenge is to keep the trains running on time. Those tasks are vital, and an institution can go downhill quickly if they're not performed well. But leaders rarely find themselves with a mandate to keep things as they are. The world keeps changing, throwing new opportunities and challenges in the path of academic leaders. Sometimes, they might do less harm if they did not try to fix what "ain't broke," but that is not always an option. Leaders are expected to make things better and to stay ahead in a rapidly changing higher education landscape. That is particularly tough whenever it means getting faculty to change. Professors generally like what they're doing and believe that the world needs whatever they do. They typically see lots of room for improvement in the world around them but less often believe it is they who need to change. Traditions of academic freedom, faculty governance, and (for some) tenure insulate them from administrative fiat. So change efforts often require bringing together autonomous players who guard their turf, defend their expertise, and insist on correct process for anything about which they have questions or doubts. Efforts to rush or force the process risk catastrophe.

A key to bringing faculty along is understanding and honoring norms of legitimate process. These vary from institution to institution, depending on history and existing agreements about who has the right to decide what. It's necessary but not sufficient to conform to formal rules and procedures—regulations, policies, faculty by-laws, and anything that faculty have voted in at some time in the past. Failure to do that, even with noncontroversial decisions, is a recipe for problems. In one professional school, the process to change the curriculum for a graduate degree program included a committee that met for several months, input from the various faculty departments, endorsement by the schoolwide curriculum committee, and discussion in the monthly faculty meeting. Somehow, though, no one took a formal vote—or, if there was a vote, it wasn't recorded in the minutes. Two years later, in a context of faculty-administration conflict, a professor noticed the missing vote and raised the cry that the curriculum was invalid because the process violated faculty governance. This raised the possibility that some students who had already graduated might not have "real" degrees. A worried dean got a ruling from the provost that the students' degrees were valid, but then some faculty complained that the administration was running roughshod over faculty control of the curriculum. Following the rules in the first place—and keeping a record of it—would have saved much time, energy, and angst. Simple adherence to established procedures is often all it takes, particularly in areas that faculty don't care very much about. For such matters, they are often content for administrators to make decisions and spare them from more meetings.

The Three P's of Change: Patience, Persistence and Process

But conforming to formal rules, while necessary, is rarely sufficient when an initiative hits faculty where they live—like a new common curriculum or changes in teaching loads. In such cases, success depends on the three P's of change for academic institutions: patience, persistence, and process. *Patience* is vital because the wheels of change rarely move very fast in colleges and universities. If time is really pressing, change agents may face a classic administrative dilemma. Is it better to be on a fast train that might jump the track, or a slow one that may arrive too late to be useful?

Persistence is the vital ally of patience. Few people in an institution will invest unlimited time or energy in promoting or opposing any single initiative, even a big item like the reform of a general education curriculum or the transformation of a campus culture. There are too many other important and interesting things to do. That is a great advantage for tenacious academic leaders. So is attention to the strategic effects of timing in introducing (and reintroducing) choices and proposals. Leaders can capitalize on the fluid participation that characterizes shared governance structures. In a world of many autonomous campus players with diverse interests and unmet needs, there are always issues, feelings, and perspectives that are trolling for opportunities—meetings and other decision arenas where they might be aired and expressed. As Cohen and March (1974) noted in their landmark study of the American college presidency, campus decision making often resembles a "garbage can" (p. 81) into which various problems, solutions, and expectations are dumped. The mix in any single can depends on who gets involved and what problems and solutions they bring with them. Garbage cans can be managed, say Cohen and March, by academic leaders who learn to see the phenomena and pace their organizational design and decision-making processes to take account of the dynamics.

The third P is *process.* It is essential to assess and adhere to faculty expectations of how things should be done. Like it or not, faculty are unforgiving when they perceive authoritarian overreach, violation of legitimate procedures, or processes that lack internal credibility—and savvy academic leaders know that it's not always even an issue of what really happened as much as what faculty think happened.[2] Legitimacy is in the eyes of the beholder, and university administrators are wise to err in the direction of overattention to perceptions of legitimate process. Faculty will often assent, albeit grudgingly, to things they don't particularly like, so long as they feel the process was legitimate. This is not to advocate bureaucracy, but a reminder that the norms of academic culture are strong—and that transparency, dialogue, and attention to process go a long way. In promoting something like a new curriculum, it's vital to ensure that faculty get to voice their views and to feel heard. A wise leader will (1) present the initiative as a proposal that is open to improvement, (2) provide ample time for good and open discussion, (3) modify in response to input, and (4) repeat the previous three steps as needed. The goal is not to satisfy everyone, but to arrive at the point that there is enough support to move forward—either because people believe that the process was legitimate or simply that they're bored and ready to move on to something else.

So, what do you do if the provost asks you to get that common curriculum initiative back on track? Heed the three P's—patience, process, and persistence—and there is good reason for optimism. Patience counsels you not to be discouraged that movement is slow. The issue is too big and too important to rush. Process tells you to focus on structuring a decision process that takes the time necessary to ensure major players are given ample opportunity to influence the decision—they may or may not use that opportunity, but it's vital that they know they can. Third, persist. You may sometimes feel like Sisyphus, pushing a boulder uphill by day only to see it roll back down by night. But over time, you'll learn what adjustments have to be made to make the initiative broadly acceptable—and better. You'll gradually attract support and, eventually, outlast or wear down many of the critics—and the cynics will find other garbage cans for their pet peeves. The innovative, student-friendly curriculum may take time and even be a little worse for wear when all is said and done. But in the end the president's signature initiative will come to fruition. If not, you'll be able to explain to her why it was a mistake in the first place.

Summary

The architecture of disconnection in higher education makes colleges and universities difficult to manage and change. Inertia is high and authority is severely constrained by norms of autonomy and shared governance. This makes it all the more important that leaders understand structure, attend to it, and get it right wherever possible. They need to attend to three interconnected levels of structure: (1) structuring their own time; (2) managing the structure of their unit or organization; and (3) structuring the change process to enhance the likelihood that the organization can adapt to a demanding, fast-changing environment. In structuring change initiatives, it is vital to honor the three P's of academic change: patience, persistence, and process.

Notes

1. Creating environments to foster creativity requires understanding something about the creative process. Suggested resources for those new to the issues include Edwards (2008), Csikszentmihalyi (1996), and Gardner (1993, 1997).

2. The symbolic frame as outlined by Bolman and Deal (2008b, Chapters Twelve to Fourteen) is helpful in understanding the power of meaning systems and why what actually happens may be less important than what key constituents believe did.

5

Respecting and Managing Differences

Leader as Compassionate Politician

Donald Quixote charged into the presidency of a research university with an aggressive vision of "transformation" to vault the institution forward in both national reputation and service to its local community. "Right now, at this university," President Quixote announced to the campus, "campus transformation is the one thing worthy of our passion."

Soon after Quixote's arrival, the transformation was launched with a series of workshops guided by outside consultants. The goal was to acquaint faculty and staff with the new vision and to fire their desire to get on "the rocket to greatness." Staff, especially those in lower-level positions, loved the workshops and relished the opportunity to get involved in shaping the university's direction—a role historically reserved for faculty and campus leaders. Many faculty and senior-level administrators, on the other hand, were skeptical and busy. The workshops and meetings felt like one more imposition atop already heavy workloads.

Noting that faculty were staying on the sidelines, President Quixote pressured deans to get their professors to attend workshops and to participate in the growing number of transformation activities on campus. Those included culture change dialogues, breakthrough projects (new initiatives to follow "energy streams" generated during the workshops), unit-specific transformation opportunities, expanded outreach centers, town-gown partnerships, and the President's Shared Leadership Council (approximately 150 people chosen from across units and ranks to advance the transformation). A few deans balked. Most did their best. All felt squeezed between presidential expectations and faculty norms of autonomy.

As pressures mounted for deans to get everyone "on the rocket," stories swirled around campus about the consequences for those who couldn't or wouldn't. Some deans resigned. Others were replaced. Junior faculty enlisted in significant numbers—partly because the campus rumor mill told them that workshop attendance and "loyalty to Don" were necessary, if not sufficient, for promotion and tenure. Of the faculty who attended, some bought into the vision. Many concluded the process was flawed and the workshops intellectual hokum, but most stopped short of saying anything publicly critical about the president's change initiative.

Over time, the transformation efforts produced fear and loathing on a deeply split campus and exacerbated historical tensions among faculty, staff, and administration. The president's supporters saw possibilities for dramatic improvement and national acclaim. Much of the faculty saw misguided efforts that threatened academic freedom and wasted precious time and scarce resources. The rocket crash-landed a few years into the transformation when President Quixote was forced out by a series of no-confidence votes.

President Quixote's intentions were admirable: increased clarity about campus mission and direction, empowerment, expanded capacity and motivation across campus, aligned reward systems, and a distinctive university brand and reputation as a recognized leader in higher education. Quixote hoped that his change process would build campus priorities from the ground up based on everyone's ideas, energy, and enthusiasm—and that a culture of optimism and participation would leverage untapped creativity and human potential. The many people involved and the projects generated were expected to produce a host of creative new efforts, programs, and contributions. It was a noble experiment. Early wins might have generated good press, good will, new donors, additional resources, and other opportunities for the campus. That did not happen—and President Quixote left a failed presidency wondering why.

A Political View of Leadership in Higher Education

The script for Donald Quixote's tragedy is a familiar one. It has befallen countless university administrators whose change efforts fail because of their inability to master the political complexities of academic leadership. There are many variations of the old saying that academic politics are so vicious because the stakes are so small. Consult fiction, humor, or the *Chronicle of Higher Education*, and you continually find colleges and universities depicted as intensely political places populated by political amateurs who keep making a mess of things because their interests are so parochial—and their political skills so limited.

One reason faculty and academic administrators play the political game so badly is that they have rarely wanted to learn to play it better. They often view politics with distaste and prefer to view themselves as rational beings with noble intentions—even if they grant that they live in an imperfect world with scarce resources where they must contend with others who seem motivated by self-interest and a lust for power. It is not uncommon for everyone in a department or a school to believe that "I'm okay, but you're only out for yourself." Such shared perceptions typically lock everyone into dismal political prospects.

The political view of academic leadership (Table 5.1) sees colleges and universities as akin to jungles: vibrant ecosystems that house a variety of different species or groups, each with its own specific characteristics, capabilities, interests, needs, and lifestyles. All live in proximity to one another, sometimes peacefully, but often not because scarce resources and conflicting interests make conflict inevitable. Academic leaders, in this view, serve as both advocates and negotiators in the inevitable bargaining over who

Table 5.1.   A Political View of Academic Leadership

Metaphor for academic institution	Jungle
Images of the academic leader	Advocate, negotiator, political strategist
Basic leadership tasks	Bargain, negotiate, build coalitions, set agendas, manage conflict
Leadership logic	Distributive justice
Leadership currency	Empowerment
Frame emphasis	Allocation of power and scarce resources
Key leadership assumptions	Differences are enduring
	Resources are scarce
	Conflict is inevitable
	Key decisions involve who gets what
Areas of analysis	Power, conflict, resources, interests, agendas, alliances

Source: Adapted from Gallos (2006, 2008c).

gets what. As advocates, they need to be credible and persuasive in promoting the interests of their unit or organization, while learning to negotiate with leaders of other organizations or groups whose help or resources they may need.

Colleges and universities *are* highly political institutions, but that is a statement of fact, not an indictment. The challenge for campus leadership is to understand and leverage the political realities that are present in every situation. Writing almost a half century ago, Richard Cyert and James March (1963) rejected the conventional view that organizations are essentially rational entities with unitary goals set at the top. Instead, they argued that organizations are better understood as coalitions composed of individuals and subgroups. In this view, goals and decisions arise from a continual process of bargaining among coalition members. Since the preferences of different participants are always at least partly divergent, decisions can rarely satisfy everyone. A coalition survives if it offers sufficient inducements to keep its key members on board and happy. While chancellor at the University of California-Berkeley, Clark Kerr (2010) acknowledged this in his memorable quip at a faculty meeting that his job amounted to providing "parking for the faculty, sex for the students, and athletics for the alumni."

At a macro level, campuses divide into broad groups like administrators, faculty, staff, students, alumni, and external constituents. Each of those groups may be subdivided in a variety of ways. In a perfect world, different groups would work harmoniously in service to the institution's mission, but that ideal is not easily achieved. Different participants often have different views of what the mission is or should be, different views of which activities or units are more important, and different ideas about how resources should be allocated. Each group makes claims on institutional decision making in the light of its own interests and understandings. The crux of the challenge is that many of an institution's most important decisions involve the allocation of scarce resources: they are decisions about who gets what. Faculty interests in higher salaries, better classrooms and facilities, and research funding, for example, conflict with parents' and students' desires for lower tuition, with board needs for a sensible budget, and with legislators' desires to keep taxes down. Whenever different groups bring divergent values and perspectives to a decision-making opportunity, it is difficult to agree on data, criteria, or analytic frameworks for assessing the relative merits of the different options. Power then becomes the key resource.

Without power, administrators can't lead because no one will follow and they can't get anything done. But power is a complex and fluid phenomenon that is often misunderstood. Like politics, in many people's minds power carries a negative connotation— something that bad people use to ride roughshod over good people. But power is simply the capacity to influence, to make things happen. If you want something to happen but can't do it, you lack power. It is important to understand that power takes many forms. Authority, or position power, is a basic tool for administrators, but it needs to be supplemented with other forms—the power that rests in having information, expertise, control of resources, personal skills, relationships, allies, the capacity to reward, and many others.

Presidents, provosts, and deans are typically seen by subordinates as having a lot of power, as was true of Quixote for much of his presidency. But power can evaporate quickly and unpredictably, and that is exactly what befell him. Quixote's transformation initiative triggered political battles in which he ultimately found himself outgunned. The opposition that gradually increased during his tenure was largely hidden because so many on campus believed that it was dangerous to have open and honest discussions about or to express public criticism of Quixote's initiatives. Disaffected faculty talked and voiced their criticisms mostly among themselves. So Quixote was able to remain optimistic even as the pillars of his presidency were eroding. The denouement was swift and surprising to almost everyone. An administrative white paper that speculated about possible futures for the campus might have drawn little attention in a less volatile context, but it became the spark that set off a firestorm. Anger and distress suddenly exploded across campus. Faculty in one school after another voted no confidence in the president by overwhelming margins. When the news hit the front page of local papers, the president's many supporters in the community were stunned and enraged—and many blamed the faculty for undermining the university's best chance to move to a new level.

A battle that no one really wanted produced tragic consequences. The president resigned under pressure, and the transformation initiatives mostly died. The university's image with external constituents was severely damaged. Campus morale and finances tanked as the institution scrambled to regain its bearings and set a new course—and those on both sides of the Quixote controversy had to learn to trust again. Variations on this tragic tale occur every year at every level in the world of higher education. The question is why so many campuses keep reenacting their own versions of *Macbeth* or *Othello* even while hoping for *All's Well That Ends Well*. This chapter addresses two major sources of such tragedy. First, we revisit the "three P's of change" introduced in Chapter Four. We then examine the politics of change in higher education, exploring how President Quixote's efforts went awry. We conclude by using Bolman and Deal's (2008a) skills of an effective politician to look for ways that President Quixote might have increased his chances of success.

Revisiting the Three P's of Change

In Chapter Four, we argued that persistence, process, and patience are essential elements in successful change. President Quixote was nothing if not persistent. He brought passion and determination to his office. Both are vital elements of effective leadership. But he neglected the other two P's—patience and process. His impatience in pushing the institution to move faster and in prodding constituents to devote themselves totally to the transformation process led to exhaustion, burnout, and growing resentment. Even strong Quixote supporters began to wonder if he understood what it took to deliver on a major research university's mission for teaching, research, and service.

Quixote also deeply misunderstood the importance of legitimate process. His thinking was plausible on the surface: if you want to transcend business as usual and transform the institution, you can't get there using traditional processes. So, with the assistance of consultants whose prior experience was in the corporate world, Quixote tried to circumvent existing lines of campus authority and governance with new structures: transformation workshops, the President's Shared Leadership Council, breakthrough project teams, and others.

The early seeds of disaster were sown at the very first work-shop, attended by Quixote and senior administrators. Some of the deans and vice presidents found the consultants' approach trou-bling. When a few of the more outspoken voiced their concerns, they were told that such critique was neither helpful nor welcome and that they were expected to support the process. A tin ear for dissent became a persistent feature of the transformation process. At subsequent workshops, faculty perceptions that they were under pressure to participate and to say only good things under-mined the legitimacy—and the quality—of the process.

For President Quixote, the workshops were a central vehicle for individual and organizational learning. But, paradoxically, he had not built learning into a process that was supposed to pro-duce it. Instead of trying to understand the sources and meaning of consumer skepticism, Quixote intensified his efforts to push his agenda and sell people on the merits of his process. He found it hard to believe that the workshops were creating more problems than they solved—or to see how the transformation process was overloading the system. The consultants' inexperience in work-ing with universities compounded the problems. The workshops constituted temporary structural additions that redefined existing roles, power arrangements, resource allocation systems, and his-torical governance relationships. Faculty, for example, were cast as the students of workshop instructors who lacked relevant infor-mation and terminal degrees and whose expertise was distrusted. Staff members chaired academic policy committees. Workshops espoused openness but discouraged normal features of academic discourse. Questioning and open debate, the cornerstones of uni-versity culture, became signs of disloyalty—and indications of the need for additional workshops and remedial coaching.

While many faculty avoided involvement in the transforma-tion activities, the majority of administrators and staff partici-pated in them. The result was that faculty were underrepresented in the process. In one case, a breakthrough team of staff, students, midlevel administrators, and a few younger faculty developed a creative proposal for revising the promotion and tenure (P&T) system. The initiative landed with a resounding and predictable thud at a meeting of the faculty senate. Members of the team were disappointed that the senate was so arrogant and closed to new ideas, while faculty across the campus were dumbfounded that people with no P&T experience would presume to know how to make it better. In neglecting to ensure that the change process was broadly seen as legitimate, President Quixote inadvertently triggered unproductive conflict, plummeting morale, and resistance to the entire process.

Political Skills for Academic Leadership

Sophisticated leaders use four key political skills: (1) setting agendas, (2) mapping the political terrain, (3) networking and building coalitions, and (4) bargaining and negotiating (Bolman & Deal, 2008b; Gallos, 2008c). Had President Quixote consistently employed these skills in his leadership efforts, the chances for success would have improved greatly.

> **Leaders who embrace a political view . . .**
>
> 1. Set agendas
> 2. Map the political terrain
> 3. Network and build coalitions
> 4. Bargain and negotiate

Setting Agendas

In reflecting on his experience as president of the University of Cincinnati, Warren Bennis (1989) arrived at a deceptively simple insight. "It struck me that I was most effective when I knew what

I wanted" (p. 20). President Quixote knew that he wanted transformation, but his approach lacked other critical elements of successful change. Organizational change expert John Kotter (1988) found that effective leaders develop a well-defined change agenda that includes (1) a clear vision that balances the long-term interests of key constituents and (2) a detailed strategy for achieving the vision that takes account of competing internal and external forces. Quixote had a vision for national prominence. But without focus, strategic direction, and a politically viable plan, a vision remains an illusion.

President Quixote got off to a strong start in his early months. He impressed constituents on and off the campus with his energy, determination, and public commitments to vault the university to new levels of attainment and reputation. He wanted to involve a broad range of constituents. Faculty, staff, students, and community were excited by the prospect of working together to chart the university's future. But when the change process itself became the agenda, Quixote's efforts broke down. With no clear parameters identifying a general direction for the change or any institutional constraints or priorities, every issue and aspect of campus life and work became fair game for change—all at the same time. Projects grew and multiplied. Study after study was launched. More and more meetings and presentations to campus leadership were added to sort proposals and to support individual initiatives. Quixote saw dynamic engagement. The system felt overload. Chaos in manageable doses is invigorating. A steady diet is no way to run a university.

Effective change agendas attend to issues of pacing, strategic priorities, constituent needs, and institutional limitations. They also appreciate the value of diversity and plan for a world of enduring differences. The first signs of trouble for President Quixote came with the early workshops that split the audience into supporters and skeptics. The doubters saw the consultants as ill prepared and condescending in response to their concerns—and oblivious to the role that disagreement and debate play in campus discourse. Quixote cast the doubters as an impediment to campus progress—an inevitable yet annoying by-product of ambitious change. As word spread that loyalty was prized and skeptics were shunned, underground opposition grew and many early supporters became disenchanted. The relatively few administrators who were more openly critical of the process were relieved of their positions. Within two years most of the deans and senior administrators had left, with or without a push from the president. Quixote reasoned he couldn't move forward without a united leadership team, but a continuous stream of new deans and senior administrators undermined campus continuity and exacerbated system overload and discontent.

Firing dissenters is a key step in many a corporate change process (Kotter & Cohen, 2002), but it is highly problematic in higher education because of the salience of certain individuals and groups—particularly among the faculty—whose combination of talent, reputation, networks, and tenure makes them quasi-independent power centers. Many on campus grew increasingly troubled by mixed messages: a process that had originally been billed as participative and energizing appeared increasingly coercive and intolerant. Rumors spread that the president's spies were scanning e-mails and taking notes in meetings to report about opposition.

Organizational scholar Jeffrey Pfeffer (1992) underscores the importance of "sensitivity" as a key political attribute. Effective academic leaders know how their stakeholders think and what they care about so that campus agendas, resource allocations, and processes can respond to those concerns.

Mapping the Political Terrain

From a political perspective, a central challenge in making change stick is mobilizing enough power to move your initiative forward. Administrators have authority over their subordinates but often overestimate how far that authority will carry them, particularly in the face of opposition from powerful individuals or constituents with strong reputations and power bases. Agendas move forward when leaders take a step back, assess the political environment, and get a feel for the full lay of the landscape and how to use it to their advantage. Three questions help to map the political terrain for any given issue:

1. *Who are the players?* (Which groups or individuals are most likely to try to influence the outcomes of a particular process or decision?)

2. *What are the interests of each player?* (What's at stake for each player and what does each player want? In simplest terms, this comes down to who is likely to be for or against the change we seek.)

3. *How much power is each player likely to wield?* (This requires assessing the potential power of any given player, the likelihood that a given player will use that power on the issue at hand, and the power of each player's webs of influence.)

These questions are rarely easy to answer. Political situations are fluid: players come and go, interests shift in response to events, and power can wax or wane over time. It takes a careful eye and savvy detective work to collect and assess available clues—and continued vigilance to notice shifts in the political winds. Quixote operated as if, implicitly, the political landscape looked like the map in Figure 5.1. It depicts almost all the players, including those with the most power, as highly supportive of his goals. The exception is the faculty, who are shown in an isolated, low-power position. That is how the situation looked to most observers, even many opponents, for much of Quixote's tenure. Growing faculty discontent bubbled quietly beneath the surface for lack of overt and orchestrated opposition—and for fear of retribution. What Quixote and his allies did not anticipate was that the map could shift toward the picture in Figure 5.2, which only

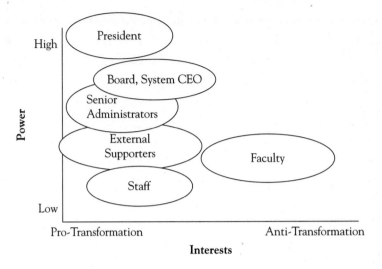

Figure 5.1   President Quixote's Implicit Map.

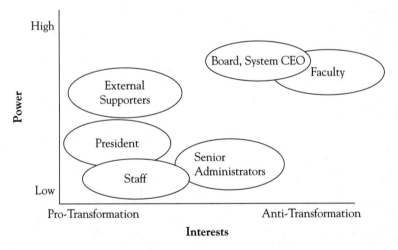

Figure 5.2   Map of the Denouement.

occurred near the end of Quixote's tenure. The series of no-confidence votes made faculty sentiment a powerful force that caused the university system's chancellor and then the board to decide that Quixote was no longer a viable leader. If President Quixote and his allies had recognized the potential power in faculty as an increasingly restless sleeping giant, they could have spent more time building linkages, courting respected faculty thought leaders, and responding to faculty concerns. The explosion that blew apart Quixote's presidency could have been averted.

Networking and Building Coalitions

In a study of senior executives, John Kotter (1982) found that networking was a key determinant of leadership effectiveness. The higher your position, the more people there are who can help or hinder you in doing your job. Kotter found that effective managers spent more time at the front end, building relationships with key constituents so that the managers had an easier time getting help when they needed it. Quixote was effective in building credibility with his boss and board and with prominent members of the community. He also had strong support among the nonacademic staff, who felt more valued and involved in campus decision making. That was a formidable coalition as long as the faculty were reasonably quiescent. But, he misjudged or underestimated the potential for faculty opposition to undermine his presidency as well as his change initiative.

A key error was failing to adapt his strategy to the realities on the ground. The workshops were intended as the primary vehicle for building campus support, but there were signs from early on that they were alienating more professors than they enlisted. Networking is all about relationships, and a key part of its value is the opportunity to listen to people, understand what they care about, and find ways to respond to their interests. Instead, Quixote discounted resistance, convinced that he was on the right track and would eventually attract the support he needed. When he met with the faculties of various schools, he often made things worse. In more than one case, when he hoped to energize faculty with the challenge "You can do much more," he instead deflated and alienated them. Faculty got the impression that he didn't understand their world, didn't care about their reality, and had little respect for them or their work.

Quixote also failed to recognize that coalition building for complex projects often requires some *horse trading*: offering desired gains irrelevant to the project itself in return for constituent support of it (Kanter, 1983). People will coalesce around a public agenda for a wide variety of private reasons. Effective leaders use this reality to their advantage and seek to meet important constituent needs in exchange for their support. Early in the transformation process, for example, Quixote missed a critical opportunity with faculty in his college of engineering.

The engineering dean was a long-term veteran who had built the school from a backwater to a research powerhouse. He was as arrogant as he was brilliant and internationally renowned, and not many of his faculty were in love with his ego or his leadership style. The dean became one of Quixote's earliest and most vocal opponents, writing biting public screeds criticizing the transformation process. Quixote concluded the dean had to go. Without consulting or warning the engineering faculty, the president announced that the dean was being relieved of his duties and that Quixote was naming an interim. A faculty that had been ambivalent at best about their dean's leadership was instantly converted into a loyal and united front by what they viewed as an attack on their college. They passed a unanimous resolution criticizing the president and urging the dean's reinstatement. Quixote concluded that he needed to hang tough. But the cost was high. He was dogged for the rest of his presidency by an angry and resistant engineering faculty. That faculty produced the first no-confidence vote against the president.

It was an avoidable tragedy. If we assume that Quixote's initial impulse—to get rid of the engineering dean—was correct, there is little doubt it could have been achieved at a significantly lower cost. Ideally, the president would have patiently negotiated with the dean and consulted with members of the engineering faculty. Those conversations would have alerted Quixote to the dangers in removing the dean, and they could have been used to build better understanding and support for the transformation process.

He and the dean might have reached a mutually agreeable deal whereby the dean would quietly resign. Failing that, Quixote might have found ways to engage the engineering faculty in a dialogue that could have identified common interests, enabled them to see how his plan dovetailed with their long-term interests in a school leadership change, and garnered enough support to move forward. Instead, Quixote's actions seemed petulant and impetuous, sending shock waves across the campus.

The faculty vote of no-confidence is a distinctive and often devastating feature of colleges and university governance. Once no-confidence missiles rained down on him from multiple faculties, Quixote's position quickly became untenable, providing further evidence for the first law of higher education leadership: *If you lose the faculty, you lose.*

Building and maintaining wide networks of relationships is the essence of political leadership, and four simple rules can guide the political newcomer.

Rule 1 says that *there are no permanent friends and no permanent enemies in a political world*: opponents today can be partners tomorrow. Effective academic leaders don't hold grudges, take names, or see opposition as personal—no matter how personal the criticism may sound. They keep their eyes focused on the issues and the prize of advancing their institutions and programs. Quixote demonized dissenters in hope of isolating resistance. His strategy backfired.

Rule 2 dates back to the sixth century BCE and Chinese military strategist Sun-Tzu: *Keep your friends close and your enemies closer.* This sounds easier than it is. The political world of the university is rough and tumble, and the daily fray is wearing. It's tempting to manage the strain by spending time with those who think and feel like us—and who will work with us to advance our goals and projects. But ignoring opposition doesn't make it go away. Like Quixote, we won't learn from it—or about it—until it is too late.

Rule 3 comes from leadership guru Ronald Heifetz: *Court the uncommitted.* Allies and opponents are important, but don't forget the silent majority in the middle. Change affects them too, and their support—or opposition—can make all the difference. They may have no substantive stake in your initiative, but they do have a stake in the comfort, stability, and security of the status quo. They have seen change agents come and go, and they know that your initiative will disrupt their lives and make their futures uncertain. You want to be sure that this general uneasiness doesn't evolve into a move to push you aside (Heifetz & Linsky, 2008). The wave of no-confidence votes became possible only after Quixote had lost the uncommitted.

The late Thomas P. "Tip" O'Neill, former Speaker of the U.S. House of Representatives, was a master politician. For O'Neill, political skills were all about enjoying and connecting with people. The things we do every day to build and maintain positive relationships expand our political capital. "Politics always was about values combined with instincts," said O'Neill. "Put those together and you get a rule" (O'Neill & Hymel, 1994, p. xi). O'Neill's famous dictum—All politics is local—is Rule 4 for the compassionate campus politician. Every interaction is an opportunity to leave a positive impression, connect with another around common interests, show respect, and learn something about someone and what he or she holds dear. O'Neill passed along a wealth of specific suggestions for how to make sure that happens: avoid bunk, remember names, don't forget the people who got you where you are, keep speeches short, memorize poetry (and use it to elevate issues), keep your word ("In politics, your word is everything")— and never get introduced to a crowd at a sporting event (p. 125).[1]

Actions that communicated genuine care, interest, respect, and appreciation—actions, not just words—could have made a major difference for President Quixote.

Bargaining and Negotiating

Academic leaders continually find themselves engaged in a complex, multiplayer game on a field crowded with other skilled players. Some are natural allies, others are likely opponents, and still others could go either way depending on the issue and the circumstances. Bargaining and negotiation are an essential part of working under those circumstances. The essence of negotiation is deal making—building agreements that enable two or more parties to unite around a particular project or initiative. Those agreements are rarely perfect, but they don't need to be. They only need to be good enough that the parties find it profitable to work together. It is important to tend to potential opponents in the deal-making process. Whenever opponents might derail your initiative, it's worth asking how you can modify your package to make it more attractive or less likely to wake sleeping dogs. The adage that *perfect is the enemy of good* is particularly true in political negotiations, where the right package is always imperfect but is the best deal you can actually implement.

President Quixote and his constituents all agreed that the university could be much better than it was, and there was almost universal support for broad goals like academic excellence, national prominence, and creating a community of learners. That consensus allowed Quixote plenty of negotiating room for a win-win understanding with the faculty. Quixote's big error was that he was open to negotiation on the *what*, but not the *how*. The what—the vision of the future and the initiatives to achieve the vision—emerged from a broadly participative process and evoked relatively little controversy. But the how—a change process that purported to be participative but felt closed, top-down, coercive, and intellectually dishonest to many—seemed to violate fundamental values of the academy.

Summary

"Politics," conclude Bolman and Deal (2008b), "is the realistic process of making decisions and allocating resources in a context of scarcity and divergent interests. This view puts politics at the heart of decision-making" (p. 190). Nowhere is this truer than in higher education, with its unique combination of diverse mission, divergent interests, competing theologies, multiple power centers, weak authority, distinct discipline-based cultures, and scarce resources. It is no accident that both film and fiction depict colleges and universities as places of intense political jockeying, often over ill-defined issues and seemingly trivial stakes.

Higher education leaders work in a political world. Success requires learning how to navigate it successfully. To do this, academic administrators first need to confront whatever distaste for politics and ambivalence about power they may have acquired. This does not mean they should lay aside ethics and principles—in fact they should cling even more tightly to their values and vision for higher education. But achieving noble values and principles in a highly political context requires political sophistication, strong skills, empowerment, and personal courage.

None of us wants to experience the kind of tragedy that befell President Donald Quixote. His story underscores the importance of the three P's of change: persistence, process, and patience. It also provides important object lessons about vital strategies, insights, and skills for everyday progress and for managing institutional change. Academic leaders who know how to develop clear and viable agendas, map the political terrain, build strong networks and relationships with key constituents, and negotiate with both allies and opponents will go far.

Note

1. Those seeking to develop their political skills can learn from studying two skilled politicians: Tip O'Neill and Lyndon Johnson. O'Neill (with Novak), 1997; O'Neill and Hymel (1994); and Caro (1990, 1991, 2003) are filled with insights and strategies.

6

Fostering a Caring and Productive Campus

Leader as Servant, Catalyst, and Coach

Christina Hernandez knew the campus priorities: increase enrollments, strengthen academic programs, and enhance community outreach. More important, she believed in them. North Bridgewood State University had launched a new five-year plan the year before she came, and Christina had been recruited as dean to advance the College of Arts and Sciences. She was proud to serve a campus that educated so many first-generation college students from Bridgewood's blue-collar community. But five months into the job, Christina's optimism was eroding. "Campus enhancement and growth?" she mused. "On most days, it's hard to keep the ship afloat and moving in any direction."

Hernandez knew the job would be tough when she accepted it. She was the fifth Arts and Sciences dean in eight years, following a history of health problems, interim appointments, and dubious hires among her predecessors. The revolving door of leadership had contributed to lingering questions about the college's quality and responsiveness. It also helped explain why her faculty and staff were so apprehensive about their new dean and why they seemed most energized when complaining about a history of unfair attacks on the school. Some feared that Hernandez would overload them with new responsibilities. Others worried that their skills were insufficient to meet new challenges. Performance evaluation practices had been largely pro forma. The arrival of a new dean, coupled with campus efforts to link rewards to performance, were making even strong performers nervous. Griping in the hallways had already begun.

"Everyone in this school needs reassurance, resources, and recognition," Hernandez concluded. She felt that she was getting a handle on the situation until the scenario took a turn for the worse with major state funding cuts. The university instituted an early retirement program and asked deans to encourage individuals to apply—revenue projections would work only if enough took the buyout. But there was risk of losing valuable people, and no guarantee that deans would be able to refill vacant positions.

Talented individuals with options elsewhere grabbed the package and looked for new jobs, fueling competitive jealousy. Others agreed to full retirement. Programs and offices took differential hits: some lost no one, others were decimated. Everyone scrambled to regroup. Retirement parties and good-bye lunches became the norm. Collective feelings of loss and confusion were palpable. Goals for school enhancement were still there, along with lingering critiques of the unit. The mandate from above was "Do more with less." Tangible progress and program improvements were the stated criteria for future funding allocations.

Faculty and staff streamed through Hernandez's office—venting, mourning, complaining, celebrating, negotiating. Many wanted answers and resources that she didn't have. No one said it directly, but she knew many blamed her for not making things better. She was, after all, The Dean. Uncertainty abounded and it complicated planning. Faculty and staff pressured Hernandez to begin hiring immediately. She wanted to but couldn't, which fueled collective angst. Everyone, including Hernandez, believed that pressures from above to advance strategic goals were unreasonable under the circumstances. Hernandez and other deans tried without success to persuade the president to allow more slack, but the president had pressures of her own. Christina's boss, the provost, coldly advised her to hunker down and deliver on the goals.

Christina Hernandez faces a difficult situation, but one not unusual in higher education. Details may change, but academic managers often face analogous challenges and demands, along with the intense personal and emotional responses they trigger. If you're in Hernandez's seat, you have been asked to take a unit forward and make strategic progress at a time of financial retrenchment. Addressing tough financial realities while advancing the organization will require change, and change brings loss and a range of human emotions (Gallos, 2007; Marris, 1986). Some of those emotions are positive: change can be exciting and energizing to individuals and systems. Many are not. Those who retire face disruption in everything from where and how to spend their days to how they will express important needs and values. Those who stay will lose long-term colleagues as well as established work patterns and norms. Skill and knowledge for a host of jobs will be gone, as will personal files, informal information networks, and institutional memory that facilitated work. Increased stress, bigger workloads, confusion, and insecurity face those left behind—as do potential health concerns. A study in Finland, for example, found that workers who survived massive staff cutbacks were five times more likely to die from heart disease or stroke in the three to five years after the cuts than employees whose workplaces were not downsized ("Job cuts hurt," 2004). A growing body of research supports the findings (Lau, 2010). No question about it: Christina Hernandez and her school are in for a tough time.

In responding to the present, Hernandez must also deal with the past. Her school's history of revolving-door leadership and external censure have produced accumulated pain and emotional turmoil that play into people's reactions and resilience in the face of more change. While every new leader dreams of a clean slate and unlimited opportunities, reality is rarely so kind. Leaders inherit a history—often one with long-buried land mines. Pent-up frustrations and disappointments may fade from institutional consciousness, but they still lie buried, along with memories of ineffective handling of the anguish. New pain rekindles old feelings. But, ready or not, academic administrators have to cope with reality as they find it—and help others navigate it successfully.

Hernandez's situation is daunting, but not hopeless. It is vain to expect quick fixes, but steady improvement is possible for leaders who bring an ethic of care and the skills to respond compassionately to the human side of organizational life. Enlightened leaders believe in the potential for human development, and they focus on creating a supportive and liberating work environment that fosters learning and growth. Their confidence in human capacity to adapt to change—no matter how daunting—fuels hope and progress.

The issues that Dean Hernandez and her school face lie at the heart of a human resource view of academic leadership which focuses on the symbiotic relationship between people and organizations. (See Table 6.1.) Organizations and people need each other. But aligning human and institutional needs is never easy, and handling people problems regularly ranks high on the list of leaders' toughest challenges.

Human resource leaders need strategies for responding to constituents' individual and collective needs and for building a work environment with characteristics akin to those found in a caring and supportive extended family. To do this work well, leaders need the combined skills of a servant, catalyst, and coach. The servant's role is to understand and respond to the best interests of both people and the institution, seeking ways to bring them into a more harmonious alignment. The work of the catalyst is empowerment—helping people get the information, resources, and leeway that they need. The coach teaches, mentors, and provides developmental opportunities to sharpen skills and understandings. The payoff, research tells us, is higher levels of employee motivation, satisfaction, and productivity (Bolman & Deal, 2008b; Pfeffer, 2007).

Table 6.1.   A Human Resource View of Academic Leadership

Metaphor for academic institution	Extended family
Images of the academic leader	Servant, catalyst, coach
Basic leadership task	Facilitate the alignment between individual and organizational needs
Leadership logic	Attending to people
Leadership currency	Care
Frame emphasis	Satisfaction, motivation, productivity, empowerment, skills development
Key leadership assumptions	Institutions and individuals need each other
	Individual-organizational alignment benefits both sides
	Productive relationships are vital to organizational health
	Learning is central to productivity and change
Areas of analysis	Needs, skills, relationships, "fit"

Source: Adapted from Gallos (2006, 2008c).

Human Resource Leadership

The bedrock of effective human resource leadership is a capacity to encourage people to bring their best talents and selves to their work. Effective leaders do this in several ways. First, they promote openness and transparency. They understand that their constituents want a leader they can trust, especially when times are tough and emotions are raw. People want to believe that their leader is telling the truth—bad news as well as good. Second, they empower by providing constituents the resources and space they need to make the best use of their talent and energy. Trust and confidence are easier to squander than to develop. Third, leaders help ensure that groups and committees function as effective teams. Fourth, they provide support, coaching, and care for their constituents. Finally, they recognize that a vital part of developing the fit between people and workplace is hiring the right people in the first place.

Leaders who embrace a human resource view build liberating campus environments through . . .

1. Open communication

2. Empowerment

3. Effective teams for collective action

4. Support, coaching, and care

5. Hiring the right people

Open Communication

The endless daily e-mails, phone calls, and meetings that threaten to overwhelm Dean Hernandez exemplify a dilemma for all campus leaders. Sitting at the intersection of multiple information flows, Hernandez can see a bigger picture because she has access to information that many of her constituents don't. But her workload keeps her so busy that it's hard to find time to figure out what to communicate to whom. If she forwards everything to everyone, people will soon tune out. But if she doesn't tell people what they want to know, anxiety and mistrust will mushroom. Information vacuums beg to be filled; and they will be, often with rumor and speculation based on fear, fantasy, misinformation, or someone else's agenda.

A perennially salient example of what people want to know is the true fiscal state of their unit—information that administrators often choose to withhold or obfuscate. Sometimes they withhold in hope of protecting their options. The shifting sands of higher education funding make even a small cushion comforting— and a cushion may be easier to preserve if no one knows about it. Other times administrators figure that constituents can't criticize what they don't know, including how much discretion the leader really has. Or they may simply feel it's better to spare people the distress of knowing how tough things are. But withholding the numbers typically generates more problems than it solves. Constituents rightly suspect that they're not getting the whole story, and they often assume that the administration is secretly hoarding resources. All this exacerbates feelings among faculty and staff that they are powerless while the administrators are in control of valuable resources. They then logically conclude that the administrators, and not they, are responsible for the overall health and success of the unit. How responsible can you feel if you don't really know what's happening and don't feel you can have an impact? Academic leaders do well to follow Mark Twain's advice: "When in doubt, tell the truth." As dean of Harvard's Faculty of Arts and Sciences, Henry Rosovsky (1980) sent a detailed annual budget letter to all faculty. He saw this as an important expression of his leadership accountability. It had the added benefit, he noted, of increasing sympathy for a beleaguered dean, since even at Harvard the financial news was usually worse than faculty expected.

The equally important flip side of transparency is listening and learning from others. Crowded calendars put a premium on efficiency and encourage focus on the issues that you're already aware of. If constituents get the message that you don't listen or don't care about things that are important to them, they will stop trying to communicate with you. At first, that might seem like a godsend—you'll have less to worry about and fewer people to deal with. But meanwhile, they'll be communicating among themselves, and research and experience teach that what you don't hear is likely to come back to bite you down the road. The no-confidence votes discussed in Chapters One and Five occurred when constituents saw their leaders as inaccessible and out of touch. Open communication is a two-way street.

Empowerment

Empowerment has become a buzzword, an often-fuzzy idea that is easy to talk about but hard to do well. That helps to explain why empowerment finished third, right below "working with idiots," on a list of annoying business practices as voted by readers of the *Dilbert* comic strip (Adams, 1995). Academic leaders need to get beyond hypocrisy or empty rhetoric to the serious and important task of finding ways to increase people's ability to make informed and consequential choices—decisions that make a difference. Research confirms that empowered employees do a better job and feel better about their work and their organizations (Biron & Bamberger, 2007).

In practice, empowerment amounts to providing people the resources they need to get their jobs done in a context of bounded autonomy and accountability. One key resource is relevant information, which is why transparency and openness are important. Other resources include money, training, staff support, organizational clearances, and whatever else individuals or groups need to work successfully. Bounded autonomy comes down to giving people freedom to find their way to the goal line while ensuring that they know the rules of the game and the boundaries of the playing field.

But freedom without responsibility is a half-empty glass, and academic institutions or units where autonomy overshadows clear systems of accountability court disaster. In his classic *Man's Search for Meaning*, Viktor Frankl (1956) talks about it this way:

> Freedom, however, is not the last word. Freedom is only part of the story and half of the truth. Freedom is but the negative aspect of the whole phenomenon whose positive aspect is responsibleness. In fact, freedom is in danger of degenerating into mere arbitrariness unless it is lived in terms of responsibleness. (p. 132)

From a human resource perspective, the central responsibility of academic leaders is to create environments where all employees—faculty, administrators, and staff—succeed. Clear roles, unambiguous expectations, regular and timely feedback, tying consequences closely to actions, and appropriate rewards for good performance all help. Empowerment is not achieved through loose management systems and practices that leave employees on their own to err, meander, or fail. Good human resource leaders are good managers of people and skilled creators of the organizational systems that support them.

Faculty members, for example, typically have wide discretion over how they teach their courses, but that freedom is never unlimited—they still have to operate within the boundaries of law and policy and to conform to such things as academic calendars, grading systems, accreditation standards, degree requirements, discipline and professional association standards, and so on. College and university leaders can be forgiven for thinking that the last thing faculty need is more empowerment, given how much autonomy and influence they already have, but that may lead them to miss important opportunities.

What all this means for new dean Christina Hernandez is that she needs to avoid colluding with constituents in assuming that she's responsible for everything and that it's her job to solve all the school's problems. If she tries, she will fail, pay a huge personal cost, and get little thanks for trying. More likely, she will become the target of endless blaming and criticism from those around her. Ronald Heifetz (1994) underscores the developmental nature of leadership: growing the adaptive capacities of individuals and groups for tackling complex challenges. His advice is simple and prudent: Create adequate support, set clear parameters, and give the work back to the people.

Effective Teamwork

Individual empowerment is critical, but so is strong teamwork—even for highly autonomous employees like faculty. Much of the freedom in the faculty role is limited to the teaching and

scholarly work of each individual instructor. Faculty tradition-
ally are empowered more to do their own thing than to contribute to collective purpose, yet unit success requires unitwide
engagement and cooperative action. When empowerment works,
much of the payoff comes from empowering groups and teams
(Chen, Kirkman, Kanfer, & Allen, 2005). But, some might ask,
Isn't higher education already riddled with too many committees that soak up too much time and energy while accomplishing
too little? Often so, but leaders can enhance the likelihood that
committees and other groups will be more productive and satisfying. Katzenbach and Smith (1993) studied successful teams in a
variety of settings. They draw a clear distinction between undif-
ferentiated groups and sharply focused teams. "A team is a small
number of people with complementary skills, who are committed
to a common purpose, set of performance goals, and approach
for which they hold themselves mutually accountable" (p. 112).
Their research identified six key characteristics of high-quality
teams:

1. *High-performing teams shape purpose in response to a demand or
   an opportunity placed in their path, usually by higher management.*
   Leaders clarify the group's charter and challenge but give it
   flexibility to work out goals and plans of operation.

2. *High-performing teams translate common purpose into specific,
   measurable performance goals.* Purpose yields an overall mission, but successful groups take the additional step of recast-
   ing purpose into more specific goals that provide concrete
   yardsticks for assessing progress.

3. *High-performing teams are of manageable size.* Committees and
   project teams in higher education are often too big and dis-
   jointed. Team leadership assignments are often vague and
   attendance erratic, so it can seem as if a team is starting over
   every time it meets. Aim for the smallest size that can get the
   job done with legitimacy.

4. *High-performing teams develop the right mix of expertise.* A faculty committee whose members know what they want to teach but not what students need to learn may develop a curriculum that is academically coherent but doomed to market failure. The first question in forming strong academic teams should be, Who has the knowledge needed for good decisions? A close second is, Who has political influence and expertise—the political capital and respect among important constituencies—to make the process legitimate and the outcomes viable?

5. *High-performing teams develop a common commitment to working relationships.* New groups often plunge into the task but skip over discussion of how they will work together. An effective team "establishes a social contract among members that relates to their purpose and guides and obligates how they will work together" (Katzenbach & Smith, 1993, p. 116). Teams succeed when members agree on who will do particular jobs, how schedules will be set and monitored, what skills need to be developed, how quality performance will be assessed, how continuing team membership is to be earned, and how the group will make and modify its decisions.

6. *Members of high-performing teams hold themselves collectively accountable.* Pinpointing individual responsibility is crucial to a well-coordinated effort, but effective teams find ways to hold the collective accountable too. "Teams enjoying a common purpose and approach inevitably hold themselves responsible, both as individuals and as a team, for the team's performance" (Katzenbach & Smith, 1993, p. 116).

Dean Hernandez needs to work with her faculty and staff to identify key challenges. She'll succeed if she then sets up strong teams or task forces to address them, ensuring that the groups have clear goals, sufficient autonomy, clear accountability, effective work processes, and resources to address the pressing issues.

Support, Coaching, and Care

Beyond transparency, empowerment, and strong teamwork, the fourth pillar of effective human resource leadership is caring for individuals and supporting their growth and development. Robert Greenleaf (1973) argued that the essence of leadership is service and that the chief responsibility of leaders is to serve the best interests of their constituents:

> The servant-leader makes sure that other people's highest priority needs are being served. The best test [of leadership] is: do those served grow as persons; do they, while being served, become healthier, wiser, freer, more autonomous, more likely themselves to become servants? (p. 7)

As Greenleaf saw it, people caring for one another is the rock on which society and institutions are built. Unlike "leader-first" individuals who seek leadership for power or possessions, those who are "servant-first" begin with care and a desire to support. Asked about the secret of her leadership, Mother Teresa replied, "Small work with great love" (Chatterjee, 1998, p. 150). Like Mother Teresa, great leaders love their work, their organization, and, above all, the people they serve. Like good coaches, they work to identify the skills and capabilities that others bring and enable them to develop and use those capacities to the best of their ability.

At its simplest, caring begins with reaching out to constituents and spending time with them to understand their needs and concerns. The packed schedules that typify administrative work make this challenging, but time spent building relationships with constituents will often save time in the long run by fostering a more trusting and collaborative climate that makes it easier to lead and get things done. Jeffrey Pfeffer (2007) attributes much of the success of Spain's IESE, one of the world's most highly ranked business schools, to its caring culture and gives a personal example to illustrate. When Pfeffer came over for a visiting stint, his wife arrived in Spain with a severe earache. IESE's dean arranged for her first to visit a clinic and then to see a prominent ear specialist. For both appointments, he sent along an English-speaking employee and paid for both taxis and the doctors. He had no contractual obligation to do any of that; but, as Pfeffer saw it, for a dean who wanted to build community and commitment to the school, "It was almost automatic to offer help to someone who was having difficulty, even if that person was just a temporary part of the organization" (p. 20).

If Dean Hernandez can find ways to make openness, empowerment, strong teamwork, support, coaching, and care consistent cornerstones of her leadership, she will go a long way to reduce the anxiety and fear that feed the toxicity in her workplace. To do this well, there are important things she needs to do for herself. Working at the boundaries of human growth and development is tough—it's easy to overidentify with individuals and their needs and to lose sight of the larger purpose of human resource leadership—the creation of an empowering work environment that facilitates productive work. To stay focused and avoid burnout, Hernandez will need the discipline to take regular breaks from the action: opportunities to step back, to take stock, and to reenergize herself. She'll never survive the leadership challenge if she doesn't.

Hiring the Right People

Dean Hernandez, like most academic leaders, inherited a workforce. She had no choice but to look for ways to develop a positive and productive environment with the people she had. In the early going, fiscal pressures kept her unit in downsizing rather than hiring mode. But sooner or later the time will come to bring on new faculty and staff. Then it will be vital to get it right. Hiring decisions are particularly critical for autonomous workers whose judgment and skill are essential to their effectiveness.

The stakes are even higher when the new hire comes with tenure, a multiyear contract, or the quasi-tenure that exists in many institutions that are reluctant to fire anyone. The autonomy that benefits good professors and professional staff in higher education also protects bad ones, and a bad hire begets others when the misfit is in a position to bring people on board who share his or her values or work standards. It's much easier and more productive in the long run to put more time and effort into getting the right person than to hope you'll be able to fix a doubtful hire down the road. Buckingham and Coffman (1999) argue that the best managers capitalize on individuals' strengths and avoid trying to fix weaknesses. "People don't change that much. Don't waste time trying to put in what was left out. Try to draw out what was left in. That is hard enough" (p. 57). The other side of the same coin is that even the best people can look bad if they're placed in a dead-end job or a situation designed for failure.

For a variety of reasons, hiring processes in higher education are often rushed and unsystematic. They may adhere closely to procedural rules dealing with affirmative action and basic background checks, but those hurdles rarely confirm that the new hire brings the necessary talent, motivation, and cultural fit. Good hiring depends particularly on three key steps: (1) knowing what you are looking for, (2) ensuring a strong candidate pool, and (3) being thorough and systematic in assessing candidates.

Step 1 in a good hire is to determine your needs. Higher education job descriptions are often cursory, and the duties and expectations for positions with the same title can vary from campus to campus. The right hires are individuals who bring the needed skills, talents, and experiences to do the job that you have in your specific work environment, context, and campus culture. The clearer you are in defining what that means—and in using the information in your advertising and in assessing potential candidates—the better the chance of a strong match. If you don't have a job description for the position, develop one that is detailed—and discuss it with relevant others to test for shared understanding. Write out a list of qualifications for the ideal candidate—needed skills and expertise, education and training, and required experiences—and include critical intangibles like preferred work style, values, leadership approach, openness to learning, motivation, collegiality, and capacity for autonomy. Prioritizing the qualifications before you begin interviewing will help you stay focused on what you really need.

Step 2 is to ensure a strong candidate pool. It is surprising how often colleges and universities take a passive approach to recruiting. Depending on the position, they may run an ad or two in the local paper or in the *Chronicle of Higher Education* and then wait to see what comes over the transom. Sometimes that works reasonably well when institutional prestige or the job market is tilted in favor of the hiring institution, but it is almost never as good as an active effort to recruit. The best candidates usually aren't looking for a job. Passive recruiting often results in a weak pool, and an inadequate candidate may look strong by comparison to weaker others.

To make matters worse, the process of assessing candidates often relies too heavily on how well they present themselves in an interview or campus visit. Step 3 is to take a systematic and thorough approach to candidate assessment. Again and again, institutions hire the individual who is best at self-marketing, but they don't do the necessary probing and homework to ensure that the candidate's track record, skills, values, and experiences are consistent with his or her impressive presentation of self. Reference checking is often cursory or neglected because deep data gathering takes time and talent. Interviews are often short and perfunctory—general conversations to get to know the candidate with time spent answering questions or selling the position or institution—with no one investing the skill and persistence to penetrate generalities and obtain a more nuanced picture of candidate strengths, weaknesses, values, or style. But doing so is vital.

More than one university has announced an important hire with great public fanfare only to discover down the road that their new recruit has skill deficits or skeletons in the closet that could have been unearthed with a little more digging or behavior-based interviewing that got the candidate talking in detailed ways about past performance and workplace choices (Hoevemeyer, 2005). Bad hires are usually unhappy and unproductive people who become a drag on both productivity and morale. They are also a major sinkhole for the leader's time and energy. It takes effort to get hiring right in the first place, but the investment will pay generous dividends down the road.

Summary

Colleges and universities are human enterprises, and people are their most important resource. People are also the biggest leadership challenge. Any institution that cannot create a positive work environment for its faculty and staff is likely to fall well short of its educational aspirations. Academic leaders succeed when they bridge the needs of the institution and its employees. They do this with basic strategies that encourage adaptive growth and development and that create work environments to unleash human creativity and contribution:

1. *Open communication*: Providing information that constituents need and value

2. *Empowerment*: Providing the resources and encouragement people need to do their work in a context of bounded autonomy and clear accountability

3. *Effective teamwork*: Setting parameters and providing support to facilitate collective problem solving and action

4. *Support, coaching, and care*: Engaging with people; understanding their concerns and needs; and helping them grow, learn, and be productive

5. *Hiring the right people*: Increasing the likelihood that the people you hire will be happy and productive by taking recruiting and the vetting of candidates seriously

Human resource leadership in colleges and universities is demanding work, and it takes an emotional toll. Academic leaders cannot satisfy everyone, and a flood of negative emotions sometimes engulfs a school or unit. Work inevitably produces frustrations and discontents that are often blamed on the leader. In order to sustain oneself in the face of the psychic demands and costs of their work, academic leaders need to understand and accept the organizational history they inherit, stay grounded through periodic breaks from the action, and persist in their efforts to create empowering environments where all can bring their full talents and motivations to the work.

7

Keeping the Faith and Celebrating the Mission

Leader as Prophet and Artist

I n his 2002 inaugural address as president of Arizona State University (ASU), Michael Crow (2002b) opened with a ceremonial nod to the glories of ASU's past and the accomplishments of his predecessors before he shifted to the heart of his message:

> As we begin a new chapter in the history of this institution, I would like to look beyond its current success. I would like to talk to you about transformation, and the further evolution of the American research university— what I want to call the new American university—and why Arizona State University is uniquely positioned to become such an institution.

A new American university was needed, he said, because universities had been following a single, tired model of excellence for too long. Fifteen universities (the Ivies and the usual suspects among elite privates and publics) had become the model that everyone else tried to emulate. "Such has been the influence of these fifteen institutions that, to this day, every university in the nation measures itself according to their standards. Make no mistake: these universities represent the gold standard—but, as I hope to explain, it is the *gold standard of the past.*"

With Harvard and its ilk yesterday's news, Crow explained, ASU was "uniquely positioned" to become the first great twenty-first-century university. Its frontier heritage gave it the legacy of "vaunted individualism" needed to pioneer a new path. Arizona was also rapidly becoming more diverse and was in an economic shift from cattle and copper to a growing "creative class" (Florida, 2003)—a microcosm of the contemporary shifts that call out for new models of teaching, learning, research, and service. For all those reasons, said Crow, ASU was called to pursue "a new gold standard, the design imperatives of a New American University." He outlined eight.

One imperative was that ASU should embrace its geographic home. A second urged activism and high impact—the university as a "force, not just a place." A third required ASU to "develop a reputation for its entrepreneurial boldness." A fourth mandated relevant and applied research that is "use inspired." Others included "a focus on the individual," "intellectual fusion," "social embeddedness," and "global engagement." Crow summarized his message with a stirring conclusion:

> The new gold standard will be represented by the university that is inclusive, rather than exclusive, the university that is fully committed to its community, the university that directly engages the challenges of its cultural, socioeconomic, and physical setting, and shapes its research initiatives with regard to their social outcomes. . . . I believe we should strive to become a true university, not a place for a few, but a force for many. There is much at stake. Our success affects the fortunes of the region, but, if we are successful, if we are able to create a true academic community in the fullest sense of the idea, then we may prove to have more influence than we suspected. . . . But I cannot do it alone. I ask you to join me in the task of redefining the

American research university. I ask you to join me in the
task of building the premier new American university—
the university that sets the new gold standard.
I ask you to join me in the task of building Arizona
State University.

Inaugural speeches are invitations for symbolic performances,
and Crow delivered a classic example. He reached back into the
history of the university, the state, and the region to find timeless
values of individualism and pioneering spirit. He depicted an institution at the crossroads, buffeted by cross-currents of change and
at risk of missing its destiny if it pursued an antiquated image of
its possibilities. He put forth a vision of greatness in the future—a
vision that was uniquely ASU's to achieve—and a plan that would
enable the university to accelerate past the lumbering dinosaurs
of the Ivy League. Displaying one of the trademarks of symbolic
leaders, he reframed ASU by offering a new and distinctive way
to think about its identity and possibilities: not just one among
many public universities, but "the premier new American university." And he ended with an invitation and exhortation: "Join me
in the task of redefining the American research university."

A Symbolic View of Leadership in Higher Education

Michael Crow's case provides an instructive example of symbolic
leadership in higher education. (See Table 7.1.)

A symbolic view of colleges and universities focuses particularly on issues of meaning and belief. It sees a college as a sacred
place whose legitimacy rests ultimately on faith in the transforma-
tional power of knowledge, and as a theater whose success derives
from staging powerful dramas that connect and communicate to
important audiences. From this view, the role of an effective academic administrator is akin to that of both a *spiritual leader* who
helps to build and sustain constituents' faith in the institution

Table 7.1.   A Symbolic View of Academic Leadership

Metaphors for academic institution	Theater, temple
Images of the academic leader	Artist, prophet
Basic leadership task	See possibilities; create common vision; manage meaning; infuse passion, creativity, and soul
Leadership logic	Building faith and shared meaning
Leadership currency	Hope and promise
Frame emphasis	Meaning, purpose, and values
Key leadership assumptions	People interpret experiences differently
	Meaning-making is a central organizational process
	Culture is an institution's emotional and intellectual glue
	Symbols express institutional identity, values, and beliefs
Areas of analysis	Culture, rituals, ceremonies, stories, myth, vision, symbols

Source: Adapted from Gallos (2006, 2008c).

and in their contributions to it and a *spirited artist* who gives audience members an inspiring performance that they will remember and endorse. The two images of leadership may have more in common than it first seems. The need to express the intangible through the concrete is deeply rooted in the human experience, and theater and storytelling have long been important vehicles for teaching beliefs and values across cultures and through the ages (see, for example, Denning, 2005, 2007). Theater as we know it had its origins in ancient Greek religious rites (Wickham, 1992). The dramaturgical image reminds academic leaders that they are always on stage, closely observed by their audience. Their success depends on how well their performance conveys the messages and evokes the responses they intend. A show that bombs on opening night tends to close soon thereafter. But a triumphant start generates buzz and ticket sales that set the stage for a long and profitable run.

From a symbolic perspective, the leader's role is generative, interpretive, and inspirational. Academic administrators who bring the imagination to envision new possibilities and the skills to convey a compelling picture of the future enable others to feel positive and hopeful about their work, their institution, and its leadership. Certain roles, like president, chancellor, dean, and director, are by their nature heavily and visibly symbolic. The dean represents the school, the president the college, the director his or her program or center, and so on. Occupants of such roles preside over more ceremonies and get more opportunities to take center stage and to play the role of public leader with gravitas and flair than those who lead informally or without executive titles. Still, the power and possibility in symbolic leadership are vital at all levels of the university. At lower levels, the stage might be less lofty and the audience smaller, but attention to symbols and a hopeful future are arguably even more important in roles carrying less formal authority and status that those at the top.

A symbol is something that stands for something else, often for something more complex, less tangible, or more difficult to articulate. Symbols serve two particularly important functions in universities, as in life. One is economy—a symbol communicates a complex message in a succinct way that saves words, time, or effort. A position announcement for faculty members typically specifies a terminal degree because that certification symbolizes advanced training, research skills, a taste for intellectual work, intelligence, tolerance for the ways of the academy, and more. A second function of symbol is interpretive and emotional. Symbols work when they influence what something means and trigger deeply embedded, nonconscious associations that affect our feelings and attitudes toward it. If the only criterion were descriptive accuracy, "typical public" might describe ASU about as well as "new American university." But the first suggests a university plodding down the same old path to mediocrity, while the second tells constituents that they have an historic opportunity to create one of America's most significant and influential institutions. Which would you prefer? We know of one business school dean candidate who borrowed from Michael Crow's script during his job interview: he offered a vision of a "new American business school," complete with elements from Crow's playbook like "use-inspired research." He got the job.

When well-chosen and artistically employed, symbols speak to both head and heart. Leaders need to do both. If they speak only to the head, they may lead institutions short on joy, creativity, and passion. If they speak only to the heart, they may turn their institutions into rockets without guidance systems. Speaking to both head and heart is particularly difficult, because university leaders continually operate on contested and ambiguous terrain. Uncertainty, diversity of perspectives, and conflict are at the core of the academic enterprise.

A good inaugural address or opening talk is only one step on a long road that will present twists, turns, ups, and downs. But even if beginnings are not everything, a leader's first steps are crucial. They set a tone, shape expectations, and define an initial trajectory. Symbolic leaders recognize this and seek to leverage the opportunity. They understand the importance of hitting the right key and sending the right messages, particularly during the fleeting period when the window of opportunity is open and constituents are eager to learn more about the leader and his or her direction. Symbolic leaders like Michael Crow offer excitement, hope, and opportunity to those willing to join in the efforts to turn a dream into reality.

Culture as Holding Environment

One of the most famous documents in the history of American higher education is the "Yale Report of 1828," developed by administrators and faculty in response to a then-controversial proposal to drop "dead languages" (Latin and Greek) from the required undergraduate curriculum. After acknowledging critics who argued that colleges "would soon be deserted unless they are better accommodated to the business character of the nation" (Committee of the Corporation and the Academical Faculty, 1828), the report countered that curriculum must respond to purpose; and the purpose of "superior education" must be, above all, to teach students how to think, to instruct them in "the art of fixing attention, directing the train of thought, [and] analyzing a subject proposed for investigation" (p. 8). After arguing that Yale's curriculum was continually changing and that change was a good thing, the committee concluded that Yale should nonetheless retain a central place for Latin and Greek because they were so well attuned to the purpose of a collegiate education.

The proposition of nothing better than Latin and Greek for teaching people how to think has subsequently drawn withering attack from historians and education scholars who have seen it as Exhibit 1 of a retrograde traditionalism that stultified higher education for decades. But Pak (2008) argues that the Yale committee's conclusions were rooted less in dogma and ideological rigidity than in realism and savvy attention to competitive pressures. The bulk of Yale's clientele, he argues, still wanted the ancient languages that had been regarded for centuries as the mark of an educated person. To draw students in the face of growing competition, Yale had to give its customers what they wanted.

The controversy over this historic decision is emblematic of the perennial uncertainty that characterizes higher education. The fact that, almost two centuries later, historians still can't agree on what happened at Yale, why, or what it means underscores the magnitude of the complexity in academic leadership. The Yale Report is one among countless examples to illustrate the same basic point: fundamental questions of purpose, curriculum, direction, and pedagogy have always been contentious and difficult to answer—and those questions are at the center of what a college or university is all about. Academic leaders must continually confront basic questions that can never be fully resolved: Who are we? What are we here to do? How should we go about doing it? Such pervasive uncertainty is a problem because a steady diet of deep and unanswerable questions is not something most people want to face every day—it is a fast track to angst, exhaustion, and burnout.

What to do? Do what humans have always done when faced with questions too important to ignore but too difficult to answer. Answer them anyway so as to ward off anxiety and get on with life. When data and logic fail, people make sense of their experiences as best they can. They tell stories and develop symbols to shape and convey meaning to themselves and to others. Over time, they infer that certain patterns of choice, action, thought, taste, values, and purpose work better than others. These gradually coalesce into a culture: "a pattern of shared basic assumptions that a group learned as it solved its problems of external adaptation and integration that has worked well enough to be considered valid and therefore to be taught to new members as the correct way to perceive, think, and feel in relation to those problems" (Schein, 1992, p. 17).

In simple terms, culture is how we've learned to think and do things around here (Deal & Kennedy, 1982). From a symbolic perspective, building and shaping institutional culture is at the heart of academic leadership. But in shaping culture, leaders never start with a blank slate. Instead, they inherit raw materials from the past—values, beliefs, artifacts, stories, heroes and heroines, rituals and practices (Bolman & Deal, 2008b). These symbolic building blocks offer academic leaders a place to start in sorting out and diagnosing their unit's or institution's culture.

In an organization with a history of success, the culture is likely to be coherent and strong, with many positive elements on which leaders can build. Organizations with more troubled pasts often present fractured and incoherent cultures in need of substantial overhaul, but be forewarned. Toxic cultures can be coherent and strongly rooted despite their dysfunction (Gallos, 2008b), and leaders need to understand the strength of whatever culture they have inherited. Strong cultures are vigorously and widely supported, and they are difficult to change. In those circumstances, leaders do better to ally with the culture and to emphasize the values, history, and legends that are most helpful in taking the institution forward, while downplaying elements that are less useful. Yale provides an illustration. It eventually dropped Latin and Greek from the required undergraduate curriculum. It no longer specifies that the main end of a Yale education is "to know God in Jesus Christ and answerably to lead a Godly, sober life." But it still retains its eighteenth-century motto, *Lux et Veritas*, and still issues diplomas in Latin that few recipients can decode (Oren, 2003). In any event, leaders have much greater opportunity to make substantial change in cultures that have little coherence or support.

Different colleges and universities—and units, departments, and programs within them—will evolve their own distinct cultures. Each of these, however, is also nested within the multifaceted culture of higher education. At the broadest level it is an international culture of shared beliefs, practices, and values that permits academics from different parts of the world to meet and work comfortably together because they all agree more or less on the rules of the game. That's why it is perfectly plausible in Roberto Bolaño's (2004) final novel, *2666*, for four academics from France, Italy, Spain, and the United Kingdom to become fast friends who delight in reconnecting at conferences around the world. Their reunions let them celebrate and reconfirm their shared faith in the value of devoting one's life to the study of an obscure German novelist whom almost no one outside the academy knows or cares about. Beneath the broad international umbrella, academic culture takes a variety of more delimited forms: national, regional, institutional, and disciplinary, among others. All this provides a broad set of cultural parameters within which academic leaders can operate without having to ask anew every day whether, say, teaching and research are good things. At the same time, these nested layers of culture create a complex web of influence and meaning that makes it harder to tease out more local and changeable elements.

Culture is always a work in progress, which is both a curse and a blessing. The downside is that culture wars are a permanent feature of colleges and universities, and academic leaders continually find themselves threading their way through hazardous and foggy battle zones. Basic questions about purpose, content, and pedagogy like those in the 1828 Yale Report continue to fuel the fires of intellectual and political combat—and academic administrators are forewarned to tread slowly and carefully into this sacred faculty ground. But the positive side of the same coin is that ambiguity and controversy create opportunities and wiggle space for adroit leaders. They can always find ways to reframe their institution—its history, its circumstances, and its possibilities:

> Symbolically, leaders lead through both actions and words as they interpret and reinterpret experience. What are the real lessons of history? What is really happening in the world? What will the future bring? What mission is worthy of our loyalty and investment? Data and analysis offer few compelling answers to such questions. Symbolic leaders interpret experience so as to impart meaning and purpose through phrases of beauty and passion. (Bolman & Deal, 2008b, p. 367)

That is what Michael Crow sought to do in his inaugural speech. He could have told his audience "ASU has been great and will be even better some day" to polite applause. But he wanted to do more. He hoped to inspire and excite action—to reshape cultural givens and persuade his audience that ASU could escape mediocrity and achieve its destiny as "the new American university." Getting there wouldn't be easy and would require difficult choices and hard work. But Crow's framing of the opportunity and choice of language elevated the task, energized key constituents, and enlisted important others with a promise of groundbreaking impact.

How Symbolic Leaders Work

During his tenure as ASU president, Michael Crow exemplified four key practices for successful symbolic leadership. Each involves decisions about how to frame the institution and its purpose, build on its current support and strengths, and position oneself to lead and advance institutional objectives and agendas.

Symbolic leaders construct meaning and foster hope and faith by . . .

1. Building on the past for an exciting, new vision of the future

2. Leading by example

3. Constructing a heroic narrative and telling it often

4. Leveraging the power in ritual and ceremony

Build on the Past for an Exciting, New Vision of the Future

Crow could have chosen to ignore or downplay ASU's history as a young institution founded as a teachers' college with Research I status only since the 1990s. He chose instead to wear that history as a badge of honor central to ASU's mission: "We hold that to be at our core. We are teachers first, teachers always, and teachers last" (Crow, 2009c). This history made ASU distinctive and a "people's university," meant not for the rich but for everyone who wanted an education. It was a natural evolution from there to build the new American university and to serve the diverse and growing population of Arizona. Savvy symbolic leaders build visions of the future that are rooted in the current attachments and meaning systems of their key constituents. Every department, unit, and institution has a history; and many are groping for direction at the moment a new leader arrives on the scene. The wise academic leader will study the history, listen to constituents, and engage them in developing a new sense of vision, purpose, and possibility.

Lead by Example

Many college and university presidents say they'd love to teach, but few squeeze it into their packed calendar. Though Michael Crow is scheduled months in advance and averages more than seventy-five meetings a week, he still mentors students and teaches a weekly seminar on science, technology, and public affairs. To give another example: most college web sites contain a presidential welcome message and texts of at least a few speeches. As we write, ASU's site goes above and beyond almost any other university, with more than thirty video clips of President Crow in action (Arizona State University, n.d.). Consider his 2008 welcome video to new students, faculty, and staff. With more than 60,000 students, Arizona State was big enough to keep its president busy, but that didn't stop Crow from extending a personal invitation to incoming students. "Every employee at ASU is here to help you. If you have issues and you're not getting the help you need, you write to me directly, michael.crow@asu.edu, and we'll find the right person to get you some help" (Crow, 2008). The point is not that Crow could intervene personally on behalf of every student with a problem, but that he personalized the institution, reminded everyone at ASU of the value of caring for students, and took personal responsibility for ensuring that the university lived up to its commitment. Strong symbolic leaders understand that they are always onstage, and they take advantage of every opportunity to use themselves as symbols of important values, priorities, and agendas. Doing that takes discipline, planning, and creativity.

3 Construct a Heroic Narrative and Tell It Often and Widely

Crow varied details of the story to fit specifics of his audience and circumstances, but his broad narrative arc was consistent—and he repeated some version of it at every opportunity. Boiled to its essence, the story said that universities had fallen from an earlier state of grace and that a new vision was needed to restore greatness. In Crow's words, "We have undertaken the task of pioneering the foundational model for what we have termed 'The New American University'—an egalitarian institution committed to the topmost echelons of academic excellence, inclusiveness to a broad demographic, and maximum societal impact" (Crow, 2009b, p. 1).

Crow's story follows the classic form that appears repeatedly in visionary performances, such as the inaugural addresses of Abraham Lincoln and John F. Kennedy, Martin Luther King Jr.'s "I Have a Dream" speech, and others. It is a story in three parts: a great past, a troubled present, and a new path to an inspiring future.

Crow's version reached back to the great universities of Europe and colonial America that bequeathed higher education a grand legacy of learning and the unfettered pursuit of truth. But higher education faces troubles today because it has "remained excessively attached to the outmoded institutional paradigms that we derive from our lineage" (Crow, 2009b, p. 3). The result is diminishing returns on investment as "increasingly specialized knowledge [is] measured in smaller and smaller ratios" (p. 3). Yet the future is bright, argued Crow, for a university that sees itself as an entrepreneurial enterprise, committed to "use-inspired" research addressing the most pressing social and technical problems of the day—an institution that will "reject the notion that excellence and access cannot be achieved in the same institution" (p. 5). ASU could be that new kind of university, and Crow's aspirations were far from modest: "If we are to advance metropolitan Phoenix as entrepreneurial, creative, and adaptive, it is the responsibility of the university to envision and guide that outcome" (p. 5).

Leverage the Power in Ritual and Ceremony

Many of the best opportunities for academic leaders to retell their stories are at institutional rituals and ceremonies. Rituals are stylized or scripted patterns of action that recur on a regular basis, such as the meetings of a class, the faculty, or a president's or dean's cabinet. Ceremonies, on the other hand, are ritualized occasions that are grander and less frequent, such as commencements, convocations, inaugurations, or ribbon cuttings to launch new initiatives or facilities.

An essential feature of ritual and ceremony is that they simultaneously signal continuity and change. A commencement ceremony, for example, certifies that graduates have transformed from child to adult, from untutored to educated, from layperson to professional. Yet the ritualized, tradition-driven nature of a graduation ceremony makes it clear that the new graduates, clad in caps and gowns modeled on those of medieval scholars, are following in the footsteps of generations before them. The fusion of transition and continuity gives rituals and ceremonies much of their power—and their capacity to strengthen bonds of loyalty and affection, to remind all present of the meaning and significance of the enterprise, to renew faith, and to build hope.

Many colleges and universities are richly symbolic institutions, infused with myth, stories, ceremony, and symbols rooted in ancient traditions. Commencements and convocations, academic regalia and archaically named degrees, maces and mascots are among the more visible symbolic vestments that adorn colleges and universities. They are vital because educational institutions survive and prosper only so long as they sustain constituents'

belief and faith in their mission and activities. This would be easier if most of those activities produced immediate, easily assessed
outcomes, as is true for many private sector businesses whose
products or services consumers can easily describe, observe, and
judge. The outcomes of teaching and research are much less certain and may not be known or fully appreciated until well into
the future. When a student graduates from college, the degree
and the accompanying ceremony are obligatory because it is so difficult to judge just how an individual has benefitted from four years
of opportunity costs. The same assessment problem is a major reason that research tends to outweigh teaching as a criterion for promotion, tenure, and status within the academy: it's easier to count
publications, grants, and projects as symbols of productivity and
contribution than to assess how much value a professor delivers to
students, the campus, or the world. This also helps to explain why
college sports play such a dominant role in American universities.
Those "scholar athletes" may or may not be delving very deeply
into the life of the mind, but boosters can immerse themselves
in the competitive drama on the field and cheer for their side. At
the end of the game, they will know who won.

Symbolic leaders take advantage of ritual and ceremony to
convene the congregants, reinforce shared beliefs, and reinspire
commitment to shared purpose. In the case of Michael Crow, one
of the clearest illustrations was also one of the most public and
controversial—ASU's 2009 commencement ceremony at which
President Barack Obama was graced with a speaking opportunity but not an honorary degree. The tempest in Tempe over
what some saw as an insult to the president of the United States
guaranteed a huge audience—not just the more than 70,000
people who filled Sun Devil Stadium, but an international audience who would read press accounts and flock to the online video.
Crow took advantage of the opportunity, using his introduction
of President Obama to tell his story and to emphasize that ASU
and the president shared a passion for an egalitarian and inclusive

approach to education. ASU, he said, would continue building itself as an "egalitarian center for advanced teaching and learning" from which "no Arizona student will be left out . . . because of his or her family income" (Crow, 2009a).

Finally, skilled academic leaders use occasions that go well beyond the annual pageantry of commencement. Crow gave speeches, made personal appearances, and put videos online for just about every audience (faculty, staff, students, alumni, community members, and beyond) and every occasion (beginning a new school year, opening of a new school, dedicating a building, launching a new program, and so on). The basic message was always the same: We've made a lot of progress in recent years, we're still on track, and there's a lot more to come. Even in the face of massive funding cuts during the fiscal crises of 2008 and 2009, Crow insisted that ASU was undaunted in its commitment to build the new American university.

Risks and Rewards of the Prophetic Leader

Prophets can be inspirational and magical as they lead toward previously unimagined possibilities. They can also be seductive and dangerous, leading their institutions to damage and disappointment. In Chapter Five, we examined the tragic story of the pseudonymous President Donald Quixote, who, like Michael Crow, entered a presidency with the goal of transforming his institution into a standard bearer for American higher education. Quixote raised the hopes of many on and off campus, but pushed too fast, accomplished too little, sent contradictory signals, and was forced out of office within a few years. He left a wounded and fractured campus and community in his wake.

Michael Crow also pushed fast, and he has been a lightning rod for controversy and criticism. Some faculty complained about what they called "Mike-Crow management" and characterized him as an autocratic manager introducing a corporate mentality that undermined faculty governance (Irwin, 2007). Yet in 2009, eight years into his presidency, *Time* magazine put Crow on its list of America's "ten best college presidents" (Von Drehle, 2009). During Crow's first eight years, ASU grew its low-income freshmen enrollment nearly ninefold annually, boosted its roster of National Merit Scholars 61 percent, and increased its minority student population by 62 percent. Fund-raising was up nearly 85 percent, and the university more than doubled its yearly research spending. Crow's new American university attracted faculty superstars, built spectacular buildings, and created numerous new interdisciplinary schools and institutes (including the world's first School of Sustainability). Though ASU made little headway in the *U.S. News & World Report* ranking of America's best colleges, it took pride in its ratings by a group in China as one of the world's top 100 universities and by *Forbes* as one of the best values in American higher education.

Why such divergent outcomes in the Quixote and Crow cases? One difference is that Crow began with a clear, substantive vision that he outlined in his inaugural speech and consistently continued to champion: he made it clear from the start where he thought ASU should go. Strong visions provide direction through their clear picture of a desirable end-state. Such clarity enables institutions to work backward from the vision in a systematic way to determine what needs to be done to take the campus forward to the promised future. Quixote's vision was ambiguous and primarily about process: the university would liberate human potential and set new standards. The content remained to be worked out—a difficult task for a campus cast of thousands to define and agree upon. Even if they did, how would they know when they got there? Crow and Quixote both generated heated discussions about change, but Crow's clear vision also triggered a productive debate about substance and tactics for accomplishment. Quixote set off a battle over decision making and governance, and the campus had difficulty ever getting past the *how* to address the *what*. Even though a substantive vision gives opponents a clear target to shoot at, it also provides potential allies more reason to get involved and potential donors a clearer reason to write a check. Crow's ideas did generate campus opposition and criticism, but they also garnered a base of political and financial support that enabled him to deliver significant early wins and to set the stage for further success.

Crow's leadership also went beyond the symbolic to include important structural and political elements. Structurally, he centralized at the strategic level but moved toward more decentralization at the operational level of schools and colleges. Three campuses that had been relatively autonomous were combined into "one university in many places," but individual schools became more autonomous fiscally and programmatically. Politically, Crow developed a strong coalition that relied heavily on external players—leaders in the business, civic, political, and philanthropic realms—to provide resources he could use in prodding his institution forward.

Symbols are powerful and evocative because they convey meaning beyond their obvious intrinsic function. A doctoral robe at its most concrete, for example, is just a not-very-functional, thin fabric coat. Yet as a symbol it evokes a wealth of meaning about the institution reflected in its colors, as well as intangibles like status, intellectual credibility, intelligence, achievement, and more. Strong symbolic leaders know their audiences and what they value, and they choose their symbols carefully to reflect that. A mismatch can turn people off quickly—and send a powerful signal of a major disconnection between leader and potential followers. The new American university was an uplifting and unifying symbol for Crow, and the rugged individualism and pioneering spirit implicit in creating it played well with the Old West imagery familiar to his Arizona audiences. Quixote spoke of rockets to greatness and quantum leaps of innovation, but offered little homegrown imagery that connected to his campus culture or to local traditions and values.

Another significant difference in the Crow and Quixote cases was where the leaders focused early investments. Crow put his bets on teaching and research—the bedrock of the university, a cornerstone of collegiate culture, and indisputable symbols of the academy. Quixote invested in consultants and workshops. When Quixote's faculty concluded that neither the consultants nor the workshops were attuned to academic ways and values, the corporate-level expenditures became an additional source of skepticism, anger, and resistance.

Summary

Colleges and universities are and should be committed to truth and reason, but they become sterile and devoid of passion unless they are also fueled by feeling and faith. Symbolic leaders understand this. First-rate intellect is a vital higher education leadership asset, but academic administrators can do more if they also serve as spiritual leaders who help to build and sustain their constituents' faith and hope, and spirited artists who stage performances that hold the interest and draw the applause of their audiences. They understand that institutions need a clear vision and mission that excite and energize constituents at the same time that they guide decision making. Symbolic leaders strive to be highly visible exemplars of their institution's values and of the vision they hope to achieve. They construct a coherent and compelling narrative—a story about the institution's past, present, and future—and continue to retell the story to keep reminding constituents where they've been, where they're going, and why. They appreciate the power of a strong and coherent institutional culture—and their role and responsibilities in creating and sustaining that culture. They treasure their institution's symbolic tapestry, and they seek to leverage ritual and ceremony in the service of the institution's larger purposes.

As powerful as it is, symbolic leadership is always risky. The show has to have substance and integrity, and it needs to be artistically executed and aligned with the hopes and expectations of the audience. If the symbols are wrong, if leaders push too far beyond the expectations of their constituents or the capacities of their systems, or if they simply deliver a bad performance, the audience boos and turns away. Failure brings pain and disappointment all around. Academic administrators augment their impact when they (1) build on the past to create a vision of the future, (2) lead by example, (3) construct a heroic narrative and tell it often, and (4) leverage the power in ritual and ceremony.

Part III

Sustaining Higher Education Leaders
Courage and Hope

If the chapters in Part Two achieved their purpose, you have developed your confidence and your capacity to reframe academic leadership—turning the kaleidoscope to view your leadership opportunities as those of an analyst and architect, a compassionate politician, a servant and coach, and a prophet and artist. You may already have begun to find that situations at work are less confusing or overwhelming, and that things are beginning to make more sense.

Part Three provides further support for your ongoing leadership development and your search for your professional best. The six chapters offer advice on how to handle a series of recurrent issues that often impede the ability of academic leaders to sustain their energy, focus, and hope in the face of the seemingly endless vicissitudes of administrative life. Chapter Eight answers a key question: How do leaders make conflict productive? Chapter Nine examines ways to survive and prosper in the face of conflicting pressures from every direction. Chapter Ten explores strategies for dealing with the bullies, backstabbers, and other challenging individuals who sometimes seem overrepresented in higher education. Chapter Eleven tackles the often overlooked issues of how to lead a boss and others at the top of the hierarchy. Chapter Twelve reminds campus administrators to take care of themselves when under constant pressure to do even more for everyone around them. Finally, Chapter Thirteen guides academic leaders in building and sustaining faith and spirit in an environment that can easily discourage or overwhelm. Academic leadership can be a wild ride, but the destination is worth the journey.

8

Managing Conflict

Leadership is an expression of oneself: one's talents, values, aspirations, and dreams. As a result, the self is always engaged—and is often at risk. Everything that leaders do is public and open to inspection by supporters and critics alike—by those who understand the realities that leaders face and those who judge uninformed from the sidelines. Leadership is about change, and change is always disruptive.

> You place yourself on the line when you tell people what they need to hear rather than what they want to hear. Although you may see with clarity and passion a promising future of progress and gain, people will see with equal passion the losses you are asking them to sustain. (Heifetz & Linsky, 2002, p. 12)

In the face of loss, people hold on. They may also lash out—with attacks intended to marginalize the leader's influence or to divert attention from the proposed change or from their own fears or inadequacies. In such a world, the leader's self needs to be nurtured and supported so that it can evolve and strengthen to do the difficult work that must be done.

A secure and grounded sense of self is also a prerequisite for building and maintaining the diverse networks of interpersonal relationships needed to lead and to withstand the everyday stresses and trials that can trigger insecurity, angst, or burnout. Academic administrators often take home at the end of the day gnawing problems that cause them to question their capacities, choices, and responses. Some eventually abandon the work. Discarding their dreams of building academic institutions or programs, they leave the university, change careers, or "go back to the faculty," often feeling frustrated, failed, and deeply wounded.

This chapter—and the five to follow—are written to provide guidance and strategies for sustaining higher education leaders in the face of recurrent issues that test the soul. We start in this chapter with what many see as the thorniest challenge: how to make conflict productive and to generate lasting solutions from difficult situations. Conflict is inevitable in the work lives of academic leaders, and studies of occupational stress in higher education over the last quarter century have identified it as a major source of concern (see, for example, Gmelch, Loverich, & Wilke, 1984; Gmelch, 1991; Pomerance, 2008). But conflict presents opportunities as well as challenges. It is a crucible that tests and gives birth to great leadership.

Making Conflict Productive

The interpersonal and emotional intensity of conflict can easily overwhelm leaders' coping strategies and psychic resources—and can produce harm for both academic administrators and their institutions. So can holding tacit assumptions that all conflict is bad. Disagreements sparked by differences in beliefs, perspectives, information, or experiences generate much of the value that comes from collaboration and shared decision making; and conflicts well managed can be sources of creative solutions and wise trade-offs among competing goals and objectives (Weiss and Hughes, 2008). The first step for academic administrators in making conflict productive is to recognize the rich possibilities in disagreements.

Equally important are basic skills in conflict management. The goal is not to eliminate conflict—not all disagreements can be fully resolved. It is to create processes that enable individuals to learn and grow from their differences and that allow organizations to extract the creative value buried in them. The critical task for academic leaders is how to orchestrate disagreements so that things don't get too hot or too cold for progress.

Orchestrating Conflict 1: Cooling the Flame

To Darya Smith, it was the toughest problem she'd faced since becoming chair of the history department at her urban university. In a course on U.S. cultural history, students—mostly of color—had dug into a number of major themes, including slavery. The capstone project was an end-of-term, student-designed dramatic presentation for an audience of family, faculty, and fellow students. As part of the performance, the students elected to stage a slave auction, intending to dramatize a painful period in American history. The instructor in the course—who was popular, energetic, and white—endorsed the student plan. When the college began to hear protests from distressed parents, the instructor defended the students' choice as powerful learning and, of course, an expression of academic freedom. The conflict reached the president, who passed the buck to the dean, who in turn ducked and passed it on to Smith, telling her that this was a department chair's decision. Smith, herself African American, felt she was in a no-win situation. If she called off the auction, she'd be accused of violating academic freedom. "The AAUP will be writing me up," she mused. But, if she let the performance go forward, she expected to be viewed as naive and insensitive.

Administrators often dislike and avoid conflict because they see it as dangerous, distrust their own skills, or are uncomfortable with the emotional turmoil that accompanies it. But conflict is an inevitable part of leadership, and savvy leaders recognize its benefits: "a tranquil, harmonious organization may very well be an apathetic, uncreative, stagnant, inflexible and unresponsive organization" (Heffron, 1989, p. 185). When leaders handle conflict well, they can stimulate innovation and organizational learning, making their institution a livelier and more effective place.

Darya Smith's dilemma is one of countless examples of the leadership challenges in orchestrating conflict. The hallmark of such situations is that conflict takes on personal and emotional overtones involving two or more parties, each of whom feels strongly that "we're right and they're wrong." These situations touch hot buttons for leaders and create the risk that their fears, raw emotions, and jangled nerves will impair their capacity to bring about a good outcome. Typically, the leader is caught in the middle, hoping to find some solution that everyone can live with. But resolution is rarely easy. It requires adaptation or learning by parties who are tied to their current stance and view of the world. Leadership and teaching share much in common. Both push the boundaries of personal growth and disrupt existing belief systems and emotional investments. Both ask others to look hard at what they know and value and to stretch their capacities to make progress on problems those values touch.

This is challenging, but Heifetz and Linsky (2002) offer an optimistic note: "The hope of leadership lies in the capacity to deliver disturbing news and raise difficult questions in a way that people can absorb, prodding them to take up the message rather than ignore it or kill the messenger" (p. 12). Several steps increase the likelihood that academic leaders and their constituents can work together to solve tough issues.

Distinguish Between Technical and Adaptive Problems

A *technical problem* is one for which existing routines can produce a solution that meets some easily accepted criteria for success. Administrators can often use their authority to resolve such problems. When leaders have the information and expertise to choose well, they do what their constituents expect—they solve problems so everyone can move on. *Adaptive problems*, however, are messier. They don't offer well-defined paths to solution, and there is little agreement about what constitutes a good outcome because of differences in values, purposes, or perspectives. For adaptive problems, any decision an administrator makes unilaterally has little chance of success because the audience isn't ready. Constituents need to learn and adapt in order to understand why the problem is so hard and to be ready to find and accept a solution. Adaptive leadership takes time and patience, and the process is different from leadership to resolve technical problems. It also evokes a different response from others (Heifetz & Linsky, 2002).

Exercising leadership from a position of authority in adaptive situations requires going against the grain—and being prepared for the predictable resistance and criticism. Rather than fulfilling others' expectations for quick answers, adaptive leaders need to pose questions. Instead of protecting people from outside threat, they let people feel the threat in order to stimulate necessary learning and growth. Instead of orienting people to their current roles, they disorient them so that new roles, relationships, and views of the future can develop. Rather than quelling conflict, they intensify it, but in ways that constituents can accept. Instead of defending norms, leaders challenge them (Heifetz & Linsky, 2002)—and talk openly and often about what they are doing and why.

Darya Smith's feeling that she's in a lose-lose dilemma is a good clue that she faces an adaptive problem. Any decision she makes will make someone unhappy. The question is, Can she lead in a way that enables others to appreciate and to learn from the challenge?

Give the Work Back to the People

It's tempting to treat an adaptive problem as if it were a technical one by making a decision and trying to impose or sell it to others. It doesn't work. Take the case of John Alden, the provost in a prestigious land-grant university. He invited his deans to participate in making significant budget cuts but acceded when they suggested he make the decision himself. After all, they told him, he had the larger institutional perspective needed for something so important. Alden developed a list of recommended cuts. When they became public, *he* became the problem. It was "Alden's plan" and "the provost's program closings." Those who liked his proposals mostly watched from the sidelines. The opponents were vocal, visible, and persistent. The ensuing firestorm marked the end of a dedicated provost's career. For Alden, it was painful and devastating—and he chose to leave the academy for a job in the private sector. Meanwhile, the campus could blame him and evade responsibility for addressing the financial realities.

Subordinates everywhere know the organizational equivalent of the hot potato game (Weiss & Hughes, 2008)—the tendency to toss thorny issues up the management hierarchy in hopes that their boss will solve things and save them from the difficulty and conflict endemic in complex problem solving. Bosses like Provost Alden, with the best of intentions, try to serve their constituents and institutions by grabbing problems and trying to fix them—and they get burned. In the process, they also encourage an unhealthy dependency. They tacitly communicate that people should send issues to them at the first sign of difficulty. They deprive others of opportunities to become better at productively managing conflict—and themselves the opportunity to become better mentors, coaches, and leaders.

In order to give the work back, leaders need to orchestrate a process that engages constituents in addressing the challenge, understanding the issues, and searching for answers (Heifetz & Linsky, 2002). Provost Alden tried to do this but backed off in response to the deans' successful effort at upward delegation. Leaders need to bring together people on different sides of an issue and facilitate conversation. Darya Smith could, for example, convene a meeting of parents, student leaders, and the course instructor. She would need to set down ground rules and be prepared to tightly manage the exchange. But if she does this well, there is a good chance the participants will learn from the dialogue and find a way out of the impasse.

Don't Personalize Criticism

It is inevitable that any academic leader will make mistakes and enemies. Even when leaders are right, some people will think they're wrong—or will react emotionally to the adaptive challenges in the situation or to the stresses in the personal growth required to respond to them. An administrative role is the wrong place to look for love, and critics will not always express their views in nuanced or reasonable ways. Many will act as if it's always open season on academic leaders and may go well beyond criticizing actions to describing you as despotic, rigid, stupid, crazy, or worse. It is important to listen to critics and to try to learn from them, though that gets harder the more intemperate critics become. But even when the criticism seems personal, painful, or unfair, remember that others are responding more to your role and title than to you. One of the hardest and most important tests of professionalism is to "keep your head when all about you are losing theirs and blaming it on you" (Kipling, 1895). When your emotions run hot, as they sometimes will, slow down and buy time before doing anything rash. Take a step back and give yourself another perspective on the action. Talk it over with someone you can trust. Stay on task, and focus on the purposes you're trying to achieve. That makes it easier to depersonalize and to avoid letting your emotions lead you into impetuous and regrettable actions.

Orchestrating Conflict 2: Turning Up the Heat

When conflict burns too hot, it makes dialogue almost impossible and increases the chances for destructive warfare. In such cases, leaders need to look for ways to cool it down. That was Darya Smith's challenge. But there are also times when leaders need to dial up the heat to get constituents to recognize the seriousness of a problem and invest the effort needed to get to a reasonable outcome.

Consider Jorge Mendez in his fifth year as director of admissions for an enrollment-driven, liberal arts college. He was losing sleep over "AAs"—alternative admits who did not meet the school's standard admissions formula. Originally conceived as a category limited to a few students with special circumstances, AAs had mushroomed to almost half of each entering freshman class in the wake of pressures from an aggressive new president to grow enrollments despite a stagnant admissions pool. For a year or two, the increase in AAs was barely noticed. But now deans and faculty were getting increasingly vocal about the "flood" of students "who can't do the work." Meanwhile, the president had made it clear that he wanted no excuses from his admissions director: if Mendez could not meet the president's enrollment targets, the college would find someone else who could.

Jorge tried to keep everyone happy. He gave the president the numbers he wanted. He reminded deans of the financial benefits of enrollment growth for their units. He assured the faculty that these AA students were deserving diamonds in the rough. But deans and faculty members were pushing back and asking why Mendez wasn't bringing in stronger applicants. Privately, Jorge feared that the college was plunging into an admissions death spiral: weaker students weakened the school's image, which hurt the admissions pool and then forced him to admit even more AAs.

Mendez's strategy for dealing with the challenges he faced is common among academic administrators: try to placate everyone while absorbing the pain and working alone to solve the problem. Seeing conflict as a problem rather than an opportunity, administrators often don't see that it can be a powerful entry point into institutional learning and collaboration. So they respond by avoiding and dampening conflict—ducking if possible and pouring oil on troubled waters when that doesn't work. Sometimes they get lucky and their avoidance strategy succeeds: the problem somehow gets solved or simply goes away. More often, things get worse. The difficulty lingers and festers; and the administrator

pays a heavy personal cost in the form of stress and eventual burnout. Taking on the worries and frustrations of everyone around is
debilitating.

Mendez's situation is a candidate for a particular form of giving work back to the people: orchestrating conflict to take it to an
optimal level. Mendez has absorbed so much of the conflict that
others have little incentive to deal with it. They see it as his problem, and he has implicitly internalized and accepted that framing.
Instead of taking sole responsibility for the situation, however, he
can externalize the conflict by raising questions and encouraging
discussion among those who have a stake in a positive resolution
of the issue.

One way to do that is to network with the key players and
engage them in conversation: make sure they all understand the
full complexity of the issues and gather their suggestions for handling the current impasse. Promising, shared options may already
exist. A second is to bring people together for problem-solving
meetings. A third is to get the issue on the agenda of campus
forums, like the deans' council and the faculty senate. The goal
is to raise the flame under the admissions issue and make it more
visible and urgent on campus. There are risks, of course. If things
get too hot, the issue might explode in unproductive ways—and
Mendez stands in the middle of it all. Another is that the president may prefer the current calm because Mendez is protecting him
from campus push-back. But Jorge is already at risk; and, even more
important, he believes the institution is at significant risk as well.

Fix It Now or Fix It Later: Self-Protection Versus Learning

Academic leaders are busy people (Gallos, 2002), and they regu-
larly have to decide what to do now and what to save for later.
Leaders often postpone work, telling themselves they're too busy.
Bill Noonan (2007) cautions that the real reason for many delays

is deeper and more personal: self-protection. Leaders put off addressing issues they know they should confront because of their own discomfort, fear of incompetence, worries of embarrassment, or desire to avoid threatening or unpleasant situations. Conflict is central to many of the thorniest concerns academic administrators face. Typically these require intense conversations on sensitive, high-stakes issues—and those are tough.

The examples in this chapter point to an uncomfortable reality: sometimes academic administrators have to find ways to engage in discussions they wish they could avoid. If they don't, the situations will continue to haunt them. Like getting the car brakes checked when they first start squeaking and grinding and before break failure sends you hurtling into the car in front of you, leaders need to think carefully—and honestly—about what to take on, what to postpone, and what to avoid.[1] If they choose to avoid the things that scare or challenge them, they may fill their days with the easy things but never quite get around to the important ones. If they're clear about the big picture—what's happening and where they want to go—they know that success means giving more time to the things that really matter, even if they're hard.

Jorge Mendez may not want to be the messenger who tells a demanding president that he's missing something important about campus admissions. But the issue isn't going away—and if things continue to go downhill, Jorge will have a lot more to explain. Darya Smith may not relish her role as referee in an open discussion about the student slave auction drama. She may worry about others confusing her leadership in the situation with her own racial identity. But ignoring the potential for an explosion will not make it go away. Engaging such issues requires both skill and courage, and those qualities are essential to great leadership.

But how? We offer three suggestions. First, remember that whatever got you into this mess won't get you out of it. Start by changing the only thing you're sure you can control—your own actions. Chart out a scenario of what someone would do if fear

---

Academic leaders manage conflict best when they . . .

1. Change their own actions first

2. Focus on learning rather than avoidance or fixing others

3. See the big picture clearly

---

and worry were not an issue and start from there. This may put you on the road to the right strategy.

Second, don't go into a difficult meeting expecting to solve the problem by fixing someone else. How well would it work to open by telling someone, "The purpose of this meeting is to get you to realize that you need to change your ways"? We know the answer to that question, yet we often hope we can do just that so long as we don't tell others what we're up to. There is an alternative: focus on learning rather than avoidance or fixing others. You wouldn't have chosen a career in higher education if you didn't believe in learning, and the same is probably true of most people you work with. Establish a simple criterion for success: If everyone learns, it was a good meeting. Then, review the message about advocacy and inquiry in Chapter Three. In preparing for a difficult conversation, plan to combine advocacy and inquiry with a goal of ensuring that each of you hears and understands the other. A good starting point is to get agreement on the purpose and agenda for the meeting.

If you're Darya Smith, for example, you could call the interested parties together, and start the meeting with something like this:

> We're all aware that there's controversy over the students' upcoming show. Some of you feel strongly that it should go as planned, and others think it needs to be changed. The university has delegated the decision to me; and I'll make it if I have to, but I hope that won't be necessary.

Let's see if we can agree first on a way to move forward. I suggest we proceed by asking students and the instructor to explain why they planned the slave auction and what they hope it will achieve. Then we'll ask those who think it's not a good idea to speak. We'll try to make sure we all understand each other. After that, we can discuss options, and see if we can find something that has broad support. Does that agenda work for everyone?

The group may buy Darya's proposed agenda or may suggest some changes. Either way, Darya signals that she is open to learning and wants a collaborative process. In the best of worlds, the dialogue will fulfill Darya's hope for a consensual solution. Even if that doesn't happen, everyone will have a better understanding of the issues and what's at stake; and Darya will have a much better chance of finding an optimal path out of the thicket and of getting support for whatever decision she ultimately makes.

The third suggestion takes us to the Heifetz (1994) image of the balcony and the dance floor. Amid the endless opportunities and messy problems that clamor for a leader's attention, it's easy to get lost and to feel an ongoing sense of inadequacy or failure because you're unsure of what to do, because you can't get enough done, or because the same chronic problems simply return. We advise persistence and courage to tackle conflicts and difficult situations head on—and periodic movement off the dance floor and up to the balcony to get you through tough times. Administrators get on the dance floor because that's where the action is, not to mention that it's exciting and fun to be engaged and in the middle of things. But it's hard to get your bearings and a larger perspective while you are focused on your own skills, space, feet, and rhythm and are surrounded by gyrating others doing the same. A trip to the balcony is needed to see the big picture. While you are there, take a breather and ask yourself some key questions: What's really going on here? What's really important? What's me in this?

Where are others? What can be done differently? What can we learn from the difficulties being addressed? With a clear sense of where you are, what you face, and how the institution can benefit from the conflict at hand, you'll find yourself better able to get back in the *flow* (Csikszentmihalyi, 2008) and to know with confidence exactly what to do.

Summary

Leadership is personal work is which the whole self is engaged. At its toughest, it can put a leader at risk. Many leadership challenges involve intense conflicts in which leaders face a Goldilocks dilemma of how to get the temperature just right. Sometimes conflict burns too hot, and leaders need ways to lower the flame. It is easier to do this when leaders distinguish technical from adaptive problems, give the work back to others, and avoid personalizing the conflict. In other situations, leaders need to turn up the heat to get people's attention and involvement in serious issues suffering from neglect. Strategies for bringing key players together in open conversation, for facilitating problem solving, and for staying focused on learning are in order.

Note

1. The car imagery and title of this section are adapted from the fictional narrative used in Noonan (2007). Noonan's work is a strong application of groundbreaking work by Chris Argyris and Donald Schön (1974, 1996).

9

Leading from the Middle

Higher education administrators juggle multiple roles and a myriad of expectations from diverse constituents. Squeezed from above and below, from inside and outside the university, they work in a world of conflicting cultures, pressures, and priorities. Spanning boundaries and cultures is a central leadership task in almost any administrative post. Student services and admissions officers sometimes struggle to respond to student needs without stepping on faculty toes. Enrollments and student satisfaction depend on it. Advancement professionals encounter clashes between donor desires and unit priorities that, at worst, generate angry alums, disgruntled donors, unhelpful media coverage, or lawsuits. Business officers try to find efficiencies without triggering battles with faculty, students, or staff. The daily pressures of a life sandwiched among colliding norms and values, local and global demands, and internal and external expectations can make it difficult for academic leaders to maintain their balance and focus. The same pressures can also make it harder for them to see and embrace the joys and opportunities of life in the middle— particularly, the potential power, satisfaction, and leverage from being well positioned to facilitate communication and agreements among divergent audiences.

Randy Applegate stumbled into these issues as he entered his third year as dean of the business school on his urban campus. For once, he was looking forward to sharing good news with his division chairs. Thanks to the chief executive officer (CEO) of a local software company, SupportwareLink, he had an opportunity to turn around recent enrollment declines. SupportwareLink was in search of professional development for its employees, and the CEO asked Applegate if his school could provide the courses. "Enrollment increases and a way to showcase the school's strengths to the business community—nice," thought Applegate. "Pleasing a potential major donor right before the launch of the capital campaign—even better."

Applegate presented an overview of the opportunity to the chairs at their regular meeting, with quick calculations of the financial implications as well as the public relations and fund-raising benefits. As Applegate saw it, the program could begin next semester. SupportwareLink employees would take regular MBA classes on campus as nondegree students. A faculty group could convene to develop additional specialty courses to be offered at the company's headquarters. Applegate knew which professors he'd ask to offer those—the CEO had already requested a few by name. The CEO had also asked Applegate to get him a proposal in a week or two.

Randy finished his overview and asked the chairs for their thoughts on how best to proceed. At first there was silence. Then they began to speak.

"Randy, we need to take this to the faculty," said one chair. "We might be able to get this on next month's faculty meeting agenda. Springing this on folks over the summer is suicide."

"We'd have to change class size policies and course caps," added another. "That's got to go through the curriculum committee."

"This is going to crowd out students who need courses for graduation," added a third. "Our students always register right before the semester begins."

"We can do it," said one chair optimistically. "But we're going to have to add more sections for a few courses. And I feel very strongly that our degree students should get first crack at our regular faculty."

"First impressions are everything. You're going to let some adjunct introduce these SupportwareLink folks to our program?" asked another chair incredulously.

"Won't all those nondegree-seeking students create a problem for our accreditation? And I don't think the new budgeting system counts nondegree students in its formulas. We won't get the budget credit anyway."

"Are these special courses going to be counted in regular class loads for faculty?" asked someone. "Or are they extra comp?"

"Extra comp!" said one chair heatedly. "I can tell you my department will go through the roof. None of this lucrative exec ed ever comes our way, and faculty raises the last three years have amounted to almost nothing. Everyone remembers, I'm sure," he added, "we couldn't get any funds for our department's new tutoring center proposal last year."

"Nondegree students change class dynamics. Who wants that?" added one of the chairs. "There are faculty who just won't teach those software people!"

"Well there's another side—we probably don't want some of our faculty anywhere near those software people," added another. Everyone laughed for the first time in the meeting.

Here we go again, thought Applegate. How was he going to proceed with the faculty? The chairs had raised important issues. How was he going to buy time with SupportwareLink to sort all this out? *Welcome*, mused Applegate to himself, *to the dean's squeeze.*

Randy Applegate's case exemplifies the myths and realities of academic leadership in the middle. He may not want an enrollment-driven budgeting system, but he has to live with one. He accepts faculty governance and control of the curriculum—and the snail's pace of decision making that can result. He also sees the importance of a timely response, by corporate standards, to the SupportwareLink CEO. How can Applegate lead well and powerfully when squeezed between different sets of important constituents? The question is important because all higher education leaders face similar challenges. Those at the top, like presidents and chancellors, may look like powerful solo players, but they sit in the middle of a complex mix—everyone on campus, of course, plus boards, donors, community groups, business and civic leaders, media, alumni, elected officials, faith-based groups, foundations, government agencies, and others. Understanding middle dynamics and knowing how to manage them can make all the difference.

As a boundary spanner, Dean Applegate is an information and culture broker situated between two groups who differ from one another but who can benefit from better understanding and working relationships. In this role, academic administrators embrace the work of an informal educator and diplomat—an emissary shuttling back and forth between two different worlds to facilitate mutual learning and productive agreements. Leaders who see the possibilities and bring the necessary skills assist their institutions in developing creative partnerships.

Leading from the middle is heroic but difficult work, and there will be moments when academic leaders wonder whether the personal and professional costs are too high. The daily demands make it easy to lose faith and perspective. But understanding the origins and reality of these challenges can keep leaders focused and on top of their game. So can strategies for moving beyond the squeeze to make things happen in a pressure-filled world.

Understanding Administrative Life in the Middle

Randy Applegate lives with large unit responsibilities, scarce resources, and limited authority. Like other academic administrators, he spends more time facilitating, selling, and encouraging than controlling and implementing. If he worked outside the university, Applegate might have had a proposal back to SupportwareLink in 48 hours. Working with his faculty and chairs, he'll be lucky if he can respond in a few weeks. He could try to push the decision through and announce it, but he might lose or pay too high a price. Even if he prevails, he would expend scarce political capital and might alienate the very people he needs to deliver the program. Wise academic leaders, like good parents, pick their battles carefully. Applegate would like to keep everyone happy—the CEO, his faculty, his department chairs, and his boss—but that requires chronic juggling of divergent expectations, perceptions, needs, and demands.

Academic leaders live with feet firmly planted in two different camps: the world of academia and the corporate-informed world of administrative performance. Each has its own values, beliefs, and expectations. Each sees its own world as the dominant reality, and Applegate is expected to adhere to the cultures of both. He needs to tend his faculty and his community partners and donors, respect faculty governance and quick turnaround times, foster a collegial environment and make tough budgetary decisions. Life in the collegiate middle is even tougher than in the corporate world, which itself has seen a growing exodus from middle management. Like many higher education administrators, middle managers there want out because the balancing act required in their jobs is "too stressful, too demanding, unmanageable, and unrewarding" (Oshry, 2007, p. 2).

Living in two worlds also means that much of the work and accomplishments of those in the middle are invisible to, or dismissed by, one constituent group or another. We all construct our social reality, seeing and valuing what our worldview allows. If Dean Applegate acts globally—devoting serious time to building the school's reputation in the larger community and to cultivating external donors, as he is doing with SupportwareLink—he risks being seen as uncaring and out of touch by his faculty and staff who complain about how hard it is to get on his calendar. They may question his loyalty and priorities—does he care more about money and business leaders than scholarship and students? On the other side, if Randy mostly tends the internal gardens, he isolates himself from vital networks of community support. He'll miss opportunities to garner resources; build programs and enrollments; identify potential collaborations; and gain seats at campus, civic, and professional tables that can serve his school. At best, it's a complex balancing act. At worst, he looks weak to everyone. The trade-offs are real. Academic leaders cannot favor one world over the other—even if the majority of their constituents wish that they did.

Veteran higher education administrators understand that faculty do not always love or appreciate them. The invisibility of academic leadership is one explanation for a chronic rift (Cohen, 1996). Administration has a different pace, focus, and rhythm from faculty life—and faculty are largely focused on their world. It's also easy for academic administrators to get caught up in the hectic pace of overfilled schedules, hoping that others recognize and appreciate all that they do. Few of Randy Applegate's faculty know how he spends his time—few have ever asked. Academic leadership is largely invisible to them when things go well: success brings "the absence of dissatisfaction" (Herzberg, 1968) but no guarantee of productivity or anything else. Knowledge of Applegate's work world is even less visible to key outside constituents who often have little patience for academic decision making. They push the campus to give them what they want when they want it. Academic leadership is a lonely and fractured job, as depicted in Table 9.1. It summarizes the internal and external work worlds for many higher education leaders. A closer look into selected dynamics offers insights into the challenges and opportunities academic administrators have as buffers and boundary spanners.

An Academic Leader's Internal World

An academic leader's internal world is shaped by two sets of factors: (1) local issues within a unit, center, or department; and (2) employee perceptions of the leader's role, responsibilities, and influence. Both sets are largely driven by what others need to get their work done. Both are informed by the strong collegial culture

Table 9.1. The Academic Leader's Work Worlds

Key Variables	Internal World	External World
Key constituents	Faculty, staff, and students	Senior campus leadership and administrators, peers, colleagues, alumni, potential faculty and staff recruits, parents, present and future students, donors, civic leadership, community constituent and partnership groups, philanthropic organizations, professional associations, accrediting bodies, media, state and local elected officials, peer and competitive institutions, government certifying agencies, all those who know the institution through the Internet
Dominant culture(s)	Collegial	Administrative culture of performance, managerial academic culture, corporate culture
Core values	Academic freedom, diversity, collegiality, consensus	Efficiency, accountability, consistency, equity, responsiveness, service, transparency
Locus of attention	Local, personal, discipline-specific	University level, regional/national/global; interdisciplinary; educational and administrative

(Continued)

Table 9.1. (*continued*)

Key Variables	Internal World	External World
Central needs	Intraschool, university, and idiosyncratic supports for individual faculty and staff; independence	Quality, responsiveness, service, partnerships, innovation, funding, enrollments, effectiveness, meeting professional and national standards, accreditation, interdependence
Governance and accountability processes	Faculty-created, -based, and -driven discussions and decision making; consensus; faculty peer review	Managerial efficiency, outcome measures, data-based decision making, administrative leadership, strategic management
Expectations for successful unit leadership	Minimal intrusion, maximum support, respect for autonomy and diversity, informal and nonhierarchical relationships, local needs for transparency	Quality, strategic planning, successful external funding, balanced budget, creativity, productivity, responsiveness, collaboration and partnerships, enrollment increases, increased funding, transparency
Definition of the leader's role	Facilitator, fountain of resources, colleague, community builder, communications conduit, scholar, "not faculty"	Administrator, campus and unit leader, policymaker/ implementer, manager of people and money, entrepreneur

Key Variables	Internal World	External World
Leader's sources of power	Resources and funding, scholarly productivity	Administrative/managerial competence, charisma, information, relationships, networks, reputation, creativity, leadership skills, important sponsors, influential mentors, funding sources, position
Leader's source of authority	Faculty given	Legal-rational, positional

Source: Adapted from Gallos (2002).

of the academy and by pervasive faculty scorn for bureaucracy, administrators, and hierarchy. This anti-administrative stance has been described as "the most collectively socialized response across the academic population" (Frost & Taylor, 1996b, p. 310). Faculty who assume administrative responsibilities are often surprised by the disdain they feel from people who used to be their colleagues and friends. (See, for example, Cohen, 1996; Fukami, 1996; Napier, 1996.)

The collegial culture of the academy emphasizes academic freedom, diversity, collegiality, and consensus (Bergquist, 1992). The inherent paradoxes and value tensions complicate an academic administrator's life. Autonomy and individuality, which are highly valued, impede consensus and collaboration—and hinder an administrator's capacity for strategic leadership, building a strong unit culture, and forging broad-based collaborations and partnerships. SupportwareLink was important to the school's larger mission, but the department chairs' responses focused on local impediments. The paradox in collegial autonomy sets the stage for recurrent conflicts. By the very nature of their jobs, higher education administrators regularly ask faculty to do things inconsistent with faculty preferences, strengths, disciplines, and even professional reward systems. Faculty often choose to say no.

Good academic leaders, like Dean Applegate, also deliberately work both sides of the paradox. They nurture the individuality and idiosyncratic strengths of others as a way to foster creativity and innovation. At the same time, they need to make sure the whole herd is moving roughly west. They need to be equitable and fair; respond in real time to opportunities and to the requests and demands of superiors and key constituents; and ensure that their academic units renew themselves through organizational learning, change, and development of fresh talent. To do all that requires different and stronger leadership than many faculty prefer.

Consciously or not, faculty often try to limit the academic leader's role to initiator of faculty governance procedures and fountain of resources. They hope for benevolent administrators who offer minimal intrusion, maximum support, and unwavering promotion of freedom and individuality. They envision the academic leader as an encouraging buddy in an environment of informal and nonhierarchical relationships. But this image ignores the educational leadership and strategic management that provosts, presidents, and major donors demand.

Seeing System Dynamics

Predictable system dynamics play a piece in all this. Scholars who study bosses and subordinates (see, for example, Bolman & Deal, 2000, 2008c; Kotter, 1985; Oshry, 1995; Sales, 2006, 2008) delineate how the world looks different depending on where you sit—and how your seat influences what you see, how you feel and act, and what others want from you. Higher education administrators and faculty get caught in what systems theorist Barry Oshry (1995) terms a *dance of blind reflex*. They instinctively enact age-old scripts that serve neither well, then blame the other for the dysfunction (Bedein, 2002; Gallos, 2002). Frustrating? Absolutely.

Unique to the academy? No. It's all in the structure: we interact role to role, not just person to person—and "much that feels personal is not personal at all" (Oshry, 1995, p. 261). A different position in the chain of command means different demands, needs, information, and reactions.

Those at the top, for example, are besieged by responsibilities, complexity, pressures, and decisions that can mean organizational life or death. The buck stops with them. As head of the business school, Dean Applegate spends sleepless nights worrying about budget and enrollment concerns that faculty rarely consider. The burdens and obligations of leaders at the top feel heavy to them. Stress, burnout, and heart attacks are chronic risks.

Middles, on the other hand, need to please both bosses and subordinates to survive: as a result, they are torn, stressed, indecisive, and unable to satisfy anyone adequately. Randy may be at the top of the business school's food chain, but he sits squarely in the middle of the university hierarchy. He bears all the responsibilities of a school head and all the constraints of a leader of a subunit within a larger institutional context.

Those at the bottom feel powerless, invisible, vulnerable, and sure that their bosses are clueless. Bottoms see little beyond the scope of their own jobs, and they regularly wonder why those above them can't seem to get it right. These behavioral scripts are recreated and played out every day in organizations around the world. The same scripts, in fact, can be powerfully and quickly recreated in simulations, despite the best efforts of participants to avoid them (Bolman & Deal, 1979; Oshry, 2007).

Schools and academic units seem like self-governing fiefdoms to those who have not sat in the top leader's chair. Each has its own goals, focus, priorities, history, budgets, internal governance structures, key constituents, and so on. Faculty and staff can interpret all this as unit independence. Likewise, they can confuse the leader's day-to-day management responsibilities with autonomy. As a result, many envision academic leaders as mini-CEOs with power and prerogatives to make sweeping decisions. The reality is less enchanting. All higher education administrators have wiggle room—which varies by the job they hold and the institution in which they work. But one constant is that academic leaders mostly propose, recommend, negotiate, and nudge. At the end of the day, all serve at the discretion of their bosses: chairs and department heads answer to their dean, deans and directors to their provost, provosts to their president, and chancellors and presidents to their boards. Randy Applegate as CEO? Hardly. There are many days when it seems as if everyone has more power and influence than he does.

The Academic Leader's External World

The expectations and pressures in an academic leader's internal world are markedly different from those that come from the outside. An administrator's external world is large and diverse. Depending on where he or she sits, it can include a variety of senior campus leaders and administrators (who may or may not directly evaluate the administrator's performance), peers and colleagues, alumni, potential faculty and staff recruits, current and future students, parents, donors, accrediting bodies, government agencies and regulators, professional associations, peer and competitive institutions, the legal community, foundations, collaborators and partnership organizations of all kind, the media, elected officials, as well as community, philanthropic, and professional groups with vested interests in the school, its personnel, or its products.

These external players swirl in and out of the work day, controlling or influencing key strategies and resources that affect a wide range of programs and activities. External constituents bring their own perceptions of an academic leader's role and responsibilities; their own demands and requests; and their own expectations (or requirements) for the leader's involvement in campus, civic, and professional activities. Some, like senior campus leaders, appreciate the traditional culture of the academy yet hold standards rooted in an administrative culture of corporate expectations for managerial efficiency and effectiveness (Birnbaum, 2001). Others, like community, government, and philanthropic leaders, typically understand little about running a college or university and use corporate values and traditions as a primary lens for understanding academic performance, process, and leadership. The diversity and number of key external constituents add to the complexity of the mix, the demands on time and attention, and the unpredictable rhythm of an academic leader's work and calendar.

Outsiders often expect work processes at odds with the collegiality and minimal intrusion that insiders demand. Everyone pushes for timely delivery of quality goods and services, and bosses expect sound management of the unit or program—fiscal solvency, fair and equitable implementation of policies, the meeting of deadlines and reporting requirements, and the creation of systems and a culture that foster and reward creativity and productivity. An almost universal definition of success is "bettering the numbers"—more students and dollars. Outcome measures are increasingly important in university administration, and abstract variables like enhancing creativity or instructional quality are hard to quantify. Students and dollars are easy to measure—but not always easy to get.

The concept of academic goods and services is ambiguous, and different constituents want different things that range from strong and relevant courses, to cutting-edge research, to solutions and resources for social and technical problems, to activities that prepare the workforce, to the delivery of faculty support for major campus initiatives and policies, and more. For the CEO of SupportwareLink, it means professional development from top-notch faculty for his employees. The ability to deliver is essential to a leader's credibility. It evokes a *logic of confidence* (Meyer & Rowan, 1983)—constituents' good faith that all goes well—and enables academic leaders to compete effectively for other scarce resources. The credibility of a unit or program is directly linked to the credibility of its leader, but on most things leaders can deliver only if their people produce good and timely work. An academic administrator's effectiveness, then, is largely judged by the products and efforts of others, many of whom are protected by the mantle of tenure.

How do academic leaders bolster external credibility when they have little control over the goods and services they are expected to produce, they encounter idiosyncratic barriers like tenure and nine-month faculty contracts, and academic outputs always take longer to design and deliver than outsiders expect? They often use themselves: as diplomats employing their time, energy, personal style, and goodwill to build key relationships and as buffers to buy time or to hold the competitive wolves (and waiting customers) at bay. Playing these two roles well with SupportwareLink serves both the university and Applegate's school—and he will need to find ways to finesse the situation and to maintain good relationships with all involved. Applegate's—and his school's—future depend on it. Every external contact or event is another opportunity to place the university's name, credibility, and needs in the public eye. Each holds the prospect for more students and dollars. Each affords another occasion to manage impressions, enhance credibility, build partnerships, and achieve the mission.

All these contacts and relationships also keep academic leaders in information loops and networks—positioned to influence agendas and decisions that can affect their units and institutions. To insiders, these public interface activities may look like fluff and free meals. For higher education administrators at all levels, they are a vital part of the job. Good academic leaders are always "on," and they keep the unit's needs and mission in mind in every exchange. They recognize the symbolic power and possibilities of their role. Much of the time, they cannot easily delegate that piece of the job to others.

The trap in the boundary spanner role, however, is the temptation to take on more and more. Shuttling back and forth between two worlds, academic leaders in the middle see things that those on either side of the boundary do not; and they want to be helpful. In their efforts to do so, they can easily blur the line between their own work and others' responsibilities—exhausting themselves and forgetting that leadership is about engaging others and supporting them in joint problem solving. We return to the sage advice of Ronald Heifetz (1994): "Give the work back to the people." The pressures of the middle role make it easy to lose sight of the distinction between being responsive and owning other people's problems and conflicts (Sales, 2006). The consequence is that academic leaders can lose objectivity, effectiveness, and the capacity to serve all sides well.

Finally, the larger higher education environment compounds life in the middle. Academic leaders live daily with the pinch of shrinking budgets, diminishing public confidence, intense competition for students, changing technology, changing student markets, and dramatic shifts in the competitive landscape with the growth of online learning and for-profit providers. They are regularly reminded that students see multiplying options and shop for convenience, speed of program completion, and price (Newman, Couturier, & Scurry, 2004). In such an environment, partnership and collaboration take on new meaning. Dean Applegate is legitimately excited about the SupportwareLink option. Contracts for custom degree programs, employee training, literacy instruction, English as a Second Language offerings, professional development, and other such activities provide a steady stream of new students and dollars. They also generate resources to invest in new courses, research, and program development; provide an impetus to review current curricula and offerings; and offer opportunities to cultivate donors, sponsors, placement sites for internships, and jobs for graduates. Corporate and civic partners, however, want real collaboration. They want to influence what they get; and they expect corporate standards of responsiveness, service to the customer, and timeliness. The stage is set for the squeeze to continue.

Course and degree content is faculty territory. Moreover, the pressures and demands of scholarly life keep faculty feeling that their plate is full and that taking on more of one thing means doing less of something else. The challenge for Applegate is to land that partnership while respecting the faculty and university procedures. It is easy to play out the tensions in the case—and they are not limited to the specifics of this scenario or to the dean's role. Internally, academic leaders coax, push, and sometimes make executive decisions: they risk being seen as ogres who overstep their bounds and tread on sacred cows. Externally, they cajole and stall: they risk looking disorganized and ineffectual. Win-win requires complex skills in shuttle diplomacy—and large chunks of time that aren't there. Sitting in the middle makes it easy to see merit on both sides. It doesn't ensure a resolution anyone accepts.

Strategies for Effective Action

The leadership squeeze in higher education is a fascinating framing phenomenon. Dean Applegate can dwell on the stress and the potential conflict inherent in his boundary spanning position, feeling the frustrations of life in the middle at each twist and turn. He can pressure the chairs to move his plan along quickly—and bemoan the curse of academic folkways that could derail a great opportunity. He can charge forward on his own and let the chips fall as they may. He can tell the CEO that the school can't respond to SupportwareLink's needs at this time. But none of those strategies enables Applegate to live out the full potential of his position—to help the school *and* the CEO of SupportwareLink understand what both have to gain through a well-forged and mutually workable partnership.

The same world can look very different through the eyes of a university administrator, a faculty member, and a community leader—and all can be right. The path to successful working relationships—and to successful academic leadership—requires bridging those frame gaps. Seeing systems helps—so does patience, tolerance, and a sense of humor. Academic leaders who recognize that their "simple request" to faculty can be seen as an intrusion on professional priorities, a hindrance to scholarly progress, and another example of "them doing it to us again" may devise better strategies for communication. Faculty who recognize the burden that their "simple request" might create for a stressed and overworked academic administrator may be more understanding about delays, dropped balls, or a response of "Sorry, but no." Community leaders who understand how faculty governance works may adopt longer time horizons when partnering with a university. It is always easier to complain than to fix things: fixing things takes energy, planning, and resources that are in short supply in most professional lives (Fukami, 1996). In higher education, we often need to complain less, talk more openly and directly, and cut each other more slack. Several strategies are helpful for managing that.

Successful academic leaders in the middle . . .

1. Listen, understand, and respect differences

2. Look for mutual gains

3. Stay alert to system dynamics and take new leadership stands

---

Listen, Understand, and Respect Differences

It is tempting as a boundary spanner to distance from one constituent in order to move closer to another. We may see one party as more reasonable or better able to serve our needs. It is also comforting to spend time with others who confirm our views of the world. But taking sides is dangerous, and we can learn much from those who see things differently or make life tough for us. Good shuttle diplomacy requires the ability to hold and respect two or more conflicting perspectives at the same time and to live with the tensions. It may be easier to take one side or the other, but the leader's job is to search for the possibilities at the intersection: to serve as a translator who puts each side's message in a form the other can understand, a mediator who represents each side to the other, and a magician who conjures rabbits from seemingly empty hats.

Look for Mutual Gains

For academic leaders in the middle, negotiating is a way of life—essential whenever two or more parties with some interests in common and others in conflict need to reach agreement. One of the most helpful and practical win-win approaches we know was developed by Roger Fisher and William Ury (1981) in their perennial bestseller, *Getting to Yes*. The genius of their approach lies in a four step strategy:

1. Separate the people from the problem.
2. Focus on interests, not positions.
3. Invent a variety of options before deciding what to do.
4. Insist on objective and mutually agreed upon criteria to make the decision.

The four steps may seem straightforward, but it takes practice to get them right. The stress and tensions in conflict can easily escalate negotiations into anger and personal attacks as negotiators lock themselves into positions that can seem like their only options. Efforts to sustain a working relationship or gain approval can lead one side to "give in"—an equally unproductive strategy. Good negotiators stay focused on their larger goal, look for new options and possibilities that bring advantages to both sides, and engage in a joint search for objective criteria—standards of fairness for both substance and procedure—that can be used to make a mutually satisfying final decision.

Stay Alert to System Dynamics and Take a New Leadership Stand

We all like to think of ourselves as independent actors, and it's often hard to remember that many of our actions and choices result from our roles and place in the chain of command. Universities are temples of knowledge but they are also human systems; and those who lead them experience the same role tensions found in other hierarchical organizations. Academic leaders may be squeezed in the middle, but there are ways for them to gain better control over their work life and their leadership.

Leaders in the middles can take new leadership stands and break the expectations that they and others have of them. Suggestions from systems theory (Sales, 2008) include:

Act like a top *when you can.* Recognize the power you have and don't be afraid to use it.

Be a bottom *when you have to.* Put aside the middle's temptation to try to please everyone, and say no when you know something is wrong or won't work.

Enlist and coach others. Help others work better instead of doing their work, making their conflicts your own, or jumping in to fix things that others have broken.

Be a facilitator. Bring people in conflict together and help them work through their issues.

Find support and solace in peers. Create opportunities to connect with others in the middle. They understand the pressures you face and can share the strategies they use to lead well.

Summary

College and university leaders face an important opportunity to use their positions in the middle of things to facilitate relationships and to bring the divergent needs of different parties together in support of institutional advancement. Life in the middle can be a squeeze. But academic administrators who understand the predictable system dynamics and pressures in the role are ahead of the game. Knowledge and the choice to take a different leadership stand will help. So will skills for working productively with differences and for conducting win-win negotiations.

10

Leading Difficult People

We don't know that colleges and universities have more idiosyncratic and difficult people than other organizations, though anecdotal evidence to that effect is buttressed by popular stereotypes in film and fiction of mad scientists, absent-minded professors, campus despots, and manipulative administrators. Faculty, in particular, are expected to be idiosyncratic. It's part of their charm and may fuel their productivity (Andreasen, 2006; Wallace & Gruber, 1989). Even if academe has no more than its fair share of challenging personalities, its employees have more autonomy and room to bring their full personal package to the workplace than do workers elsewhere. As a result, there are fewer guard rails to keep individuals from going off the road or crashing head-on into someone else. Most academic administrators have to deal with at least a few unusually difficult or prickly people who cause a disproportionate share of their headaches. How ready are you?

Our focus here is not on everyday cranks, critics, and gadflies. They may be irritating but are often valuable and productive citizens. Wise academic administrators honor and protect these industrious and candid curmudgeons. Think of them as a special kind of ally—and make them your best friends, not enemies. They offer early warning signs of trouble because they voice what others are thinking and feeling but not saying. Recognizing this can save a lot of energy and aggravation—and yield valuable information to inform your leadership choices. We will not address poor performers or folks who routinely promise more than they deliver. We recommend clear performance goals, consistent feedback, coaching, and assessment processes that hold people accountable for meeting stated expectations. Our major concern here is preparing you to handle individuals who spread toxicity and misery wherever they go, while draining away everyone's time and energy from getting work done. You need a workable strategy for handling these individuals before they erode collective morale—and your sanity.

We begin with a set of seven rules to help you stay grounded in the face of the range of cases you may encounter. Handling difficult people takes a combination of strategy, confidence, and calm—and some good training in counseling basics. We then apply the guidelines to two types of difficult people common in the academy: bullies and backstabbers.

The Seven Rules for Dealing with Difficult People

Academic leaders handle difficult people best when they . . .

1. Assess the full situation

2. Look in the mirror

3. Befriend their challenge

4. Unhook

5. Set expectations

6. Get help

7. Divorce, if necessary

Rule 1: Assess the Full Situation

A first step in dealing with difficult people is to assess the situation so that you know what you have before you. It helps to differentiate between a genuinely difficult person and a work situation that is bringing out the worst in someone. This is important because it's often easier to change the circumstances than the individual.

Branding another person as difficult is tempting as a way to local-ize blame, but jumping to conclusions can block you from identi-fying situational adjustments to curtail the bothersome behavior.

A key test of a difficult person is whether the problematic behavior is chronic and consistent or situational. Does the indi-vidual's behavior vary with different people or circumstances? Does the individual ever learn or adapt in response to feedback or open discussion? Was there a particular incident that triggered the behavior pattern? Indications that the behavior is situational or influenceable offer hope that a solution to the troublesome behav-ior can be found with learning for all involved (Bramson, 1981).

Rule 2: Look in the Mirror

When others seem unreasonable or uncooperative, it's impor-tant to remember that they may see you as the problem—and sometimes they could be right. There may be feedback on your leadership or your choices that you are not hearing. You may be over-responding to behavior that you perceive as troublesome. Or you may be reading unresolved issues from painful circum-stances in your past into the current relationship, fearful that an unpleasant or challenging situation will repeat itself. It is human nature to respond defensively when feeling threatened or under pressure—and this is often the case in dealing with people we find difficult. Ask yourself or someone you trust if there's anything you're doing that might be causing or maintaining the difficulty. Even if there isn't, you'll have taken time for a useful check on your own leadership. The opportunity to take a step back and look at the big picture is always helpful.

Rule 3: Befriend Your Challenge

It often feels counterintuitive, but reaching out to those who cause you pain can go a long way in solving the problem—and it's a good way to get the data you need to assess the situation. In the process, you may learn from them that there are reasonable things you can do to meet their needs or reduce their frustration, and the two of you may discover new ways to work together. Reaching out is also a good diagnostic device to see whether you are dealing with someone who can respond to rational dialogue, as opposed to a candidate for separation or professional intervention.

For example, a new dean in a professional school inherited a tenured faculty member, Professor Amo, who brought a reputation as a competent scholar and teacher but perennial malcontent. Amo had issued occasional broadsides harshly critical of the previous dean and soon appeared in the new dean's office to complain that his raise from the prior year was entirely too low. For a variety of reasons, the dean concluded that she could not and should not change the raise. But she probed to understand the sentiments behind the request and learned that Professor Amo had special family circumstances that were causing significant financial pressures. The new dean listened and empathized. She told Amo that she couldn't do anything about the raise, but she promised to keep her eye out for ways that the school could help. Later in the year, she was able to steer a modest amount of extra compensation to Amo for a small project. For the first time Professor Amo felt that a dean had listened and responded to his concerns. He became a more productive citizen and loyal supporter of the dean, and many of his colleagues were pleasantly surprised by the uptick in his outlook on life and work.

Rule 4: Unhook

The hardest people to deal with are those who push our emotional buttons. If, for example, you still carry the pain of a relationship with a parent who was never satisfied with anything you did, a demanding boss or colleague can inadvertently evoke feelings of rage and helplessness you've been trying to bury for years. Your colleagues and constituents have their own unresolved life issues, and leaders are perfect targets for their projections and negative feelings. When someone attacks you for something you didn't do, if you stay grounded and unhooked, you can learn a great deal about the attacker from his or her projections (Carter, 1989).

The first step in unhooking is to recognize that you're getting hooked. *Know thyself* is a ground rule for effective academic leadership—and a life saver for dealing with difficult coworkers. Step 2 is to understand the pattern: What does the other person do and in what circumstances that sets you off? Once you know that, you are ready for step 3: develop and rehearse alternative ways of responding that help you manage your feelings and stay on task. In the same way that professional musicians practice for hours so that muscle memory carries them through moments of forgetfulness or stage fright—and more important, builds their confidence that they won't be shaken if either happens—academic leaders who rehearse and prepare alternative responses to difficult situations increase their likelihood of staying grounded. They also expand their repertoire of interpersonal options.

Suppose, for example, a colleague's sarcastic digs cause you to seethe inside, which undermines your concentration on the task at hand. What are your alternatives the next time the sarcasm comes your way? You could ask a question, like "Is there something you're trying to say that I'm missing?" You could say, "Thanks for the feedback," take a deep breath, and move on. You could confront the other person: "That stings. Was that your intention?" You can probably think of others. You're looking for responses that do two things. First, you want something that lets you script yourself as a calm and confident professional so that you can control your feelings rather than let them control you. Second, you want something that breaks the recurring pattern by responding in a way that your difficult person isn't expecting. Surprise disrupts old routines and opens opportunity for a productive conversation.

Rule 5: Set Expectations

Sometimes people who seem difficult are simply doing what comes naturally in the absence of clear norms of conduct or expectations for performance. For example, most institutions have developed a code of conduct to deal with romantic or sexual involvement between employees and students. Those codes will not deter every instance of inappropriate contact, but they make it more likely that people know the rules and the potential costs of breaking them. The codes also make it easier to intervene when someone has gone off track. Setting standards, communicating them clearly (including in writing), and then holding people accountable for meeting those standards can make a world of difference.

Rule 6: Get Help

You don't want to be alone in dealing with unusually difficult people. Consult with your boss, your human resource department, a trusted colleague, a professional coach, your campus counseling center, or a good friend. Ask for advice, and look for allies. Someone who troubles you is likely to bother others as well; and working with others makes it easier to mount an effective, coordinated response. Seeking support is not admitting defeat. It is a sound professional strategy for managing a complex institutional problem.

Rule 7: Divorce, If Necessary

Not every relationship problem can be solved, and not every individual is coachable. Some people are closed to learning. Others may have psychological or personal problems too deep to tackle with a workplace intervention. Offering others opportunities to reflect on their behavior and to expand their interpersonal competencies is not therapy, and a threshold of psychic stability is essential for professional growth (Argyris, 1968).

If a sincere attempt to use rules 1–6 doesn't produce improvement, it's time to consider reassignment or discharge. This is rarely easy, particularly in the case of tenured faculty, and always requires careful attention to documentation and process. But when it becomes necessary, accept reality and move forward. Do it with as much grace and sensitivity as possible, but get it done. During Henry Rosovsky's tenure as dean of Harvard's faculty of arts and sciences, one of his tenured professors became so erratic he no longer regularly met his classes. After multiple meetings failed to produce progress, Rosovsky (1990) put the professor on medical leave "with pay and very much against his will" (p. 281). The individual felt so insulted he resigned and left Harvard. It was a personal tragedy for the professor, but the dean did what he had to do.

Two Classic Archetypes: Bullies and Backstabbers

The seven rules provide generic guidelines that should help in most cases but will need to be adapted to the specifics of any given situation. We discuss how to do that by exploring two classic archetypes: bullies and backstabbers.

Bullies

Bullies are arrogant or narcissistic individuals who enjoy power and are willing to beat up or bulldoze anyone who gets in their way. They are sometimes high performers whose track record gives them substantial credibility and influence. If they also happen to be smarter and more combative than many of the people around them, they can be a destructive presence in a unit or institution. Recent studies of higher education document the growth of an academic bully culture (Schmidt, 2010b; Twale & DeLuca, 2008; Westhues, n.d.). The growth is fueled by a variety of forces: the rise in corporate culture mentalities and practices on college campuses, institutional shifts from a mission-driven to a market-driven focus that make things like rankings and status so important, and higher education practices such as courting and appointing winner-take-all superstars. Big egos, weak faculty governance structures, a culture of individualism, and tolerance within the academy for behaviors not accepted elsewhere also play a role.

Take the case of Professor Burly. The chemistry department in a prestigious research university was thrilled when it succeeded in recruiting him to fill a newly endowed chair. He was one of the most highly regarded scientists in his field—many saw a Nobel Prize in his future. His research record was extraordinary, and he was an energetic teacher and mentor. Some of his protégés were becoming prominent in their own right through their associations with him. Once on board, Burly did the things people had hoped he would. His presence immediately elevated the image and reputation of the chemistry department and of the college. He brought in major grants to support the lab that had been built for him, and he began to recruit highly talented young scholars and doctoral students to build his program.

Down the road, the university began to realize that Burly had a darker side. He was relentless in building his program and reputation, but he seemed oblivious to anyone else's needs. He became a major source of stress for his department chair, who dreaded meetings because Burly was continually demanding something more and rarely took "No" for an answer. If he didn't immediately get what he wanted from the chair, Burly took his case to the dean, the provost, the president, and even members of the board. Everyone in the administrative chain struggled to find ways to keep Burly happy because the university had tied its own image—and resources—so publicly to his reputation. Even more troubling, stories began to spread about Burly's abusive behavior toward staff, students, and junior faculty. Most never got beyond the rumor stage because many of the aggrieved individuals left the university. But some made it to the human resource department as informal complaints or formal grievances. An administrative assistant grieved Burly for creating a hostile work environment. A fired lab assistant filed a complaint of gender and age discrimination. Burly was unrepentant. He insisted that any such claims were falsehoods generated by jealous people who blamed him for their own incompetence.

Talented bullies like Burly create a knotty and perplexing dilemma for academic leaders. A faculty or administrative star is a scarce and valuable asset, but no college or university can indefinitely tolerate an individual who poisons the atmosphere and undermines important institutional values. The dilemma is so painful that it's tempting for academic leaders at the top to push the problem down in hopes that deans and division chairs can contain the mess—but the latter may have thrown up their hands and backed off in hope that things will somehow get better with time. Unfortunately, at work as on the playground, bullies rarely stop of their own accord because, for them, their strategies work. Burly's university needs to acknowledge the problem and move aggressively to deal with it. That will only happen when academic leaders with a stake in the larger issues come together in support of a consistent action plan.

When they apply our rules for dealing with difficult people, leaders at Burly's university need to start by assessing the situation and then looking in the mirror. What's *really* going on? How did things get to this point? Was the university careless in the hiring process? Were they willing to sacrifice institutional values in exchange for a rise in status? Answering those questions won't solve the Burly issue, but it fosters organizational learning and shared ownership of a complex dilemma—and it might prevent similar disasters in the future. Is the university colluding with Burly's destructive behavior? Has a lack of courage or skill caused campus administrators at multiple levels to coddle him? Could Burly legitimately believe that the only thing that matters to the university is the reputation of his research and his program? Has the department chair been given the assistance and support she needs to supervise an unusually challenging subordinate? What are the university's options for resolving the current situation?

Rule 3 is to ask if the university has done all it could to befriend Burly: Has anyone invested in getting to know him better and in trying to learn more about his needs, concerns, goals, and feelings? This is often difficult with bullies; and it typically requires persistence, sensitivity, and skill. You don't want to give the impression that you are colluding or condoning inappropriate professional behavior. But a university leader who develops a rapport with Burly has a better chance at influencing him and of gathering the information needed for a lasting solution. Even bullies listen better to their friends.

Rule 4 is to unhook. Burly has been creating ambivalence and emotional turmoil that has blocked campus administrators from developing a strategy and sticking to it. They need to acknowledge the feelings that have gotten and kept them hooked and to develop specific ways of dealing with Burly that let them move on. Bullies persist when permitted to do so.

The fifth rule says to set clear ground rules for Burly. The basic principle of standing up to bullies without fighting with them is the key to successfully coping with their aggressive behavior (Bramson, 1981). Burly needs to know what's expected and what the consequences will be if he doesn't meet those expectations. Consequences need to be carefully planned and consistently monitored. The penalties may be relatively minor at first, but Burly needs to understand that they will become more severe if he does not rein in his troublesome behavior. Discussing these issues is not a mission that the department chair should undertake alone. She will need coaching in advance and support during the meeting, as well as clear confirmation that the university—from the dean through the president and the board—will stand behind her and support the consistent implementation of the ground rules. If Burly reforms briefly and then reverts to his old pattern, the university needs to intervene quickly or Burly will be back in the saddle again.

Backstabbers

Combat is natural for bullies, and they fight head on. That makes them easier to deal with than backstabbers, who are more insidious. They are guerrillas who shoot from behind trees or assassins who poison the coffee. They prefer to work in the dark where their attacks are hard to see or trace. A young assistant professor up for tenure was stunned when his department chair told him that the evaluation committee had done him a favor by not mentioning that he had offered sex in exchange for promotion. He had no clue as to where the slander came from. Another case involved a dean who was asked by his provost to dismiss a department chair because of reports that the chair's insensitivity might have been a factor in the unexpected death of a senior faculty member. The dean investigated and concluded that reports were false and probably instigated by a longtime malcontent in the unit, but the damage was done. A student services director began to hear stories from multiple sources that one of his key subordinates, Brenda, was spreading stories around the campus about his poor leadership and inability to do his job. When the director asked Brenda, she expressed surprise and demanded to know exactly who had said what about her.

Backstabbers may be difficult to identify (authors of anonymous poison pen letters are a case in point), and they will often deny any charges against them when confronted. But backstabbers are close cousins to bullies with their clandestine hostility, and the same general steps for dealing with difficult people—assess the full situation, look in the mirror, befriend, unhook, set expectations, get help, divorce—still provide useful guidelines for a constructive response to their inappropriate behavior. The assistant professor might have been guilty of nothing more than being talented, young, and handsome; but he might start by assessing what's been happening in the department and by asking himself what he might have done in his relationships with colleagues to have triggered such a hostile story. Befriending is difficult when it's hard to be sure who's undermining you, but it is worth a try if you have one or more suspects. In this case, it is wise to unhook before you befriend. The idea is not to accuse the other of anything, but to approach them as a colleague with whom you'd like to develop a relationship and seek advice. That may be all it takes to end the backstabbing—or not. At least you've done your part. Brenda's boss could set expectations by telling her, for example, "We need to work as a team. If you have concerns about me, come to me. It will be bad for your reputation if there continue to be stories that you're working to undermine your boss and the department." If the behaviors continue, termination might become the right step.

Whether a backstabber is rehabilitated or released, it is important for academic leaders to recognize and to respond to the lingering damage caused by his or her sinister behaviors. Once information enters a social system—whether it is accurate or fictitious—it circulates and influences the perceptions that others have of the backstabber's target and of the unit. Skilled backstabbers can do more damage to their victims than to themselves, and wise academic administrators avoid colluding in their plots by following a key leadership rule: Keep an open mind in the face of criticism of any people or programs and look for opportunities to test and validate what you hear before acting on it.

Targets of backstabbing need not be passive victims. They need to keep an ear to the ground and to recognize when misinformation is damaging them, their work, or their credibility. When this occurs, the best defense is a strong offense: actively communicate accurate information to relevant parties about the unit's directions, activities, and choices—and elicit help from allies in doing the same. Becoming personally defensive or attacking the backstabber won't help, but emphasizing the good leadership choices that have been made and unit or program accomplishments will. Backstabbers will only stop when their tactics no longer work: when they know that others recognize their game and that they are hurting themselves more than they are harming their targets.

Summary

Into every higher education administrator's life an occasional difficult individual will fall, and these relatively few people often generate a disproportionate share of challenges while draining substantial amounts of time and emotional energy. There are no quick fixes, but there are things academic leaders can do to cope with the situation and to increase the chances that difficult people become valued and productive members of the team. Start by assessing the situation and asking if there's anything you're doing as a leader that might contribute to the difficulties. You will learn important things about your organization, about your leadership, and about the other. Look for ways to befriend even those who seem negative or outrageous—you may learn something significant that helps you make life better for those who have been making yours harder. Pay attention to any emotional buttons of your own that others are pushing, and look for ways to unhook. If people are consistently behaving in unproductive ways, make sure that you communicate clear expectations about what's expected of them and the consequences for violating those expectations. Finally, be prepared for the possibility that divorce may be the best option.

11

Managing Your Boss

Jeffrey Hall's heart sank as he picked up the phone. It was the president again. "What does she want now?" Hall wondered.

"Jeff, I've sent you an e-mail with a letter of reprimand for that guy—what's his name—the union rep. Print it out. Sign it. And send it to him."

Before Hall could even say that he needed to look at the letter, the president hung up.

There had been an initial surge of enthusiasm when Louise Fulsome arrived as the new president of Riveredge Community College, but the wave crashed after a few months. Her lean communication style and curt, autocratic management left many on campus angry and pessimistic. Among them was "what's his name," Willie Kacmarsky, a longtime instructor at Riveredge. A talented and passionate teacher as well as a popular faculty union representative, Kacmarsky was a perennial critic of administrative malfeasance and a chronic thorn in President Fulsome's side.

As dean of instruction, Jeffrey Hall often found himself in a bind. He didn't have to read the letter to know what the president was unhappy about. It had to be the recent broadside Kacmarsky had sent to everyone on campus criticizing the president and the campus administration for fiscal mismanagement. Hall understood Kacmarsky's agenda: position the union for salary negotiations and cement support among the members. Hall and Kacmarsky had been colleagues for years. Historically, they had also been friends, but their relationship had become more strained since Fulsome came on the scene. Hall had tried to convince the president that a combative posture toward Kacmarsky and the faculty union did more harm than good, but Fulsome had little patience for such talk. In her mind, being tough was the only way to keep the union at bay.

Hall pulled up President Fulsome's e-mail and read it carefully. "Typical," he thought. "The president is mad as hell, but she wants me to say it for her. This letter would just give the union new ammunition. Why would I want to send this? Well, because the president told me to. Now what?"

Why Leading Up Is Important

Leadership is often equated to managing the people who report to you, but savvy academic administrators understand that leading up is every bit as important. In the culture of the academy, where resources are scarce and relationships are vital for opening doors, the ability to understand, influence, and work closely with your boss and other senior players is one of the most important tasks in administrative work.

There are wonderful bosses and terrible ones in any line of work. Many of us have worked for both types over the course of our careers. Jeffrey Hall does not have the boss of his dreams, but he needs to do the best he can with the boss he has (at least until he or the boss moves on). Fulsome expects her subordinates to salute and follow orders. But Hall's responsibilities to her and to the college require him to lead both up and down, developing productive ways to work with those above and below. Otherwise, he is in a no-win situation. If he can't meet his boss's expectations, he'll look ineffective or treacherous. But if he follows orders regardless of the consequences, he'll betray his institutional responsibilities.

Despite what cynics might think, leading up does not equate to self-serving manipulation or becoming a lackey. It is instead a strategic and orchestrated approach for developing clear expectations and communication patterns that enable you and your supervisor to work productively together on behalf of both personal and institutional goals. The support and friendship of those above you makes it easier to get the resources you need, the projects you enjoy, and the opportunities you want for advancement. It gives you cover when you are under attack—and the confidence to think long term and to take risks on behalf of your unit's mission. Without support from above, your wings are clipped—whether you realize it or not.

If you are blessed with a wise and supportive boss, nurture that relationship. If not, do your best to move your relationship to a more positive and productive footing. Waiting for your boss to change or reach out amounts to an abdication of leadership—success requires a proactive stance. In their book *Managing Up*, Michael and Deborah Dobson (2002) liken it to the ongoing work needed for a strong marriage: assessing and then accommodating personal behaviors to sustain and improve an important relationship. If you want your job and you want to do it well, you need a strong and productive working relationship with your boss.

Goals for the Relationship

Three overarching goals—partnership, open communication, and credibility—help you develop a productive relationship with your boss (Carlone & Hill, 2008). A partnership is a cooperative venture with mutual objectives. Building partnership requires conversation and shared agreement about roles, expectations, and assessment standards. The ideal time to begin that conversation is before you accept the job, but it is never too late to start. The goal is to clarify what each of you needs from the other. You need things like information, counsel, support, protection, resources, and mandates from your boss. Your boss needs information, support, accountability, integrity, and reliable performance from you. Smart subordinates look for ways to help achieve their manager's goals while keeping the boss in the loop. It's all about reciprocity: you deliver for your boss, and your boss is likely to do the same for you. Wise subordinates are also generous in acknowledging and expressing public appreciation of their boss's contribution to their success.

A second goal is to develop open communication. That can be challenging with someone like President Fulsome, but Jeffrey Hall still needs to work on developing ways to communicate with his boss so that they understand one another. Hall can improve his chance for open communication with President Fulsome by working to see the world through her eyes, so that he can position his ideas and suggestions from the perspective of her interests and needs. Fulsome may not want to hear that her letter to Kacmarsky is a mistake. But if things blow up with the union, she'll likely blame Hall for letting things get out of hand.

The third goal is to establish the credibility needed to negotiate key work priorities with your boss. "Credibility is the cornerstone of persuasion and negotiation," conclude Carlone and Hill (2008, p. 40). It has two equally important components: expertise and trustworthiness. You may have solid experience and business acumen, but if people don't believe in you as the messenger, they won't believe in your message (Kouzes & Posner, 2003). Academic leaders build their credibility when they consistently demonstrate their integrity and reliability in achieving or exceeding their stated objectives. Bosses listen to and trust employees who have their best interests at heart: making your boss look good is a proven formula for establishing credibility in any organization (Carlone & Hill, 2008). Be forewarned: Credibility may take time to build, but it can be quickly lost.

So what do you do if, like Jeffrey Hall, you have a dominating, noncommunicative boss like Louise Fulsome? You've probably seen people like her in senior jobs and wondered how they got to where they are. Sometimes bosses like that are individuals with high IQ but low EQ (emotional quotient)—they're very smart and strong on substance, but they're short on people skills and the capacity to understand social nuance. In other cases, difficult bosses are ambitious individuals who are very good at keeping their bosses happy, but who are also prone to bullying their subordinates to get what they want. Whatever the cause, you need a strategy for responding to them. Some basic guidelines can help to ensure a relationship that works for both parties.

Leaders forge productive working relationships with their boss when they . . .

1. Know themselves

2. Understand the boss

3. Give the boss solutions, not problems

4. Use the boss's time wisely

5. Avoid surprises

6. Keep promises and deliver on commitments

7. Speak up when necessary

Know Thyself

In Chapter Ten we suggested that a look in the mirror is a good first step in dealing with difficult people, and the same holds for bosses—difficult or not. The plethora of books about bad bosses (see, for example, Graham Scott, 2005; Kellerman, 2004; Kets de Vries, 2003) tells you something: lots of people have worked for one—or thought they did. But it's critical to know how much is you and how much is the boss. If your relationship with your boss is rocky, what's your contribution to the strife? If you want more influence in negotiating with your boss, what can you do to increase your credibility? If you feel overwhelmed by a continuous stream of demands, like Jeffrey Hall, how are you responding to them? If you are frustrated by a boss who seems overwhelmed and reluctant to use the power of position, how do you react to the leadership vacuum? The answers to such questions are at the heart of an honest diagnosis of your situation.

A relationship with a boss carries a special twist because power differences are a central feature of the relationship (Carlone & Hill, 2008). Your boss almost always has more power than you, up to the ultimate sanction of firing you. Tenure, if you have it, may offer job security as a faculty member, but does not ensure your right to continue to enjoy the resources and rewards of administrative work.

In the face of power differences, Gabarro and Kotter (2008) advise understanding and avoiding two common reactions to authority. One is overdependence—responding to a boss in a fearful or overly compliant manner. Jeffrey Hall could just print and sign anything the boss tells him to, but that will not serve him or the president well. The alternative stance is counterdependence—resistance to being controlled—which often leads subordinates to reject, resent, or battle authority. If Hall simply balks at signing the letter, he may not teach Louise Fulsome anything about the situation or about the impact of her leadership. That's no favor if she is unintentionally digging herself into a leadership hole. The key to leading up effectively is the development of a collaborative relationship of mutual respect and influence—despite the reality of uneven power. Knowing something about your response to authority—and where you fall on a continuum between the two extreme reactions of overdependence and counterdependence—is baseline information for determining how your predispositions might affect your relationships with bosses. Many of us gravitated to careers in college and universities because we like autonomy and independence, but those characteristics can hinder our ability to deal with difficult and demanding bosses. Reflect on the bosses you have had during your career. Which have worked best for you? Why? Your answers are a clue to what you need from your boss.

Understand the Boss

Good working relationships with a boss require an appreciation of the boss's pressures, problems, and working style (Kotter, 1985). It's a mistake to wait for your boss to fill you in on his or her reality. Take the initiative and ask about it. Like you, your boss has goals to achieve in a context of constraints and pressures that you may not be aware of. You need to understand the boss's priorities and problems so you can better gauge how your performance makes your boss's life easier—or harder. Demanding, needy, or oblivious subordinates tend to have a short shelf life, even for the most patient and nurturing bosses. It's also important to understand how your boss wants to work with you. You may enjoy long meetings and lots of face time or maximum autonomy to run your own show, but that doesn't mean your boss does. Find out how your boss likes to communicate so that you can deliver messages in a format that works. Don't project your needs on your boss—or expect that the boss you have will be the one of your dreams. Jeffrey Hall has strong feelings about President Fulsome's stance toward the union, but it's less clear that Hall has given significant attention to trying to understand the problems and pressures that Fulsome is experiencing or why she believes her strategies will get her what she needs. Knowing those can help him craft his message and develop a stronger and more open relationship with her.

Give the Boss Solutions, Not Problems

As much as possible, make your boss's job easier, not harder. Your boss probably has at least as many problems and pressures as you do and doesn't need you to make life harder than it already is. It is wise to consult with your boss on issues that might wind up on her desk anyway, but she is likely to be grateful and to have more confidence in you if you arrive with well-researched and thoughtful solutions. When your implicit message is "Solve this problem for me," you raise red flags about your initiative and your strategic capacities. When you say, "Here's what I see. Here's what I've done. Here's what I've learned. And here's my plan. Any advice?" you keep your boss in the loop without putting one more problem on her plate. If Jeffrey Hall tells President Fulsome that sending the letter to Kacmarsky is a bad idea, he's offering a problem without a solution. But if, for example, he drafts an alternative letter and offers a rationale for why this will produce better outcomes for the college, he makes it easier for the president to say yes.

Use the Boss's Time Wisely

You're busy, and your boss is probably busier. You want to maximize the value of the time you spend together. That means using it on the things that are important to both of you. Bosses, of course, vary; and the better you know what your boss expects, the better the choices you can make. As a general rule, busy bosses don't want to be besieged with lots of tactical questions and small logistical issues—unless they have asked for that. They want the big picture stuff and want to know that you are working within the goals, parameters, constraints, values, and expectations they have set for you. Use your boss-time to show that you are focusing on the things that matter—or to check in if you aren't sure. Meetings oriented around ensuring that you and your boss are in sync on values and goals are likely to be winners. Unless you know in advance that it's a brainstorming session, come prepared to meetings with your own prioritized agenda. You'll keep yourself on track to get what you need. You'll also show that you respect your boss's time and that you have done your homework.

Avoid Surprises

If you can help it, never let your boss be blindsided! If there's something developing in your unit that could produce an explosion or generate a negative story in the local media, alert your boss immediately. You want your boss to understand the issues, know the risks, and, ideally, to support whatever you're doing to deal with the problem at hand. It may go without saying, but it's important enough that it can never be said too often: All your choices should be clear, clean, and ethical. Transparency is increasingly important in higher education and elsewhere. Live by the old adage: Everything you do at work should be something you—and your boss—would be proud to see described on the front page of the *New York Times* or the *Chronicle of Higher Education*.

Keep Promises, Deliver on Commitments

You build credibility and trust by doing what you say you'll do. The more your boss trusts you and is confident that you will consistently deliver on your commitments, the easier it is to get the support and resources you need to go forward.

Speak Up When Necessary

Useem (2001) notes that the biblical prophets Abraham and Moses sometimes pushed back and persuaded their God to change course when they felt the Almighty was about to make a big mistake. Bosses are not infallible and are not well served by subordinates who hesitate to tell the truth about potential fallout from their judgments and decisions. An important test of leadership capacity is willingness to speak truth to power. Even tenured faculty sometimes fail this test because they cannot overcome their fears or excessive deference to authority and voice uncomfortable truths. Mindless attacks and reckless personal insults are unproductive. But both authors, even as untenured junior faculty, had occasions to tell senior administrators that we thought some idea or initiative was wrong. Contrary to conventional wisdom, the candor increased our credibility.

The same was true for General George C. Marshall, who became one of the most revered and trusted military leaders in American history. On more than one occasion everyone around him thought he was committing career suicide by telling his commanders the truth that they did not want to hear. He did this as a young colonel in confronting General Pershing during World War I, and later with President Franklin D. Roosevelt in the run-up to

World War II. In both cases, the bosses concluded that Marshall was someone that they could trust.

Jeffrey Hall needs to be able to speak up effectively with President Fulsome if he is to develop a relationship of influence and mutual respect. When speaking up seems risky, it is often a good time to experiment with inquiry. You can argue directly with some bosses; it's futile with others. But asking the right questions can often accomplish the same result. In Jeffrey Hall's case, there is no shortage of significant and provocative questions he could ask President Fulsome. "So what do you think the fallout would be if we send this letter and Kacmarsky spreads it all over campus?" "Would you want to send the letter if it gets the faculty and the media saying that we don't believe in academic freedom?" "What if this letter makes Kacmarsky a hero to his members and costs us at the bargaining table?" Such questions could help Hall understand Fulsome's thinking and might provoke her to think again. Saying what needs to be said is risky and from time to time may leave a few battle scars. But leaders need to hear the truth, and telling it is a way to be authentic and to have influence and opportunities in areas that you care about. That's what leading up is about.

Not all bosses present the same impatient, damn-the-torpedos approach of President Louise Fulsome, but the same seven steps for managing your boss can help develop a more productive working relationship with those who lead in other ways. Occupying a very different niche on the leadership spectrum, for example, is the cautious, hard-to-read boss who communicates sparingly, responds slowly, studies issues excessively, and rarely takes initiative. Subordinates' teeth may grind as they wait for their boss to stand up and do something—almost anything. They wonder whether to hold back or charge forward in the absence of clear signals about what the boss wants (or doesn't) and will support (or not). If you find yourself with such a boss, it is urgent to take initiative to avoid playing in an endless version of *Waiting for Godot*.

Such bosses need their subordinates' help, whether they know it or not. The trick is learning to do that in a way that does not raise your boss's fears or defenses.

Start with *Know thyself*. It helps to ensure that you have a clear understanding of your own contribution or collusion in the relationship. Taking initiative to *understand the boss* by spending time and asking questions is particularly helpful with undercommunicative bosses. *Give the boss solutions, not problems* works well with passive bosses who often find it easier to approve your suggestions than to come up with their own solutions. *Avoid surprises* responds to a basic concern of timid bosses, whose inaction often stems from fear that anything they do might cause something bad to happen. A strong track record and your capacity to *keep promises, deliver on commitments* will build trust and reduce anxiety. The courage to *speak up* and the willingness to find a voice that facilitates relationship building are particularly important and powerful with bosses who are themselves reluctant to say what they're thinking and feeling. Your openness and compassionate professionalism will model a different approach to academic leadership—and can help your boss to learn and grow in the role.

Summary

Leading up is as important as anything else academic administrators do. Their capacities to take risks, make a difference, and survive in their jobs depend on support and mandates from above. Wise campus leaders attend carefully to relationships with more powerful players in their institution, pursuing goals of partnership, open communication, and credibility. They try to ensure that they understand themselves as well as their superiors' concerns and interests, and they do their best to make things easier rather than harder for their bosses. They rely on the basic proposition that if you deliver for your bosses, he or she is likely to return the favor.

A seven-step strategy can guide academic leaders in developing a more productive relationship with their bosses:

1. Know thyself.

2. Understand the boss.

3. Give the boss solutions, not problems.

4. Use the boss's time wisely.

5. Avoid surprises.

6. Keep promises and deliver on commitments.

7. Speak up when necessary.

12

Sustaining Health and Vitality

Deans and other academic leaders are natural magnets for others' emotions. Michael Maccoby (2004) and Manfred Kets de Vries (2003) remind us how easily humans project onto leaders their early life disappointments, ambivalence about power, and disdain for dependency. Part of the unstated contract between leaders and followers is the leader's willingness to accept followers' current and past emotion-laden projections—and more. Followers, after all, give a leader authority in exchange for the leader's willingness to hold and respond to their fears and needs. This is especially true under conditions of confusion, complexity, or overload.

> In times of distress, we turn to authority. To the breaking point, we place our hopes and frustrations upon those whose presumed knowledge, wisdom, and skill show the promise of fulfillment. Authorities serve as repositories for our worries and aspirations, holding them, if they can, in exchange for the powers we give them. (Heifetz, 1994, p. 69)

William Kahn (2005), in his study of caregivers, identifies an important paradox in compassionate service that is relevant to the psychosocial challenges of healthy leadership. Caring professionals who serve individuals in need require simultaneous openness to and distance from those they seek to aid. They need clear boundaries to sustain objectivity, protect themselves from the stress of the work, and nurture autonomy in others. At the same time, good caregivers, like good academic leaders, need to understand others at a deep level in order to respond in appropriate ways to the unique realities of situations over time. This only happens, concludes Kahn, when caregivers "take in" those in need of their services—fully grasp others' fears, capabilities, limitations, needs, wishes, and knowledge base—*and* simultaneously practice the skill of "detached concern" to limit the closeness. This is difficult: even the most skilled risk the strain of absorption— accumulated stress from close relationships with those in need and from toiling with "constant waves of emotion" washing up against them in the course of their everyday work. Over time, "compassion fatigue" (Figley, 1995) is hard to avoid. In the leadership and management literature, we call it *burnout*. Learning about, understanding, bearing witness, and working close to strong emotion take a toll.

It is tempting for leaders to try to ignore the emotional costs of their work. They feel pressures to produce, and the demands of the situation often keep them attending more to others' needs than their own. Followers expect that, but nonetheless remain leery. John Gardner (1990) describes a universal ambivalence. People want leaders who are powerful and capable of results. At the same time, they hate dependence and giving power to others. Ambivalent and scared when leaders can't—or don't—deliver quickly enough, followers often accelerate their dependence. They can project even stronger expectations for their leader to shoulder more responsibility and to alleviate their mounting distress. The stage is set for an escalating cycle of anguish for leaders and for followers.

Conceptions of heroic leadership—commonly accepted myths of the solitary superhero whose brilliance and strength save the day—seduce leaders into stoic acceptance of the added pressures and responsibilities. But rising expectations often join hand-in-hand with rising disappointment. Leaders, after all, are only human. Mounting frustrations can lead followers to cross a more dangerous line when disappointment morphs into toxic anger and ill will directed squarely at the leader.

Newcomers to academic administration are often unprepared for what they find: emotion-heavy work contexts and pressures that can include long-term angst and toxic memories deeply rooted in their institution's culture (Gallos, 2002). Leaders often hope that optimism, good will, a few quick wins, and some new things to celebrate will dissolve the lingering bitterness or distress. Not always true. Often, the anguish just smolders underground, ready to erupt at unexpected times and places. Persistence, patience, process, and time are needed to work it through. What can protect and support academic leaders during this demanding work?

Five Steps to Healthy Academic Leadership— and Healthy Academic Leaders

On reflection, college and university leaders are sometimes struck by the openness and naiveté that they have brought to their work, opening themselves to burnout—or cynicism. Nobel laureate Herbert Simon once noted that universities are places run by amateurs to train professionals. There's a cost in that. Many academic leaders learn the administrative ropes mostly by muddling through. This can be disconcerting—and humbling—for those accustomed to consistent professional success and acclaim within their disciplines or classrooms. As a relatively new dean noted, "It's a shock for us highly successful Type A's to recognize that we'll never bat 100% or go 12–0 with our faculty no matter how much we want to—or what we do. Surviving as a dean has required me to accept that." The missions, talents, idiosyncrasies, and potential of those who populate universities make academic leadership a tough ride. Strategies for sustaining confidence and leadership resolve during the darkest hours require attention to five key areas: boundaries, biology, balance, beauty, and bounce (Gallos, 2008b).

> **Healthy leaders care for self and build vitality by attending to . . .**
>
> 1. Boundaries
>
> 2. Biology
>
> 3. Balance
>
> 4. Beauty
>
> 5. Bounce

Boundaries

Writer and poet Gertrude Stein (1935) offered good advice: "It is awfully important to know what is and what is not your business." Leaders need to distinguish between their own business and the baggage and work of others. Boundary management occurs at a number of critical interfaces: self-other, personal-professional, self-work role, leader-follower. Monitoring and managing each interface is an ongoing process, but the stresses and strain of leading may numb leaders to the necessity for vigilance and the costs of boundary violations.

Daniel Goleman (1995) and others assert a human predisposition to absorb the feelings of others, especially negative emotions. On a simple level, it's the reason we feel better around positive, high-energy people. People vary in their empathic capacities. Cognitive scientists have identified hard-wiring in the brain that makes certain individuals more attuned to others' affect (Restak, 2003). Caring leaders often fall into this category. At a 2004 conference, for example, Dr. Maureen O'Sullivan described research about individuals so interpersonally sensitive that they can detect liars by noting extremely subtle emotions that flick across a fibber's face ("Researcher finds fibbers," 2004). These "wizards," as O'Sullivan calls them, pick up clues that a majority of others never notice, employing a natural rapid cognition that surpasses the skills of trained professionals. For emotionally open and sensitive leaders, handling intense affect in the workplace without adequate detachment is especially hazardous. Before they know it, the professional turns deeply personal.

Before his death, the late Peter Frost (2003) provided a cautionary tale. As an associate dean, he repeatedly interacted with frustrated individuals—the majority of those who came to his office. Frost was long unaware that those repeated exposures penetrated his defenses—despite his experiences as a private sector manager, professor, and management scholar. Only in hindsight did he see a clear change in himself over his years in administration. He took in more of others' pain—and felt it more deeply, personally, and longer. He increasingly replayed emotion-laden exchanges in his mind, searching for better ways to handle and respond to problems and complaints. He experienced sleeplessness and feelings of depletion at the end of each day. In the face of all this, he just kept on keeping on. Another academic administrator described to us the personal toll in stark terms: "I had a complete meltdown and couldn't understand what was happening. I ended up taking some time off to put myself back together."

An equally important boundary for academic leaders to manage is the distinction between self and work role. Leaders need to remember that others' reactions to them are largely responses to the role they occupy rather than to them as individuals. Those reactions are often transferences, projections, and other psychic assaults from distressed or disappointed others. This does not exempt leaders from paying attention to feedback and seeking better ways to lead, but it cautions them not to personalize the many reactions their work inevitably provokes. All leaders have to make decisions that not everyone likes. Constituents routinely personalize those actions, attributing them to nefarious motives, character defects, or incompetence. Leaders should not respond in kind or let their feelings lead them to precipitous action. Managing the boundary between self and work role goes to the heart of professionalism and executive judgment. If they blur the distinction between leader and follower work, academic administrators may try to carry too much on their own shoulders and challenge others too little. That is a road to burnout and failure.

Biology

Remaining vigilant to boundary management takes concentration and stamina that are strengthened by conscious attention to self-care and good health. Commonsense strategies like exercising, eating sensibly, staying hydrated, limiting caffeine and alcohol, maintaining blood sugar levels with well-paced meals and healthy snacks, and developing regular sleep patterns are essential for managing the demands of the work. So is early attention to mild, stress-related symptoms, like sleeplessness or back pain—possible warning signs of a boundary breach. Too many academic leaders find after a few years in the job that they are sleeping less, eating poorly, drinking more, and experiencing psychological and physical signals that something is awry.

Mind-body expert Joan Borysenko (1988) reminds us how easy it is under stress—physical or emotional, personal or professional, real or imagined—to settle into a primitive fight-flight stance while ignoring healthier routes. Humans are well adapted to respond to imminent danger through complex physiological responses involving hormones and inflammatory chemicals that prime the body for rapid defense. People are less prepared for life's steady stream of low-level annoyances that evoke the same biochemistry. Fight-flight reactions continuously bathe mind and body in the stress hormone, cortisol, raising blood sugar to levels perfect for emergency action. At the same time, the adrenal glands ramp up heart, breathing, muscle tension, and blood pressure—just right for arms and legs that need an extra boost of energy to battle or escape. Chronic activation of this physiological stress response, however, wears a body down. One senior university administrator joked that his grey hair was a battle scar, acquired during his years of shoring up an abusive boss and protecting others from her wrath. He may have been right, but the wounded healer cannot minister well or muster the care and empathy to attend to others' pain (Siegel, 1993).

Balance

Strong boundaries and health require balance—retaining one's equilibrium and perspective in the face of challenge or frustration. Balance flows from grounded appreciation of life's richness and willingness to attend to the diverse needs of mind, body, and soul. Experts have differed on the path to balance. Sigmund Freud (1920/1975) proposed love and work. Psychiatrist Lenore Terr (1999) adds play. Rohrlich (1980) sees it as resolution of the tension among work, family, and leisure. Lawrence and Nohria (2002) argue for four innate, independent human drives: acquire, bond, learn, and defend. A Chinese proverb depicts the elements of happiness as something to work on, something to hope for, and someone to love. The path, however defined, shapes human choices and becomes a measure of life satisfaction. Balancing energy and efforts among priorities brings meaning, purpose, and joy to the human experience.

College and university administrators stay centered when they have identified their life priorities and the steps to keep themselves on a balanced life path. Two simple suggestions are (1) counterbalance stress with relaxation techniques, and (2) neutralize toxic affect with positive emotions. Academic leaders can't stop the waves, but they can learn to surf (Kabat-Zinn, 1994). The "relaxation response" is a learned state of mental calm where heart, breathing, muscle tension, and blood pressure rates drop (Benson & Klipper, 1976). Soothing, simple repetitive activities, like meditation, deep breathing, yoga, tai chi, prayer, practicing a musical instrument, or even knitting can elicit physiological benefits. New Age guru Ram Dass suggests crocheting (Lipstein, 1992).

Academic administrators can also balance the emotional maelstrom of campus leadership with a conscious focus on positive sentiments, such as appreciation, love, care, forgiveness, and compassion. Researchers at HeartMath (2007) report immediate benefits: positive changes in heart rhythms, as well as neural, hormonal, and biochemical reactions that drop blood pressure, muscle tension, and stress hormones. Scientists at UCLA found that optimism and hope strengthened immune functioning in HIV-positive men (Benson, Corliss, & Cowley, 2004). Forgiveness—the letting go of resentment for a perceived offense—decreases blood pressure, cortisol, and other negative hormones associated with heart disease, immunity disorders, and more (Lewis & Adler, 2004). The evolving field of positive organizational scholarship offers a wealth of evidence on the generative impact of positive processes like embracing organizational virtue, gratitude, positive deviance, courage, meaningfulness, appreciative inquiry, and more (Cameron, Dutton, & Quinn, 2003).

Beauty

Maintaining balance also suggests identifying activities and events that feed the soul. The beauty and recuperative power of the arts make them obvious choices. Ronald Heifetz (1994) discusses the importance in seeking sanctuary—in leaders finding respite from the fray for perspective and rejuvenation. Many wise leaders make the arts their sanctuary—and immerse themselves in music, crafts, writing, or good fiction during especially stressful times. "Without art, the crudeness of reality would make the world unbearable," said playwright George Bernard Shaw. We agree. The arts are a powerful tonic.

There is considerable evidence, for example, that music enhances health and healing. Music's ability to alter emotional states has been long known experientially and documented in the music therapy literature and elsewhere. (See, for example, Jourdain, 2002; Levitin, 2007; McCraty, Barrios-Choplin,

Atkinson, & Tomasino, 1998; and Storr, 1992.) Music's benefits are diverse—from slowing down brain waves and equalizing neuronal firing patterns to boosting immunity; increasing memory; raising endorphin levels; reducing heart and pulse rates, blood pressure, muscle tension, and stress-related hormones; and more (Campbell, 1999). Robert Jourdain (2002) asserts that music—any kind enjoyable to the listener—guides the brain to higher levels of integration of the right and left lobes and their diverse functions. Its rhythms and patterns speak to the brain in primitive ways and "lift us from our frozen mental habits" (p. 303). For academic leaders, this elevating sanctuary may be exactly what the stress doctor orders.

Literature and creative writing have historically been used for renewal in the health sciences. William Carlos Williams, Anton Chekhov, W. Somerset Maugham, and John Keats were all trained physicians. Prestigious clinical journals, like the *Journal of the American Medical Association* and the *Annals of Internal Medicine*, regularly publish literary works by physicians. Many health care clinicians are poets (see, for example, the work of clinician-poets in Breedlove, 1998; Campo, 1994, 1996)—a promising avocation for higher education administrators, too. Robert Coles (1989) reminds us that fiction and storytelling deepen inner life for those who work on life's emotional boundaries. Literature also nurtures skills in observation, analysis, empathy, communication, and self-reflection—capacities essential for leadership effectiveness in any situation. In addition, good fiction is healthy escapism.

Bounce

Leadership requires resilience: the ability to adapt and strengthen in the face of challenge, trauma, or stress. How can academic leaders increase their odds of quickly bouncing back in the face of setbacks? Practice makes perfect. Resilience and bounce are learned skills that strengthen with use (American Psychological Association, 2007; Murray, 2003). They include recognizing that we always have choices in interpreting and responding to events, keeping things in perspective, trusting one's instincts, practicing new behaviors and responses, and reflecting on the consequences. Learning to *reframe* helps—an organization's disappointments and struggles, for example, are also a gift if viewed as an impetus for growth. So do regular mistakes, plenty of laughter, and a good nap! Mistakes provide needed interruptions for a pulse check on choices—and on the status of one's bounce. The benefits of a good sense of humor speak for themselves. And a nap is both opportunity for physical rejuvenation and psychological diagnosis: rest restores physical exhaustion from hard work but does nothing to relieve the fatigue of burnout (Siegel, 1998). Asked the secret of compassion, the Dalai Lama answered, "Water. And sleep" (Miller, 2005). Resilience, after all, comes from learning to "wear life loosely" (Siegel, 1998)—wise advice for us all.

Summary

Developmental psychologist Robert Kegan (1994) makes a poignant observation about today's fast-paced world. Over a growing portion of our lives, there is a mismatch between the complexity of today's "curriculum"—all that we need to know and understand to function effectively and productively—and the human capacity to grasp it. The result is increased stress across the life span and the need for more sophisticated levels of human consciousness and learning to satisfy contemporary expectations for love and work. From a developmental perspective, modern living is just too darn hard. Whether we realize it or not, Kegan concludes, most of us are psychologically in over our heads. For better or worse, academic leadership is a quintessential example of his point. It is demanding and unpredictable work, requiring stamina and resolve in the face of stress, challenge, ambiguity, or blame. We can never fully prepare for all that we will face; and those who turn to us for leadership will inevitably feel disappointment and project their frustrations, discontent, and disillusionment on us. Survival requires strategies for maintaining the health and vitality essential for sustaining our efforts.

Learning is at the heart of effective leadership, and sometimes what academic administrators must learn is deeply personal: how to strengthen their resilience in the face of failure, how to understand and manage the psychic demands and costs of their work, how to set limits, and how to care for themselves. They do that by attending to the key issues of boundaries, biology, balance, beauty, and bounce.

13

Feeding the Soul

Leaders need not only the technical skills to manage the external world but also the spiritual skills to journey inward toward the source of both shadow and light.

Parker Palmer (2000, p. 79)

W hen academic leaders are at their best, certain qualities are typically present in their relationships with their constituents. One is *focus*, a clear sense of what's important and where the group needs to go. A second is *passion*, a deep emotional investment that is rooted in love—for the work, the people who do it, the students who benefit, and the institution. Focus and passion enable and promote *courage*, a willingness to take calculated risks and to face danger in order to advance the cause. A fourth quality is *wisdom*, an ability to appreciate the complexity of our world without getting lost or immobilized. A fifth is *integrity*, a sense that the leader is authentic and worthy of trust—and research consistently shows no leadership quality more important to constituents than a perception that leaders tell the truth and keep their promises (Kouzes & Posner, 2007).

These vital leadership qualities do not come from a particular personality type or leadership "style"—and they are hard to fake. Rather they arise from the deep sense of calling and commitment that leaders bring when they know in their hearts that they are doing what they are meant to do and making the contributions that are uniquely theirs to make. How can academic leaders uncover these important understandings for themselves? How do we find our true calling?

Leaders bring a deep sense of commitment and contribution to their work when they . . .

1. Embark on a developmental journey

2. Recognize that inner growth matters

3. Embrace a sense of calling

4. Accept that the journey is the challenge

5. Lead with soul

6. Demonstrate the courage to learn

The Developmental Journey

Joseph Campbell's work on the hero's journey offers a fertile suggestion. Campbell (2008) argues that there is one great story—*the monomyth*—that humans in every time and culture have told one another. It is a simple story at its essence: a hero ventures forth into an unknown world to meet and defeat tremendous forces and returns from the adventure with self-knowledge and gifts to offer to others. It is a deeply spiritual story: a developmental journey that, if undertaken willingly and courageously, brings a life into focus and unleashes passion and wisdom that can lead others toward greatness. The hero's journey is every great leader's destiny—and if we are to rise to our full potential, it is our story as well. The hero's journey reminds us that to continue to grow and learn, we too must leave the comfort of what we know and love and must embark on our quest. That quest will be difficult and dangerous, because we will have to confront both enemies without and the darkness within ourselves. But if we persist and prevail, we return stronger and wiser—and with gifts that we can bring to our communities. Educator and activist Parker Palmer provides an instructive example.

Bringing a new Ph.D. and a spirit of activism from his days at Berkeley, Palmer arrived in Washington, D.C., ready to tackle the ills of America's urban crisis. His work as a community organizer grew into a faculty appointment at Georgetown, and he was elated. He found joy in returning to the teaching that he loved and in involving students in the community engagement that he felt "morally compelled" to do (Palmer, 2000, p. 20). Returning to the university also put him back on track to fill the expectations that he and many others had for him: that he would one day "ascend to some sort of major leadership," like a college presidency (p. 21). Yet five years later, it all turned to ashes. He was burned out.

> My vocational reach had exceeded my grasp. I had been driven more by the "oughts" of the urban crisis than by a sense of true self. Lacking insights into my own limits and potentials, I had allowed ego and ethics to lead me into a situation that my soul could not abide. I was disappointed in myself for not being tough enough to take the flak, disappointed and ashamed. (Palmer, 2000, p. 22)

Palmer took a sabbatical that began a long and difficult period of deep reflection. "This was a step into darkness that I had been trying to avoid—the darkness of seeing myself more honestly than I really wanted to" (2000, p. 28). The journey was not easy—and Palmer hit bottom in a struggle with depression that he openly discusses in his wise and wonderful book, *Let Your Life Speak: Listening for the Voice of Vocation* (2000). Daunting as it was, the journey was ultimately transformative. There is no easy path to soul—hardships and detours are integral to the developmental nature of the work. Palmer's courage and determination enabled him to continue his journey and to discover the career path and contribution that were right for him. What did he learn, and what can we learn from his journey to strengthen and sustain our own leadership?

Inner Growth Matters

The heart of leadership lies in the hearts of leaders.
Lee Bolman and Terrence Deal (2001, p. 17)

In recent years we have seen a steady stream of stories of malfeasance, deception, and moral turpitude among leaders in every sector—business, government, religion, social services, and, sad to say, higher education. It's easy to feel as if we're engulfed in a growing moral wasteland, yet research tells us that the majority of leaders in corporate America and elsewhere believe that inner spiritual growth matters (Delbecq, 2008; Mitroff & Denton, 1999; Tisdell, 2003): that leaders must build a strong sense of identity and ethical maturity so as to align their values with their choices and actions. If not, they lose their way in the daily grind—and many sell their souls. Our experiences and our work with higher education leaders—professionals deeply committed to education and to the development of human possibility—confirm this. Leaders sustain themselves and make the contributions to which they aspire when they know themselves and can bring that fully to their work and relationships. "Our deepest calling," says Palmer, "is to grow into our own authentic selfhood, whether or not it conforms to some image of who we *ought* to be" (2000, p. 16).

On his spiritual journey, Palmer realized that he was living a career built on a distorted sense of self and fueled by "a grim determination" (2000, p. 4) that he could will everything in his life to go the way he wanted—and the way that others had wanted for him. Palmer found that he had talents and gifts, but they were not always the ones he wished for—or told himself that he had. Basing a professional life on personal illusions is like building castles in the sand.

If you seek vocation without understanding the mate-
rial you are working with, what you build with your life
will be ungainly and may well put lives in peril, your
own and some of those around you. "Faking it" in the
service of high values is no virtue and has nothing to
do with vocation. It is an ignorant, sometimes arrogant,
attempt to override one's nature, and it will always fail.
(2000, p. 16)

Palmer also saw how easy it was to externalize his frustrations and disappointments in himself and to blame those around
him and the institutional constraints of the academy—and how
much energy he had wasted on anger.

Whatever half-truth about the university my complaints may have contained, they served me primarily
as a misleading and self-serving explanation of why
I fled academic life. The truth is that I fled because I
was afraid—afraid that I could never succeed as a
scholar, afraid that I could never measure up to the
university's standards for research and publication. And
I was right—though it took many years before I could
admit that to myself. Try as I may, try as I might, I have
never had the gifts that make for a good scholar—and
remaining in the university would have been a distort-
ing denial of that fact. (2000, pp. 26–27)

Once able to admit all this to himself, Palmer was free to
define a professional life and career path that fit him. His impact
and success as a writer, independent educator, and activist—
"another kind of educational mission" (2000, p. 28)—confirm the
wisdom of his choice.

Like all of us, Parker Palmer has diverse and special talents.
But he could only discover them when he removed the veil of

"false bravado" (2000, p. 26) and faced head-on the fundamental life questions that are at the heart of the hero's journey—and of the human experience: questions of *identity* (Who am I? What are my strengths and my limitations?), *values* (What do I believe in, cherish, and defend?), and *contributions* (What am I here to do? To what will I direct my energy and efforts?). These questions are never easy—nor ever fully answered. We may find that, like Parker Palmer, our hopes for contribution are in conflict with the reality of our skills or that we have constructed a life calling that is commendable but not one upon which we can realistically deliver.

> So I lined up the loftiest ideals I could find and set out to achieve them. The results were rarely admirable, often laughable, and sometimes grotesque. But always they were unreal, a distortion of my true self—as must be the case when one lives from the outside in, not the inside out. I had simply found a "noble" way to live a life that was not my own, a life spent imitating heroes instead of listening to my heart. (2000, p. 3)

We all have our own inner worlds and inner turmoil that need attention if we are to identify our true talents and to use those to craft a satisfying professional life. The demands of academic administration regularly pull us outward toward the relentless flow of challenges, opportunities, possibilities, and responsibilities. The overload, ambiguity, and dynamics of the university will always give ample reason to externalize our frustrations and to blame our problems on features of the academy that can drive us to distraction. While it may be satisfying and even therapeutic to grumble about our work environment, our real hope for a satisfying life and for making contributions that matter lies in the strength of our inner core. The heart of successful academic leadership rests there.

A Sense of Calling

Is that what they call a vocation, what you do with joy as if
you had fire in your heart, the devil in your body?
                    Josephine Baker (Hillman, 1996, p. xii)

In his work with senior executives, management educators, health
care professionals, and theologians, Andre Delbecq (2008), a
scholar and former business school dean, set out to explore the
role of spiritual intelligence in organizational leadership. His key
finding was the importance of vocation in its original sense of
calling. Calling has been known by many names over the centuries. The Greeks referred to it as one's *daimon* (Plato, trans. 1992,
p. 289). For the Romans, it was genius. Quakers see it as the
inner light. Humanist traditions speak of living with integrity or
authenticity. Theologian Thomas Merton saw a hidden wholeness
(Palmer, 2004), and psychologist James Hillman (1996) termed it
the "soul's code"—akin to the acorn as seed to the mighty oak.
For Parker Palmer, calling is a birthright and gift: the use of self
that "comes from a voice 'in here' calling me to be the person I
was born to be, to fulfill the original selfhood given me at birth"
(2000, p. 10). Choose your own label to describe it, but remember
three things: (1) common to all the definitions of calling is the
importance of listening to one's life and surrendering to a deep
sense of mission; (2) there is energy and passion in aligning our
action with our deepest talents and strengths; and (3) we touch
and inspire others when we lead with an authenticity rooted in
our best gifts.

How do we learn to listen to our lives? Neurobiologists suggest monitoring our spontaneous reactions to situations around us.
These top-of-mind responses, wrote Marcus Buckingham and the
late Donald O. Clifton (2008), reveal strong mental connections
and hints to deep talents. These need not be responses to extreme

stress situations—although we learn much about ourselves from these times because our defenses are at their lowest. Consider, for example, what you can learn from watching your natural choices at a conference or a large social gathering where you know few people.

> Who did you spend the majority of your time with, those you knew or those you didn't? If you were drawn to the strangers, you may be a natural extrovert, and your behavior may well reflect the theme that we call *woo*, defined as an innate need to *win others over*. Conversely, if you actively sought out your closest friends and hung out with them all evening, resenting the intrusions of strangers, this is a good sign that *relater*—a natural desire to deepen existing relationships—is one of your leading themes. (Buckingham & Clifton, 2008, pp. 80–81)

Buckingham and Clifton (2008) suggest three additional signs to guide a search for deep talents: yearnings, rapid learning, and satisfactions. What activities and experiences have you always been drawn to? What interests and passions have stayed with you from childhood? The architect Frank Gehry, for example, recalls his joy at age five in making intricate, avant-garde structures with wood scraps from his father's hardware store. At age ten, Ben Affleck and Matt Damon met regularly in the school cafeteria to plan their latest artistic project. Mozart had written his first symphony before he turned twelve.

> These childhood passions are caused by the various synaptic connections in your brain. The weaker connections manage little pull, and when well-intentioned mothers (or other circumstances) force you down a particular path, it feels strange and makes you cry. By contrast,

your strongest connections are irresistible. They exert a magnetic influence, drawing you back time and again. You feel their pull, and so you yearn. (Buckingham & Clifton, 2008, p. 82)

For a host of reasons, we may not hear—or heed—the early life call from talents within. But keeping an eye on current situations where we learn something quickly and effortlessly or where we feel deep satisfaction can fix that: an unexpected experience can spark new discoveries. The painter Henri Matisse, for example, was a sickly law clerk who felt no artistic yearnings until his mother gave him a box of paints during one of his many illnesses. The rest, as they say, is history.

Almost instantly both the direction and the trajectory of his life changed. He felt a surge of energy as though released from a dark prison and seeing the light for the first time. Feverishly studying a "how to paint" manual, Matisse filled his days with painting and drawing. Four years later, with no schooling but his own, he was accepted into the most prestigious art school in Paris and was studying under the master Gustave Moreau. (Buckingham & Clifton, 2008, p. 83)

Finally, honest satisfaction is powerful evidence of deep ability. "Your strongest synaptic connections are designed so that when you use them, it feels good. Thus, obviously, if it feels good when you perform an activity, chances are that you are using a talent" (Buckingham & Clifton, 2008, p. 84). Think about your work day. If you figuratively—or literally—watch the clock and wonder when the day or an activity will end, that's a tip-off to something amiss. When time flies and hard work leaves you tired yet smiling—waiting for the next opportunity to do more—there's a good chance a deep talent is at play.

The Journey Is the Challenge

*The journey of the hero is about the uncanny discovery that
the seeker is the mystery which the seeker seeks to know.*
            Joseph Campbell (Campbell and Cousineau, 2003 p. xix)

Leadership always looks easier when viewed from the outside.
"Most of us," reminds Palmer, "arrive at a sense of self and vocation only after a long journey through alien lands" (2000, p. 17).
Internal struggles, conflicting passions, plenty of mistakes, hidden
fears, and doubts of the soul are all par for the course. Delbecq
(2008) tells us that the notion of calling is empty unless understood within the complex unfolding of a full life's journey. Plain
and simple, finding one's calling takes time. There is "a complex
developmental process of *becoming* that precedes the *doing* that we
label a leader's calling"—and that process involves long periods
of preparation and study, skills development, "watchful waiting,"
setbacks, public and private failures, periods of false confidence,
and plenty of delayed gratification (p. 490). Successful academic
leaders often forget this reality.

Many individuals in higher education have risen to university
leadership because they do some very important things very well.
But being good at something—and being promoted and praised
because of it—doesn't always mean it brings deep joy or fulfill-
ment. Parker Palmer talks of the freedom in recognizing how he
lost his way by clinging to a false sense of his talent. Having many
talents brings its own distractions. It can lull academic leaders
into believing that their journey has been completed when it may
have just begun. The variety of opportunities available to talented
people offers an endless string of interesting detours that can fill
the travel days but take leaders no closer to their destination. A
growing list of accomplishments and contributions, especially
those viewed positively by important others, can lead to hidden
frustrations and self-disappointment. With all these options and

accomplishments, like Parker Palmer we may ask ourselves, How can we still feel so lost?

In the tradition of ancient pilgrimages, Palmer's "journey to a sacred center" required him to travel in the dark before he could "come to that center, full of light" (2000, p. 18). While in the midst of the struggles, it is easy to forget that the challenges that can bring us the most important learning are often those that can strip our confidence. In his darkest moments, Palmer was convinced that he "had developed a unique and terminal case of failure" (p. 19). He chose to tell his story as a service to others who might miss the sacred nature of the odyssey.

> The experience of darkness has been essential to my coming into selfhood, and telling the truth about that fact helps me stay in the light. But I want to tell that truth for another reason as well: many young people today journey in the dark, as the young always have; and we elders do them a disservice when we withhold the shadowy parts of our lives. When I was young, there were very few elders willing to talk about the darkness; most of them pretended that success was all they had ever known. As the darkness began to descend on me in my early twenties . . . I did not realize that I had merely embarked on a journey toward joining the human race. (pp. 18–19)

Leadership expert and former university president, Warren Bennis, concludes that one of the most reliable predictors of success is a leader's capacity to find meaning in negative events and to learn from the most trying and frustrating situations. "Put another way, the skills required to conquer adversity and emerge stronger and more committed than ever are the same ones that make for extraordinary leaders" (Bennis & Thomas, 2008, p. 504). Bennis calls these powerful, sometimes traumatic experiences "the crucibles of leadership": life-changing experiences through which leaders come to a new or deeper sense of identity and purpose.

> For the leaders we interviewed, the crucible experience was a trial and a test, a point of deep self-reflection that forced them to question who they were and what mattered to them. It required them to examine their values, question their assumptions, hone their judgment. And, invariably, they emerged from the crucible stronger and more sure of themselves and their purpose—changed in some fundamental way. (Bennis & Thomas, 2008, p. 506)

We look at and admire successful leaders and are tempted to believe that they have known only success. Reflecting on our own lives would suggest otherwise, and Delbecq (2008) offers a list of examples to verify that success is almost always built on persistence through failure, doubt, disappointment, and reversal:

> Winston Churchill as failed Secretary of the Navy could not have envisioned himself someday holding the destiny of Great Britain in his hands during the Battle of Britain. Gandhi as a failed London attorney could not have foreseen himself as the liberating leader of a free India. Eisenhower as an administrative staff officer learning what we now call supply chain logistics—hardly the glamorous side of a military career!—probably did not foresee himself becoming the Supreme Allied Commander during World War II. Early in her public life, Eleanor Roosevelt, who perceived herself as an unattractive woman in a dysfunctional marriage, painfully shy, and in despair from her move to Washington, could not have envisioned herself one day introduced as the most admired woman in the world when named the first Secretary General of the United Nations.

Martin Luther King, Jr. as a minister in a small Southern Baptist Church could not have conceived of himself as the father of a Civil Rights movement. As Henry Ford struggled with auto assembly in his small company, he probably did not focus on initiating a manufacturing revolution. (p. 489)

There is paradox in the complexity of this kind of developmental journey. Only when profoundly lost in deep challenge can we find our true selves. The difficult nature of the work can make us afraid—or tempt us to throw in the towel. On some deep level, we may choose to fill our days with busy work as a way to avoid the inevitable pain and disappointment in accepting that who we are may not be who we thought we were. While he clung to his illusions, Parker Palmer was ignoring obvious signals that his mind, heart, and body were giving him. So long as he did that, he was stymied and bottled up—and he couldn't do the great work he was capable of doing. Moreover, he paid a huge psychic price: depression, prolonged inner turmoil, and self-loathing.

Leading with Soul

> When we live our life fully, our life becomes what Zen Buddhists call "the supreme meal." We make this supreme meal by using the ingredients at hand to make the best meal possible, and then by offering it.
>
> Bernard Glassman and Rick Fields (1996, p. 1)

Soul can be understood as a deep sense of clarity about identity, values, and contribution. Without that, we lack the courage and conviction to lead. Many who become academic leaders may have chosen the work because they have some version of what Martin Luther King once described as "the drum major instinct"—the desire to be out in front of the parade where everyone can admire us. That's fine, King said, but remember that the real measure of greatness is service—and everyone can be great because everyone can serve. "You don't have to have a college degree to serve. . . . You only need a heart full of grace. A soul generated by love. And you can be that servant" (King, 1968).

How does one cultivate grace and soul? Amram and Dryer (2007) suggest three dimensions of spiritual intelligence as one way to answer the question:

1. *Embrace the spiritual.*

   - Use ways of knowing beyond linear thought—prayer, meditation, silence, intuition.

   - Align with a sacred or universal life force.

   - Sense and seek unity and the interconnection among things.

2. *Live mindfully and authentically.*

   - Live with intention and be mindful of each moment.

   - Embrace curiosity and accept reality, including the negative and dark sides of life.

   - Act with integrity and a clear code of values.

   - Work to free the self from negative conditioning, attachments, and fears.

3. *Live generously.*

   - Appreciate and express the positive: faith, hope, gratitude, and optimism.

   - Nurture relationships with respect, empathy, and compassion toward self and others.

   - Live with humble receptivity, openness, and acceptance. (Adapted from materials in Amram & Dryer, 2007 and Amram, 2007)

Exploring the concept of mindfulness is helpful in translating spiritual intelligence into daily practice, and it is well worth examining Ellen Langer's work on the topic (1989, 1997, 2005, 2009). Langer sees mindfulness as a process of paying close attention to ongoing experience and staying open to new information about it. Mindfulness helps us escape the human predisposition to cling to our self-made, overly limited views of the world around us. Langer's research demonstrates that how we think about ourselves has dramatic effects on satisfaction and health. In one study, for example, she and Judith Rodin showed that nursing home residents who were encouraged to make more decisions and to take responsibility for a simple task like watering a plant not only felt happier, they lived longer (Ruark, 2010). As Marge Piercy wrote, "Live as if you liked yourself, and it may happen" (1972, p. 18).

Cultivating spiritual intelligence is distinct from clarifying religious beliefs—although religious practices like prayer and meditation can be helpful. David Whyte, for example, proposes poetry as a vehicle for cultivating soul at work: poetry "can help us remember what is most important in the order of priorities and what place we occupy in a much greater story than the one our job description defines" (2002, p. 300). Delbecq reports that engagement in meditation and other spiritual disciplines has a powerful impact on multiple dimensions of leadership effectiveness (2008, p. 495):

- Growing abilities to listen
- Increased patience with others
- Greater adaptability
- Greater focus and less self-occupation when under stress
- More hope and joy—and less cynicism and pessimism— in difficult times

- Greater overall serenity and trust—and fewer feelings of frustrations

- More confidence in one's competencies

Rabbi Harold Kushner adds the importance of fellow travelers on the spiritual journey. He once wrote that people attend services to find a congregation, a group of others who are embarked on the same search as they. In coming together, they "overcome the isolation and solitude with which each of us ordinarily lives" (quoted in Berman, 1985, p. 164). In the search for soul, there are many things we can do on our own. But the journey will be surer and more productive when we find others who can join—and sustain—us in our travel.

Secure in what we believe and value, soul gives us a moral compass. Leaders often face tough choices that can be immobilizing because almost anything they do will generate criticism and disapproval from some corner. But when they know that they are true to their calling and aligned with their values, they can be at peace amid the storm. They know they have done their best— and they forgive themselves and others for their imperfections. Leaders who willingly accept the rigors of the spiritual journey and appreciate its fruits nourish their soul and attain a secure base from which to approach the gritty and emotionally charged work of academic leadership.

The Courage to Learn: What Got You Here Won't Get You There

Death closes all; but something ere the end,
Some work of noble note, may yet be done.
                                   Alfred Lord Tennyson (1842)

All of us who invest our professional lives in colleges and universities believe in learning and, in our own ways, work to promote it.

Yet we can easily forget to invest in our own learning. Marshall Goldsmith (2007), a leading executive coach, describes a story that he sometimes tells himself and that he frequently sees his clients telling themselves, as well. The story line is basically, *I'm incredibly busy and overcommitted right now. It should get better in a few months. Then, I'll have time to step back, look at the big picture, get organized, and change the things I really need to change.*

But we never find that better time in the future. It's a mirage, a product of self-delusion. In theory, we're all for learning. In practice, we often kid ourselves. That's a mistake. Instead, be generous to yourself in support of your own development. You wouldn't be reading this book if you didn't want to learn. Be thankful for all you've learned in the past, but recognize it won't be enough to get you where you really aspire to go. Recognizing and accepting this is important to your own future, but it's not just about you. It's about the people and the institutions you serve. They need more than your current best—they need you to keep getting better.

Summary

A theme throughout this book is that leadership in higher education is harder and less glamorous than it may seem from the outside. The pace of work is swift and steady, and decisions are often made in the face of ambiguity and conflict. Resources are scarce, and there is constant pressure to do more with less. Campus characters and academic culture often mean that higher education administrators will find more leaders than followers on any issue, yet they are expected to deliver seamlessly and without fuss.

The work of academic leadership has excitement—and capacity to change lives. But it is dangerous and exhausting—a recipe for failure and burnout. To sustain themselves academic leaders need to develop and tap inner psychic and spiritual resources. They do this by embarking on a journey in search of soul—a deep sense of who they are, what they value, and what they are called to do. That journey requires facing unpleasant realities, including the shadows, fears, and imperfections that lurk within us all; but it can take us to greater confidence and conviction that we are on the right path and are doing what we are supposed to do.

The most basic task of leaders is to foster hope. Hope, Andrew Razeghi (2008) reminds us, is more than wishful thinking. Hope takes courage: strong faith, solid thinking, creativity, willful action, and persistence in the face of the unknown. The call for more and better leadership is often a plea for those who can help us see a path to a better and more hopeful future. Choose hope, advises Razeghi. We agree. Nothing motivates followers—or sustains leaders—like recognition of a brighter world.

Epilogue

The Sacred Nature of Academic Leadership

In writing about the contemporary college presidency, Harold Shapiro, former president at both Michigan and Princeton, frames academic leadership as a noble venture—a proactive social and educational activity that constitutes a form of moral action. He writes that leadership in the modern university has "evolved from a more strictly delimited and almost rule-governed activity" of institutional management into the more complex and powerful role of "helping to set the moral tone for the academic community—and beyond" (Shapiro, 1998, p. 92). In Shapiro's view, visible, moral leadership is accomplished through a combination of the leader's choices, actions, policies, and words. It "involves not only the assertion of a 'vision' of the contemporary academic enterprise and its legitimate social functions but also the energy to pursue this vision and the capacity to inspire others—including faculty—to support this remarkable venture despite the inevitable criticism that arises when an institution's success often includes leaving the familiar for new territory" (p. 68). As Shapiro defines it, the president's work is multidimensional, its impact goes well beyond campus boundaries, and it always requires the courage to embrace change.

Shapiro's perspective is consistent with our own sense of the scope and impact of contemporary academic leadership. Those who are successful—and it is difficult, Shapiro (1998, p. 68) admits, to know how many leaders actually meet this challenge—embrace the multiple dimensions of the work and enact each with skill and focus. They see the merits in reframing academic leadership and have learned to do it well. They know their job requires the skills of a good *analyst* and *social architect* who can craft a high-functioning institution where all the parts contribute to the whole, a *political leader* who can forge necessary alliances and partnerships in service of the mission, a *prophet and an artist* who can envision a better college or university and inspire others to heed its call, and a *servant* both to the institution and to the larger goals of higher education and society.

It is hard yet vital work, as exemplified in the career of Father Theodore "Ted" Hesburgh, president of Notre Dame from 1952 to 1987. Hesburgh inherited an institution much stronger on the gridiron than in the classroom, and he set out to transform it into something that was almost an oxymoron at the time—a university that was both great and Catholic. Like all academic leaders, he had ups and downs, including the campus turmoil of the late 1960s that was devastating to so many presidents. Hesburgh reflected ruefully:

> Perkins at Cornell got fired because he didn't call the cops, and Nate Pusey at Harvard got fired because he did call the cops. It seemed like irrational improvisation. There were no rules. But I can tell you it was stressful, and there were many times when I wondered why I was doing it, why I was president. You just wondered why any intelligent person would want to be a university administrator. (Padilla, 2005, p. 160)

As we write this book, many academic leaders are asking the same question: Why indeed would any intelligent person want to do such difficult and sometimes thankless work? Higher education is in a period as chaotic and challenging as the 1960s were for Hesburgh and his peers. Our teaching and research have never been needed more, yet it seems that they are supported less and less. Even a cursory look at the challenges facing our planet make it hard to be optimistic about the prospects for humanity without more knowledge and better-educated citizens. But the global economic meltdown that began in 2008 has devastated endowments at private institutions and produced a dizzying plunge in public funding across America and beyond. In many places student demand is increasing even as dollars disappear. We witness the tragedy of plans ruined and dreams deferred as some institutions have shut down and others have been forced to turn away students for lack of funds to support the instructors and classrooms to serve them. Leading in a time of shrinking budgets, program cuts, furloughs, and staff layoffs is debilitating. Many higher education leaders are struggling with levels of pain, pressure, and uncertainty beyond anything they ever imagined.

Yet there is ample reason for hope. Ted Hesburgh survived the 1960s and became an eloquent advocate for his university and for higher education. He remained passionate about his calling and never lost his faith in the mission. After thirty-five years as president, he left Notre Dame a vastly stronger university. We can do the same in our time for our institutions. Not all of us will rise to a university presidency, nor achieve a place among the legends of higher education leadership. But whether we lead the parade or work in the shadows, we are needed to move our institutions forward and to make the case for higher education. The work that we do—and the vital teaching, research, and outreach that it facilitates—transforms lives, organizations, industries, communities, and nations. We could not ask for a more compelling contribution. Colleges and universities are in the business of creating the future every day. As academic leaders, we can help that happen when we bring deep insight into the dynamics of our institutions and the requirements to lead them, confidence in ourselves, clarity about our vocation, and commitment to purpose. That is a worthy and sacred legacy and an emblem of a life well spent.

References

Adams, A. (1780). *The quotations page*. Accessed July 26, 2007, at www.quotationspage.com/quote/3072.html.

Adams, S. (1995). *Annoying business practices*. Available at www.birdfarm.org/dilbert.html.

Altbach, P. G., Gumport, P. J., & Johnstone, D. B. (2001). *In defense of American higher education*. Baltimore: Johns Hopkins University Press.

American Psychological Association. (2007). *The American Psychological Association's road to resilience*. Accessed May 18, 2010, at www.apahelpcenter.org/featuredtopics/feature.php?id=6.

Amram, Y. (2007). *The seven dimensions of spiritual intelligence: An ecumenical grounded theory*. Accessed March 7, 2010, at www.yosiamram.net/papers/.

Amram, Y., & Dryer, C. (2007). *The development and preliminary validation of an integrated spiritual intelligence scale*. Accessed March 7, 2010, at www.yosiamram.net/papers/.

Andreasen, N. C. (2006). *The creative brain: The science of genius*. New York: Penguin.

Argyris, C. (1968). Conditions for competence acquisition and therapy. *Journal of Applied Behavioral Science, 4*(2), 147–177.

Argyris, C. (1982). *Reasoning, learning and action: Individual and organizational.* San Francisco: Jossey-Bass.

Argyris, C. (1986, September). Skilled incompetence. *Harvard Business Review, 64*(5), 74–79.

Argyris, C. (1990). *Overcoming organizational defenses: Facilitating organizational learning.* Englewood Cliffs, NJ: Prentice-Hall.

Argyris, C. (1994, July–August). Good communication that blocks learning. *Harvard Business Review, 72*(4), 79.

Argyris, C., & Schön, D. A. (1974). *Theory in practice: Increasing professional effectiveness.* San Francisco: Jossey-Bass.

Argyris, C., & Schön, D. A. (1996). *Organizational learning II: Theory, method, and practice.* Reading, MA: Addison-Wesley.

Arizona State University. (n.d.). Office of the President. Accessed July 25, 2010, at http://president.asu.edu/search.

Aziz, S., Mullins, M., Balzer, W., Grauer, E., Burnfield, J., Lodato, M., & Cohen-Powless, M. (2005). Understanding training needs of department chairs. *Studies in Higher Education, 30*(5), 571–593.

Bedein, A. G. (2002, December). The dean's disease: How the darker side of power manifests itself in the office of dean. *Academy of Management Learning and Education, 1*(2), 164–173.

Bennis, W. (1989). *Why leaders can't lead: The unconscious conspiracy continues.* San Francisco: Jossey-Bass.

Bennis, W. (1996). *The unconscious conspiracy: Why leaders can't lead.* New York: Amacom.

Bennis, W. (2003). *On becoming a leader.* New York: Basic Books

Bennis, W. G., & Thomas, R. J. (2008). Resilience and the crucibles of leadership. In J. V. Gallos (Ed.), *Business leadership* (2nd ed., pp. 504–515). San Francisco: Jossey-Bass.

Benson, H., & Klipper, M. Z. (1976). *The relaxation response*. New York: HarperTorch.

Benson, H., Corliss, J., & Cowley, G. (2004, September 27). Brain check: Can we teach ourselves to be healthier? *Newsweek*, pp. 45–47.

Berdahl, R., & McConnell, T. R. (1999). Autonomy and accountability: Who controls academe? In P. Altbach, R. Berdahl, & P. Gumport (Eds.), *American higher education in the twenty-first century: Social, political, and economic challenges* (pp. 70–88). Baltimore: Johns Hopkins University Press.

Berg, D. N. (1999). The characters change, the plot remains the same. In M. Edelson & D. N. Berg (Eds.), Rediscovering groups: A psychoanalyst's journey beyond individual psychology. *International Library of Group Analysis* (Vol. 9, pp. 116–126). London: Jessica Kingsley.

Bergquist, W. H. (1992). *The four cultures of the academy: Insights and strategies for improving leadership in collegiate organizations*. San Francisco: Jossey-Bass.

Berman, P. L. (1985). *Courage of conviction*. New York: Ballantine.

Birnbaum, R. (1988). *How colleges work: The cybernetics of academic organization and leadership*. San Francisco: Jossey-Bass.

Birnbaum, R. (1992). *How academic leadership works: Understanding success and failure in the college presidency*. San Francisco: Jossey-Bass.

Birnbaum, R. (2001). *Management fads in higher education: Where they come from, what they do, why they fail*. San Francisco: Jossey-Bass.

Biron, M., & Bamberger, P. (2007). Managerial-enacted empowerment: Dimensionality and effects on the wellbeing and performance of service workers. *Academy of Management Proceedings*, pp. 1–6. (AN 26523200) Available at http://web.ebscohost.com/ehost/pdf?vid=1&hid=7&sid=313eb259-1488-456d-94820ccb737a1557%40sessionmgr12.

Bolaño, R. (2004). *2666*. New York: Farrar, Strauss & Giroux.

Bolman, L. G., & Deal, T. E. (1979). A simple but powerful power simulation. *Exchange: The Organizational Behavior Teaching Journal, 4*, 38–42.

Bolman, L. G., & Deal, T. E. (1984). *Modern approaches to understanding and managing organizations*. San Francisco: Jossey-Bass.

Bolman, L. G., & Deal, T. E. (2000). *Escape from cluelessness: A guide for the organizationally challenged*. New York: Amacom.

Bolman, L. G., & Deal, T. E. (2001). *Leading with soul: An uncommon journey of spirit*. San Francisco: Jossey-Bass.

Bolman, L. G., & Deal, T. E. (2006). "Reframing change: Training, realigning, negotiating, grieving, and moving on." In J. V. Gallos, *Organization development*. San Francisco: Jossey-Bass.

Bolman, L. G., & Deal, T. E. (2008a). The leader as politician: Navigating the political terrain. In J. V. Gallos (Ed.), *Business leadership* (2nd ed., pp. 336–348). San Francisco: Jossey-Bass.

Bolman, L. G., & Deal, T. E. (2008b). *Reframing organizations: Artistry, choice and leadership* (4th ed.). San Francisco: Jossey-Bass.

Bolman, L. G., & Deal, T. E. (2010). *Reframing the path to school leadership* (2nd ed.). Thousand Oaks, CA: Corwin.

Borysenko, J. (1988). *Minding the body, mending the mind*. New York: Bantam.

Bramson, R. M. (1981). *Coping with difficult people*. New York: Dell.

Breedlove, C. (1998). *Uncharted lines: Poems from the Journal of the American Medical Association*. New York: Ten Speed Press.

Bryan, L. L., & Joyce, C. L. (2007). *Mobilizing minds: Creating wealth from talent in the 21st century organization*. New York: McGraw-Hill.

Buckingham, M., & Clifton, D. O. (2008). The traces of talent. In J. V. Gallos (Ed.), *Business leadership* (2nd ed., pp. 79–86). San Francisco: Jossey-Bass.

Buckingham, M., & Coffman, C. (1999). *First break all the rules: What the world's greatest managers do differently*. New York: Simon & Schuster.

Cameron, K. S., Dutton, J. E., & Quinn, R. E. (Eds.). (2003). *Positive organizational scholarship: Foundations of a new discipline*. San Francisco: Berrett-Koehler.

Campbell, D. (1999). *The Mozart effect: Tapping the power of music to heal the body, strengthen the mind and unlock the creative spirit.* New York: Avon.

Campbell, J. (2008). *The hero with a thousand faces.* Novato, CA: New World Library.

Campbell, J., & Cousineau, P. (Ed.). (2003). *The hero's journey: Joseph Campbell on his life and work.* Novato, CA: New Work Library.

Campo, R. (1994). *The other man was me: A voyage to the new world.* New York: Arte Publico.

Campo, R. (1996). *What the body told.* Durham, NC: Duke University Press.

Carlone, K., & Hill, L. A. (2008). *Managing up: Expert solutions to everyday challenges.* Boston: Harvard Business School Press.

Caro, R. A. (1990). *The path to power: The years of Lyndon Johnson,* Vol. 1. New York: Vintage.

Caro, R. A. (1991). *Means of ascent: The years of Lyndon Johnson,* Vol. 2. New York: Vintage.

Caro, R. A. (2003). *Master of the Senate: The years of Lyndon Johnson,* Vol. 3. New York: Vintage.

Carter, J. (1989). *Nasty people: How to stop being hurt by them without becoming one of them.* New York: Barnes and Noble Books.

Chatterjee, D. (1998). *Leading consciously: A pilgrimage toward self-mastery.* Boston: Butterworth-Heinemann.

Chen, G., Kirkman, B. L., Kanfer, R., & Allen, D. (2005). A multilevel, quasi-experimental study of leadership, empowerment, and performance in teams. *Academy of Management Proceedings,* pp. D1–D6, 6p. (AN 18780372). Available at http://web.ebscohost.com/ehost/pdf?vid=3&hid=7&sid=08c94fd4-ca55-4577-a63b-acfb5b3f0b60%40sessionmgr113.

Cohen, A. (1996). Becoming an administrator: The education of an educator. In P. Frost & M. S. Taylor (Eds.), *Rhythms of academic life: Personal accounts of careers in academia* (pp. 325–332). Thousand Oaks, CA: Sage.

Cohen, M. D., & March, J. G. (1974). *Leadership and ambiguity: The American college president.* New York: McGraw-Hill.

Coles, R. (1989). *The call of stories: Teaching and the moral imagination.* Boston: Houghton Mifflin.

Collins, J. C. (2001). *Good to great: Why some companies make the leap and others don't.* New York: HarperCollins.

Committee of the Corporation and the Academical Faculty. (1828). *Reports on the Course of Instruction in Yale College.* New Haven, CT: Yale University. Available at http://collegiateway.org/reading/yale-report-1828/.

Crow, M. (2002a). Facebook profile. Accessed November 16, 2009, at www.facebook.com/presidentcrow.

Crow, M. (2002b). A new American university: The new gold standard. *Inaugural address, Arizona State University.* Available at www.asu.edu/inauguration/address.

Crow, M. (2008). *Fall welcome message.* Accessed March 3, 2010, at http://president.asu.edu/library/video/fall2008_welcome.

Crow, M. (2009a). *Introduction of President Barack Obama.* Available at http://president.asu.edu/sites/default/files/Commencement%20Intro%20President%20Obama%20051309.pdf.

Crow, M. (2009b). *The research university as comprehensive knowledge enterprise: The reconceptualization of Arizona State University as a prototype for a new American university.* Address to the seventh Glion Colloquium, Montreux, Switzerland. Accessed November 13, 2009, at http://president.asu.edu/sites/default/files/Glion%20Colloquium%20062209%20Univ%20as%20Comp%20Knowledge%20Ent.pdf.

Crow, M. (2009c, April). *Welcome.* Origins conference, ASU. Accessed November 15, 2009, at http://thesciencenetwork.org/programs/origins-symposium/michael-crow.

Csikszentmihalyi, M. (1996). *Creativity: Flow and the psychology of discovery and invention*. New York: Harper Collins.

Csikszentmihalyi, M. (2008). *Flow: The psychology of optimal experience*. New York: HarperCollins.

Cyert, R. M., & March, J. G. (1963). *A behavioral theory of the firm*. Upper Saddle River, NJ: Prentice Hall.

de Geus, A. P. (1988, March–April). Planning as learning. *Harvard Business Review, 66*(2), 70–74.

Deal, T. E., & Kennedy, A. A. (1982). *Corporate cultures*. Reading, MA: Addison-Wesley.

Debowski, S., & Blake, V. (2004, February 9–10). The developmental needs of higher education academic leaders in encouraging effective teaching and learning. In *Seeking Educational Excellence*. Proceedings of the 13th Annual Teaching Learning Forum. Perth: Murdoch University. Accessed March 17, 2010, at http://lsn.curtin.edu.au/tlf/tlf2004/debowski.html.

Delbecq, A. L. (2008). Nourishing the soul of the leader: Inner growth matters. In J. V. Gallos (Ed.), *Business leadership* (2nd ed., pp. 486–503). San Francisco: Jossey-Bass.

Denning, S. (2005). *The leader's guide to storytelling: Mastering the art and discipline of business narrative*. San Francisco: Jossey-Bass.

Denning, S. (2007). *The secret language of leaders*. San Francisco: Jossey-Bass.

Dobson, M., & Dobson, D. S. (2002). *Managing up: 59 ways to build a career-advancing relationship with your boss*. New York: Amacom.

Dotlich, D. L., Noel, J. L., & Walker, N. (2008). Learning for leadership: Failure as a second chance. In J. V. Gallos (Ed.), *Business leadership* (2nd ed., pp. 478–483). San Francisco: Jossey-Bass.

Drucker, P. (1965). The new productivity challenge. *Classic Drucker: Essential wisdom of Peter Drucker from the pages of the Harvard Business Review*. Boston: Harvard Business School Press.

Drucker, P. (2006). *The effective executive*. New York: Harper Paperbacks.

Edwards, D. (2008). *Artscience: Creativity in the post-Google generation*. Cambridge, MA: Harvard University Press.

Figley, C. R. (Ed.). (1995). *Compassion fatigue: Coping with secondary traumatic stress disorder in those who treat the traumatized*. New York: Brunner/Mazel.

Figley, C. R. (2007). *Compassion fatigue: An introduction*. Accessed June 29, 2007, at www.giftfromwithin.org/html/cmpfatig.html.

Fisher, R., & Ury, W. (1981). *Getting to yes*. Boston: Houghton Mifflin.

Florida, R. (2003). *The rise of the creative class: And how it's transforming work, leisure, community and everyday life*. New York: Basic Books.

Frankl, V. E. (1956). *Man's search for meaning*. Boston: Beacon Press.

Freud, S. (1975). *Group psychology and the analysis of the ego*. New York: Norton. (Original work published 1920).

Freyd, J., & Johnson, J. Q. (2010). *References on chilly climate for women faculty in academe*. Available at http://dynamic.uoregon.edu/~jjf/chillyclimate.htm.

Frost, P. J. (2003). *Toxic emotions at work*. Boston: Harvard Business School Press.

Frost, P. J., & Taylor, M. S. (1996a). *Rhythms of academic life: Personal accounts of careers in academia*. Thousand Oaks, CA: Sage.

Frost, P. J., & Taylor, M. S. (1996b). Becoming a department chair and an administrator. In P. J. Frost & M. S. Taylor (Eds.), *Rhythms of academic life: Personal accounts of careers in academia* (pp. 309–312). Thousand Oaks, CA: Sage.

Fukami, C. V. (1996). Herding cats part deux: The hygiene factor. In P. J. Frost & M. S. Taylor (Eds.), *Rhythms of academic life: Personal accounts of careers in academia* (pp. 321–324). Thousand Oaks, CA: Sage.

Fullan, M., & Scott, G. (2009). *Turnaround leadership for higher education*. San Francisco: Jossey-Bass.

Gabarro, J. J., & Kotter, J. P. (2008). *Managing your boss* (HBR Classic). Boston: Harvard Business School Press.

Galbraith, J. R. (2002). *Designing organizations: An executive guide to strategy, structure, and process.* San Francisco: Jossey-Bass.

Gallos, J. V. (1991). *An instructor's guide to effective teaching: Using Reframing Organizations.* San Francisco: Jossey-Bass.

Gallos, J. V. (1993a). Developmental diversity and the management classroom: Implications for teaching and learning. In C. Vance (Ed.), *Mastering management education: Innovations in teaching effectiveness.* Newbury Park, CA: Sage.

Gallos, J. V. (1993b, November). Understanding the organizational behavior classroom: An application of developmental theory. *Journal of Management Education, XVII*(4), 423–439.

Gallos, J. V. (1997). *An instructor's guide to effective teaching: Using Reframing Organizations* (2nd ed.). San Francisco: Jossey-Bass.

Gallos, J. V. (2002). The dean's squeeze: Myths and realities of academic leadership in the middle. *Academy of Management Learning and Education, I*(2), 174–184.

Gallos, J. V. (2003). *An instructor's guide to effective teaching: Using Reframing Organizations* (3rd ed.). San Francisco: Jossey-Bass.

Gallos, J. V. (2005, Spring). Career counseling revisited: A developmental perspective. *Career Planning and Adult Development, 21*(1), 9–23.

Gallos, J. V. (2006). Reframing complexity: A four-dimensional approach to organizational diagnosis, development, and change. In J. V. Gallos (Ed.), *Organization development* (pp. 344–362). San Francisco: Jossey-Bass.

Gallos, J. V. (2007). Review of Joan Didion's *The Year of Magical Thinking*—Loss and change: A developmental opportunity for teaching wisdom, compassion, and respect for the human condition. *Academy of Management Learning and Education, 6*(2), 286–292.

Gallos, J. V. (2008a). *An instructor's guide to effective teaching: Using Reframing Organizations* (4th ed.). San Francisco: Jossey-Bass.

Gallos, J. V. (2008b, December). Learning from the toxic trenches: The winding road to healthier organizations and to healthy everyday leaders. *Journal of Management Inquiry, 17*(4), 354–367.

Gallos, J. V. (2008c). Making sense of organizations: Leadership, frames, and everyday theories of the situation. In J. V. Gallos (Ed.), *Business leadership* (2nd ed., pp. 161–179). San Francisco: Jossey-Bass.

Gardner, H. (1993). *Creating minds: An anatomy of creativity.* New York: Basic Books.

Gardner, H. (1997). *Extraordinary minds: Portraits of four exceptional individuals and an examination of our own extraordinariness.* New York: Basic Books.

Gardner, J. (1990). *On leadership.* New York: Free Press.

Gladwell, M. (2005). *Blink: The power of thinking without thinking.* New York: Little Brown.

Glassman, B., & Fields, R. (1996). *Instructions to the cook: A Zen master's lessons in living a life that matters.* New York: Bell Tower.

Gmelch, W. H. (1991, April). *Paying the price for academic leadership: Department chair tradeoffs.* Paper presented at the Annual Meeting of the American Educational Research Association.

Gmelch, W. H. (2002, February). *The call for department leaders.* Paper presented at the annual meeting of the American Association of Colleges for Teacher Education, New York. ERIC full text accessed on March 18, 2010, at www.eric.ed.gov/ERICWebPortal/custom/portlets/recordDetails/detailmini.jsp?_nfpb=true&_&ERICExtSearch_SearchValue_0=ED460098&ERICExtSearch_SearcType_0=no&accno=ED460098.

Gmelch, W. H., Lovrich, N. P., & Wilke, P. K. (1984). Sources of stress in academe: A national perspective. *Research in Higher Education, 20*(4), 477–490.

Gmelch, W. H., & Miskin, V. D. (1993). *Leadership skills for department chairs*. San Francisco: Jossey-Bass.

Gmelch, W. H., & Miskin, V. D. (2004). *Chairing an academic department*. Madison, WI: Atwood.

Goldsmith, M. (2007). *What got you here won't get you there*. New York: Hyperion.

Goleman, D. (1995). *Emotional intelligence*. New York: Bantam.

Good, I. (1965). *The scientist speculates: An anthology of partly-baked ideas*. New York: Capricorn.

Goodyear, R., Reynolds, P., & Gragg, J. B. (2010, April 30–May 4). *Faculty experiences of classroom incivilities: A critical incident study*. Presentation at the American Educational Research Association, Denver, CO. Accessed May 14, 2010, at www.redlands.edu/Docs/PR/AERA_presentation_2010_%28U_of_R%29.pdf.

Graham Scott, G. (2005). *A survival guide for working with bad bosses: Dealing with bullies, idiots, back-stabbers, and other managers from hell*. New York: Amacom.

Greenleaf, R. K. (1973). *The servant as leader*. Newton Center, MA: Robert K. Greenleaf Center.

Groopman, J. (2000). *Second opinions*. New York: Viking Penguin.

Groopman, J. (2007). *How doctors think*. Boston: Houghton Mifflin.

Heartmath. (2007). *Empowering heart-based living*. Accessed July 10, 2007, at www.heartmath.org/index.html.

Heffron, F. (1989). *Organization theory and public organizations: The political connection*. Upper Saddle River, NJ: Prentice Hall.

Heifetz, R. A. (1994). *Leadership without easy answers*. Cambridge, MA: Belknap/Harvard University Press.

Heifetz, R., & Linsky, M. (2002). *Leadership on the line*. Boston: Harvard Business School Press.

Heifetz, R. A., & Linsky, M. (2008). A survival guide for leaders. In J. V. Gallos (Ed.), *Business leadership* (2nd ed., pp. 447–462). San Francisco: Jossey-Bass.

Heracleous, L., & Jacobs, C. D. (2008). Developing strategy: The serious business of play. In J. V. Gallos (Ed.), *Business leadership* (2nd ed., pp. 324–335). San Francisco: Jossey-Bass.

Herzberg, F. (1968). One more time: How do you motivate employees? *Harvard Business Review, 46*(1), 53–62.

Hillman, J. (1996). *The soul's code: In search of character and calling*. New York: Random House.

Hoevemeyer, V. A. (2005). *High-impact interview questions: 701 behavior-based questions to find the right person for every job*. New York: AMACOM.

Hogan, R., Curphy, G. J., & Hogan, J. (1994). What we know about leadership. *American Psychologist, 49*, 493–504.

Irwin, M. (2007). ASU Inc. *Phoenix New Times*. Accessed February 24, 2010, at www.phoenixnewtimes.com/2007–04–26/news/asu-inc/2.

Job cuts hurt another way. (2004, October 19). *Kansas City Star*, p. E–8.

Jourdain, R. (2002). *Music, the brain, and ecstasy: How music captures our imagination*. New York: Quill/HarperCollins.

Kabat-Zinn, J. (1994). *Wherever you go, there you are: Mindfulness meditation in everyday life*. New York: Hyperion.

Kahn, W. (2005). *Holding fast: The struggle to create resilient caregiving organizations*. New York: Brunner-Routledge.

Kanter, R. M. (1983). *The change masters: Innovations for productivity in the American corporation*. New York: Simon & Schuster.

Katzenbach, J. R., & Smith, D. K. (1993). *The Wisdom of teams: Creating the high-performance organization*. Boston: Harvard Business School Press.

Kegan, R. (1994). *In over our heads: The mental demands of modern life*. Cambridge, MA: Harvard University Press.

Kellerman, B. (2004). *Bad leadership: What it is, how it happens, why it matters*. Boston: Harvard Business School Press.

Kennedy, J. F. (1963). Speech prepared for delivery in Dallas the day of Kennedy's assassination, November 22, 1963. Available at the Kennedy Library at www.jfklibrary.org/Historical+Resources/Archives/Reference+Desk/Speeches/.

Kerr, C. (2001). *The uses of the university*. Cambridge, MA: Harvard University Press.

Kerr, C. (2010). Accessed February 13, 2010, at http://berkeley.edu/news/media/releases/2003/12/02_kerr.shtml.

Kets de Vries, M.F.R. (2003). *Leaders, fools and imposters: Essays on the psychology of leadership*. New York: Universe.

Keyes, R. (2006). *The quote verifier: Who said what, where, when*. New York: St. Martin's Griffin.

Kezar, A. J., Chambers, T. C., Burkhardt, J. C., and Associates. (2005). *Higher education for the public good*. San Francisco: Jossey-Bass.

King, M. L. (1968, February 4). *The drum major instinct*. Sermon delivered at Ebenezer Baptist Church, Atlanta, Georgia. Available at www.blackwebportal.com/wire/DA.cfm?ArticleID=513.

Kipling, R. (1895). If. Accessed April 4, 2010, at www.everypoet.com/archive/poetry/Rudyard_Kipling/kipling_if.htm.

Klein, A. (2007, July 13). A gate crasher's change of heart. *Washington Post Online*. Accessed February 10, 2010, at www.washingtonpost.com/wp-dyn/content/article/2007/07/12/AR2007071202356.html.

Kotter, J. (1982). *The general managers*. New York: Free Press.

Kotter, J. (1985). *Power and influence: Beyond formal authority*. New York: Free Press.

Kotter, J. P. (1988). *The leadership factor*. New York: Free Press.

Kotter, J. P., & Cohen, D. S. (2002). *The heart of change: Real life stories of how people change their organizations*. Boston: Harvard Business School Press.

Kouzes, J., & Posner, B. (2003). *Credibility: How leaders gain and lose it, why people demand it*. San Francisco: Jossey-Bass.

Kouzes, J. M., & Posner, B. Z. (2007). *The leadership challenge* (4th ed.). San Francisco: Jossey-Bass.

Kruger, J., & Dunning, D. (1999). Unskilled and unaware of it: How difficulties in recognizing one's own incompetence lead to inflated self-assessments. *Journal of Personality and Social Psychology, 77*, 1121–1134.

Lang, J. (2010, May 6). Fare thee well, year from hell (Until next time). *Chronicle of Higher Education*. Available at http://chronicle.com/article/ Fare-Thee-Well-Year-From-Hell/65354/

Langer, E. (1989). *Mindfulness*. Cambridge, MA: Merloyd Lawrence/Perseus Press.

Langer, E. (1997). *The power of mindful learning*. Cambridge, MA: Merloyd Lawrence/Perseus Press.

Langer, E. (2005). *On becoming an artist: Reinventing yourself through mindful creativity*. New York: Random House.

Langer, E. (2009). *Counterclockwise: Mindful health and the power of possibility*. New York: Ballantine.

Lau, F. (2010, February 24). At plant closing, ordeal included heart attacks. *New York Times Online*. Accessed March 21, 2010, at www.nytimes.com/2010/02/25/ us/25stress.html.

Lawrence, P. R., & Nohria, N. (2002). *Driven: How human nature shapes our choices*. San Francisco: Jossey-Bass.

Levitin, D. J. (2007). *This is your brain on music: The science of a human obsession*. New York: Plume.

Lewis, J., & Adler, J. (2004, September 27). Forgive and let live. *Newsweek*, p. 52.

Lipstein, O. (1992, March). Sex and crocheting in Burma: A conversation with Ram Dass. *Psychology Today*, pp. 24–30.

London, S. (2002, April). *Higher education for the public good: The role of public understanding, public support, and public policy in reflecting and shaping the covenant between higher education and society*. Kellogg Foundation National Leadership Dialogue Series. Accessed July 25, 2007, at www.kelloggforum.org/NDLSmaterials/ndls%20final%20reports/wyeriver_dialogue1.pdf.

Maccoby, M. (2004, September). The power of transference. *Harvard Business Review*. Reprint R0409E.

Machado, A. (1996). *Proverbios y Cantares XXIX. Caminante*. In *Poesías Completas*. Madrid: Editorial Espasa Calpe, pp. 239–240. Translated from the original: *Caminante, no hay camino. Se hace camino al andar*.

March, J. G., & Simon, H. A. (1958). *Organizations*. New York: Wiley.

Marris, P. (1986). *Loss and change*. London: Routledge.

McCall, M. W., Lombardo, M. M., & Morrison, A. M. (1988). *Lessons of experience: How successful executives develop on the job*. New York: Free Press.

McCraty, R., Barrios-Choplin, B., Atkinson, M., & Tomasino, D. (1998). The effects of different types of music on mood, tension, and mental clarity. *Alternative Therapies in Health and Medicine*, 4(1), 75–84.

McLaughlin, J. B. (1996). *Leadership transitions: The new college president*. San Francisco: Jossey-Bass.

Meyer, J. W., & Rowan, B. (1983). The structure of educational organizations. In J. W. Meyer & W. R. Scott (Eds.), *Organizational environments: Ritual and rationality*. Thousand Oaks, CA: Sage.

Miller, J. (2005, September 12). A call to turn bad to good: Dalai Lama urges seeking the positive. *Kansas City Star*, p. A–13.

Mitroff, I., & Denton, E. A. (1999). *A spiritual audit of corporate America: A hard look at spirituality, religion and values in the workplace*. San Francisco: Jossey-Bass.

Murray, B. (2003). Rebounding from losses. *APA Monitor, 34*(9), 43.

Napier, N. K. (1996). Alice in academia: The department chairman role from both sides of the mirror. In P. Frost & M. S. Taylor (Eds.), *Rhythms of academic life: Personal accounts of careers in academia* (pp. 313–320). Thousand Oaks, CA: Sage.

Newman, F., Couturier, L., & Scurry, J. (2004). *The future of higher education: Rhetoric, reality, and the risks of the market*. San Francisco: Jossey-Bass.

Noonan, W. (2007). *Discussing the undiscussable: A guide to overcoming defensive routines in the workplace*. San Francisco: Jossey-Bass.

O'Neill, T., & Hymel, G. (1994). *All politics is local: And other rules of the game*. Holbrook, MA: Bob Adams.

O'Neill, T. (with W. Novak). (1997). *Man of the house: The life and political memoirs of speaker Tip O'Neill*. New York: Random House.

Oren, D. (2003, January). Stamp of approval. *Yale Alumni Magazine*. Available at www.yalealumnimagazine.com/issues/01_03/seal.html.

Oshry, B. (1995). *Seeing systems: Unlocking the mysteries of organizational life*. San Francisco: Berrett-Koehler.

Oshry, B. (2007). Power in the middle. *Boston: Power and Systems*. Accessed July 30, 2007, at www.powerandsystems.com/power_in_middle.htm.

Padilla, A. (2005). *Portraits in leadership: Six extraordinary university presidents*. Westport, CT: ACE/Praeger.

Pak, M. S. (2008). The Yale report of 1828: A new reading and new implications. *History of Education Quarterly, 48*(1), 30–57. Accessed December 3,
2009, at http://www3.interscience.wiley.com.ezproxy.mnl.umkc.edu/
cgi-bin/fulltext/119391216/PDFSTART.

Palmer, P. (2000). *Let your life speak: Listening for the voice of vocation.*
San Francisco: Jossey-Bass.

Palmer, P. (2004). *A hidden wholeness: The journey toward an undivided life.*
San Francisco: Jossey-Bass.

Pfeffer, J. (1992). *Managing with power: Politics and influence in organizations.*
Boston: Harvard Business School Press.

Pfeffer, J. (2007). *What were they thinking? Unconventional wisdom about
management.* Boston: Harvard Business School Press.

Piercy, M. (1972). The seven of pentacles. *University Review, 22,* 17–18.

Plato. (1992). *The Republic.* Translated by G.M.A. Grube & C.D.C. Reeve.
Indianapolis: Hackett.

Pomerance, S. (2008). The stress of academe. *University Affairs, 49.*
Available at http://findarticles.com/p/articles/mi_7762/is_200804/
ai_n32269777/?tag=content;col1.

Preskill, S., & Brookfield, S. D. (2009). *Learning as a way of leading: Lessons from
the struggle for social justice.* San Francisco: Jossey-Bass.

Razeghi, R. J. (2008). Choose hope: On creating a hopeful future. In
J. V. Gallos (Ed.), *Business leadership* (2nd ed., pp. 516–518). San Francisco:
Jossey-Bass.

Researcher finds fibbers can be found out: A few "wizards" can detect clues to
lies, professor says. (2004, October 15). *Kansas City Star,* p. A–4.

Restak, R. (2003). *The new brain: How the modern age is rewiring your mind.*
New York: Rodale.

Richardson, R. D., Jr. (2006). *William James: In the maelstrom of American modernism*. New York: Mariner.

Riger, J. (n.d.). Chilly climate studies regarding women faculty. Accessed May 14, 2010, at www.mith2.umd.edu/WomensStudies/GenderIssues/ChillyClimate/list-of-reports.

Rohrlich, R. (1980). *Work and love: The crucial balance*. New York: Harmony.

Rosovsky, H. (1990). *The university: An owner's manual*. New York: Norton.

Ruark, J. (2010, January 3). The art of living mindfully. *Chronicle of Higher Education*. Available at http://chronicle.com/article/The-Art-of-Living-Mindfully/63292/.

Sadler, B. (n.d.). *The chilly climate*. Accessed May 14, 2010, at http://www.bernicesandler.com/id4.htm.

Sales, M. J. (2006). Understanding the power of position: A diagnostic model. In J. V. Gallos (Ed.), *Organization development* (pp. 322–343). San Francisco: Jossey-Bass.

Sales, M. J. (2008). Leadership and the power of position: Understanding structural dynamics in everyday organizational life. In J. V. Gallos (Ed.), *Business leadership* (2nd ed. pp. 180–198). San Francisco: Jossey-Bass.

Schein, E. H. (1990). *Career anchors: Discovering your real values*. San Francisco: Jossey-Bass/Pfeiffer.

Schein, E. H. (1992). *Organizational culture and leadership* (2nd ed.). San Francisco: Jossey-Bass.

Schmidt, P. (2010a, May 4). Chief targets of student incivility are female and young professors. *Chronicle of Higher Education*. Accessed May 14, 2010, at http://chronicle.com/article/Chief-Targets-of-Student/65396/.

Schmidt, P. (2010b, June 10). Workplace mediators seek a role in taming faculty bullies. *Chronicle of Higher Education*. Accessed June 10, 2010, at http://chronicle.com/article/Workplace-Mediators-Seek-a/65815/.

Schön, D. (1983). *The reflective practitioner*. San Francisco: Jossey-Bass.

Schön, D. (1987). *Educating the reflective practitioner*. San Francisco: Jossey-Bass.

Schwartz, P. (1991). *The art of the long view*. New York: Doubleday.

Scott, G., Coates, H., & Anderson, M. (2008). *Learning leaders in times of change*. Sydney, Australia: Australian Learning & Teaching Council. Accessed March 7, 2010, at http://acer.edu.au/documents/UWSACER_CarrickLeadershipReport.pdf.

Senge, P. (1990a). *The fifth discipline: The art and practice of the learning organization*. New York: Currency/Doubleday.

Senge, P. (1990b). The leader's new work: Building learning organizations. *MIT Sloan Management Review, 32*(1), 7–22.

Shapiro, H. T. (1998). University presidents—then and now. In W. G. Bowen & H. T. Shapiro (Eds.), *Universities and their leadership* (pp. 65–100). Princeton, NJ: Princeton University Press.

Siegel, B. (1993). *How to live between office visits*. New York: HarperCollins.

Siegel, B. (1998). *Prescriptions for living*. New York: HarperCollins.

Smith, H. (1988). *The power game*. New York: Random House.

Stein, G. (1935). What is English literature? *Lectures in America*. Accessed February 15, 2010, at www.brainyquote.com/quotes/authors/g/gertrude_stein_3.html.

Storr, A. (1992). *Music and the mind*. New York: Ballantine Books.

Tennyson, A. L. (1842). Ulysses. *Poems by Alfred Tennyson*. London: Edward Moxon.

Terr, L. (1999). *Beyond love and work: Why adults need to play*. New York: Scribner.

Thelin, J. R. (2004). *A history of American higher education*. Baltimore: Johns Hopkins University Press.

Tisdell, E. J. (2003). *Exploring spirituality and culture in adult and higher education*. San Francisco: Jossey-Bass.

Twale, D. J., & De Luca, B. M. (2008). *Faculty incivility: the rise of the academic bully culture and what to do about it*. San Francisco: Jossey-Bass.

Useem, M. (2001). *Leading up: How to lead your boss so you both win*. New York: Three Rivers.

Van der Heijden, K. (2005). *Scenarios: The art of strategic conversation*. New York: Wiley.

Von Drehle, D. (2009, November 11). The ten best college presidents: Michael Crow. *Time OnLine*. Accessed February 24, 2010, at www.time.com/time/specials/packages/article/0,28804,1937938_1937933_1937917,00.html.

Wallace, D. B., & Gruber, H. E. (1989). *Creative people at work*. New York: Oxford University Press.

Weick, K. (1995). *Sensemaking in organizations*. Thousand Oaks, CA: Sage.

Weiss, J., & Hughes, J. (2008). Want collaboration? Accept—and actively manage—conflict. In J. V. Gallos (Ed.), *Business leadership* (2nd ed., pp. 349–361). San Francisco: Jossey-Bass.

Westhues, K. (n.d.). *Twenty-five articles since 2006 on mobbing in academe*. Accessed June 10, 2010, at http://arts.uwaterloo.ca/~kwesthue/recentarticlesmobac.htm.

Whyte, D. (2002). *The heart aroused: Poetry and the preservation of the soul in corporate America* (rev. ed.). New York: Currency/Random House.

Wickham, G. (1992). *A history of the theatre* (2nd ed.). New York: Phaidon.

Wilson, R. (2006, February 24). The fall of Summers: Lawrence Summers never won over Harvard's faculty, and that cost him his job. *Chronicle of Higher Education*, p. 1. Assessed July 3, 2007, at http://chronicle.com/daily/2006/02/2006022403n.htm.

Name Index

Subject Index

A

Academic administrators: and alignment between calendar and priorities, 54; and Bennis's "First Law of Academic Pseudodynamics," 54; and damage to credibility, careers, and institutions, 23; and reflection-in-action, 25–26; and development of skills in reframing, 24; effective change agendas of, 78–79; role system in, 56

Academic leaders/leadership: and change agenda of clear vision and strategy for achieving the vision, 78; and effective change agendas, 78–79; and development of well defined change agenda, 78; key step in political view of, 71–72*tab5.1*; and map of the denouement, 81*fig5.2*; and need to get control of schedules and priorities, 54; and questions to help map the political terrain, 80; symbolic view of, 110*tab7.1*; using key political skills for setting agendas, mapping the political terrain, and bargaining and negotiating, 77

Administrative authority: for setting broad parameters and managing administrative details, 58; and hierarchy, 58

Advocacy and inquiry: and assumptions that can lead to learning, 44; and complexity of improving the quality of, 45; and paying attention to patterns, 44–45

B

Backstabbers: academic leaders' need to recognize and respond to, 174; and befriending, 173–174; as classic archetypes, 172–173; as close cousins to bullies, 173; and damage to themselves and their work, 174; guidelines for constructive response to, 173

Bargaining and negotiating: and building agreements, 86; and President Quixote's win-win understanding with the faculty, 86

Bullies: basic principle of standing up to, 172; as classic archetypes, 169–172; and need for assessing the situation, 171; needs, concerns, and goals, 171–172; role of big egos and weak faculty governance structures in, 169; and studies documenting academic bully culture, 169

F

Faculty: and conviction that administrative authority is not always helpful, 57; and challenges for administrators, 7; and development of change agenda, 78; and leaders' role as generative, interpretive, and inspirational, 111; and learning to make deep, accurate, and quick situational diagnoses, 24; and need for diverse skills, strategies, and understandings, 47; operating with tacit consent of, 58; power and possibility in symbolic leaderships of, 111; serving as advocates and negotiators in bargaining, 71–72; and staff seen as constrained and bureaucratic, 59; structural view on, 50*tab4.1*; and their preference to view themselves as rational beings, 71; and getting the right structure in place to maximize support and minimize barriers, 59–60

Feedback: and asking as easiest way to encourage others, 42, 43; as the only way to determine whether our intentions match our actions, 42; and persistence and skill in framing the right question, 42–43

Feeding the soul: and the crucible experience, 212; and the hero journey, 202; and inner spiritual growth, 204; and leaders at their best in relationship with their constituents, 201; and the monomyth, 202; and powerful and traumatic experiences, 211–212; and qualities of focus, passion, wisdom, and integrity, 201; and the leader's capacity to find meaning in negative events, 211; and search for deep talents, 208–209;

and persistence, 212–213; and vital leadership qualities, 201. *See also* Leading with soul; Palmer, Parker.

G

Goals for relationship with boss: and avoidance of surprises, 184–185; and building credibility and trust, 185; and clarifying needs, 179; and developing open communication, 180; establishing credibility, 180; appreciation of pressures, problems, and working style, 182; and understanding the priorities and problems, 183; overarching goals of partnership, communication, and credibility in, 179; overdependence in responding to a boss and counterdependence in resistance to being controlled, 182; and partnership requiring conversation and shared agreement about role and expectations, 179; power and differences in relationship with a boss, 182; and speaking up when necessary, 185–187; and using the boss's time wisely, 184; and ways to help achieve manager's goals while keeping the boss in the loop, 179–180; and willingness to speak truth to power, 185–186

Good to Great, (J. Collins), 16–17

H

Higher education: and academic leaders empowering themselves, 9; and basic structural challenges facing the institution, 50; firing dissenters as problematic in, 79; and its distinctive combination of goals, tasks, employees, and governance structures, 5; and its educational mission, 5;

Higher education (*continued*)
and leadership preparation for, 9;
and learning as subtle and varying
process, 6; and major challenges in the
academy, 10; and mission requiring
key employees to be teachers and
scholars, 7; political view of leadership
in, 71–75; and strategies for sustaining
yourself and your leadership, 10;
symbolic view of leadership in, 109;
and two reasons for leaders going awry,
9–10

Hiring decisions: as critical for
autonomous workers with judgment
and skills, 101; ensuring a strong
candidate pool in, 103; and hiring
process as rushed and unsystematic,
102; and key steps to good hiring,
102–103; and stakes for new hires,
102; taking a systematic and thorough
approach in, 103–104

Human resource leadership: as capacity
to encourage people to bring their
best talents to their work, 93; and
fourth pillar of caring for individuals
and supporting their growth, 100;
and effective leaders' promotion of
openness and transparency, 93; and
hiring the right people, 101–102; and
listening and learning from others,
95; promotion of openness and
transparency in, 93; and provision
for support, coaching, and care for
constituents, 93–94; rushed and
unsystematic hiring processes in,
102; and "servant-first" individuals,
100; and steps to ensure a strong
candidate pool, 103; and fiscal
truth, 94–95; and working at the
boundaries of human growth and
development, 101

L

Leader as prophet and artist: and
academic culture with delimited
forms, 115–116; accomplishments
of Crow's first eight years, 123; and
ASU, 108; and building on the
past for new vision of the future,
117–118; and colleges and university
culture, 115, 120–121; and proposal
to drop "dead languages," 112–113;
and constructing a heroic narrative,
119; and Crow as ASU president,
122–123; and culture as likely to be
coherent and strong, 114; and culture
wars, 116; and the fundamental
questions of purpose, curriculum,
direction, and pedagogy, 113–114;
and giving ritual and ceremony power,
120; and function of symbols as
interpretive and emotional, 111; and
issues of meaning and belief focused
on higher education leadership,
109–113; key practices for successful
symbolic leadership, 117; and leaders'
opportunity to make substantial
change in cultures, 115; and leader's
role as generative, interpretive, and
inspirational, 111; and leading by
example, 118–119; new models of
teaching, learning, research, and
service in, 108; and personalization
of the institution, 118; and the power
and possibility in symbolic leadership,
111; and reframed ASU, 109; rituals
and ceremonies in, 120; role of
effective administrator as akin to a
spiritual leader and artist, 109–110;
and sensemaking by telling stories
and developing symbols, 114; and
steps in setting a tone and shaping
expectations, 112; and symbolic